Cultural Variation in Conflict Resolution: Alternatives to Violence

Cultural Variation in Conflict Resolution: Alternatives to Violence

Edited by

Douglas P. Fry
Eckerd College
Åbo Akademi University

Kaj Björkqvist
Åbo Akademi University

1997

LAWRENCE ERLBAUM ASSOCIATES, PUBLISHERS
MAHWAH, NJ

Lawrence Erlbaum Associates, Inc., Publishers
10 Industrial Avenue
Mahwah, NJ 07430

Cover design by Kristin Alfano

Library of Congress Cataloging-in-Publication Data

Cultural variation in conflict resolution : alternatives to vio-
lence / [edited by] Douglas P. Fry, Kaj Björkqvist.
     p. cm.
  Includes bibliographical references and index.
   ISBN 0-8058-2221-6 (alk. paper). — ISBN 0-8058-
2222-4 (pbk. : alk. paper)
   1. Conflict management—Cross-cultural studies. 2.
Violence—Prevention—Cross-cultural studies. I. Fry,
Douglas P., 1953- II. Björkqvist, Kaj.
  HM136.C93 1996
  303.6'9—dc20   96-7823
                                        CIP

Books published by Lawrence Erlbaum Associates are printed
on acid-free paper, and their bindings are chosen for strength
and durability.

Printed in the United States of America
10 9 8 7 6 5 4 3 2 1

Dedication

To Sirpa and Karin

Contents

          to the Prevention and Mitigation
          of Violence and Aggression in Inner-City Youth
          Nancy G. Guerra, Leonard D. Eron,
          L. Rowell Huesmann, Patrick H. Tolan,
          and Richard Van Acker

19   Tackling Peer Victimization   215
          with a School-Based Intervention Program
          Dan Olweus

          Part VI: Conclusions   233

20   On Respecting Others and Preventing Hate: 243
          A Conversation with Elie Wiesel
          Elie Wiesel and Douglas P. Fry

21   Conclusions: Alternatives to Violence   243
          Kaj Björkqvist and Douglas P. Fry

          Author Index   255

          Subject Index   261

Foreword

The foundation of human culture is verbal speech. There is only one human characteristic, whether behavioral, physiological, or anatomical that is truly unique, and that is the capacity to convey information through words, whether spoken or written. Speech gives humans the power to convey information regarding the making of tools. Among those archeologically preserved are flint arrow and spear points, as well as knives. These must have been used for hunting but easily could have been used to injure and kill fellow humans. As a result of our developing these tools, we have become the most dangerous species on earth, both to ourselves and to other species.

But humans also have the capacity to invent tools that serve for conflict resolution. As with all sciences, one of the major tools in the study of conflict resolution is a descriptive and comparative one. Thus this book contains a group of chapters that describe cultural differences. This evidence of cultural differences not only shows major variation in the expression of aggression and conflict resolution but also suggests that new ideas might be transmitted across cultures.

One of the interesting results from such cross-cultural studies is the fact that with respect to individual homicides, industrially organized cultures are sometimes more peaceful and stable with respect to killing individuals than are tribally organized societies. Paradoxically, industrially organized cultures are able to wage extremely destructive wars, and they have waged two World Wars within living memory. The hope is that, similarly to conflicts within cultures, this situation can be controlled by world-wide organization, but the issue is still in doubt.

This brings up another major problem: How is desirable cultural change brought about? A primary function of scientific research is to discover accurate information, and to make it available to those who can profitably use it, as is being done in this volume. Accurate knowledge about conflict resolution is the best hope for freeing humanity from destructive conflict.

As we know, it is relatively easy to change individual behavior through early and continuing education and training. Bringing about institutional change that affects whole populations is far more difficult. Obviously, we should start with educational institutions whose function is to pass along information from generation to generation. But changing an institution is not easy and often takes many generations. We need more research on the processes of bringing about institutional change.

Information that goes unnoticed or unused has little effect. As well as research on primary phenomena, we need research on the application of cultural remedies. It is my impression that this sort of science is still in its infancy.

At the 1994 meetings of the International Society for Research on Aggression (ISRA), the editors invited me to attend a symposium in order to further explore ideas about conflict resolution with many of the contributors to this volume, which was then in preparation. This ISRA symposium on conflict resolution was one of the most important presented in recent years. It is obvious that written culture can have much more lasting effects than verbally transmitted information. I am delighted that this exploration of conflict resolution, as an alternative to violence, is now published. In that way it can have a potentially long lasting effect.

I am also very pleased that this collection of chapters is both interdisciplinary and international, including many insights from non-Western cultures as well as Western ones. As Saul Rosensweig and I discovered when we founded ISRA in 1972, solving the problems of conflict resolution is not possible within a single academic discipline, but it can be accomplished by cooperation among many of them. I am pleased to see that sort of cooperation and interaction that we envisioned is taking place and bearing fruit in this volume.

—John Paul Scott
Co-Founder, International Society
for Research on Aggression

Preface

Enhanced conflict resolution resources, skills, and institutions are an absolute necessity as humanity enters the 21st century. Given current patterns of interpersonal violence, a growing international arms trade, human rights abuses, the development of computerized battlefields, and ever more lethal weaponry, violence is simply too dangerous a strategy to pursue or permit.

This volume explores possibilities for resolving conflicts without violence. The endeavor is multidisciplinary. We have invited scholars from fields such as anthropology, psychology, and political science to gain broader perspectives than any one discipline can offer on its own. Our hope is to bring together in one volume conflict resolution descriptions and approaches from diverse academic perspectives and from different cultures and nations, in order to facilitate comparisons and syntheses within the young but rapidly developing conflict-resolution field. In introductory and concluding chapters as well as in the short section introductions, we, as editors, attempt to explicitly form linkages among the contributions and to highlight certain themes and subthemes.

We emphasize three overall themes, each of which could be derived from a consideration of the title of the volume. The first theme is that alternatives to violence do exist. One reason for making this theme explicit is because of prevalent beliefs in Western culture that aggression is a biological, innate drive, and that warfare, accordingly, is inevitable. Human nature and human institutions are flexible, and levels of violence vary from one cultural setting to the next, with some cultures expressing extremely low levels of violence. The contributions in this volume provide various examples of conflict-resolution processes that lead away from violence.

A second theme reflected in the title and throughout the book is the importance of culture. Culture is critical in shaping the manner in which people perceive, evaluate, and choose options for dealing with conflict. Conflict resolution, as a cultural phenomenon, is highly connected with and dependent on a society's relevant norms, practices, and institutions. Different cultures develop their own formal and informal ways of handling conflict. This fact becomes ever more important when people from different ethnic, religious, racial, and social backgrounds attempt to solve their conflicts.

As a third theme, we suggest that by studying conflict resolution from different cultural settings, it will be possible to enhance the repertoire of alternatives to violence and to discover general conflict-resolution principles. Conflicts are often categorized according to a variety of criteria along several dimensions such as: Conflict between groups versus interpersonal within-group conflict; dyadic, triadic, and n-party conflict; symmetric versus asymmetric conflict; conflict about vital resources versus ideologically based conflict; conflict between nations versus ethnic conflict within nations; overt conflict versus latent or institutionalized conflict; and so on. Likewise, conflict resolution may be categorized in accordance with different criteria as, for example: Interest-based, rights-based, or power-based; bilateral or trilateral; formal or informal; involving conciliators, mediators, arbitrators, judges, or repressive peacemakers, and so on; problem solving involving integrated solutions, compromises, or determining a procedure for who wins; topic-focused or emotional-focused; and so on. The contributions in this volume contain a wealth of ideas for dealing with conflict and when viewed as a collection we think they also suggest certain conflict resolution principles that may be applied over a variety of settings.

Virtually every chapter in this volume touches upon the diversity and the importance of cultural factors on conflict-resolution practices. Since learning and enculturation processes are of critical importance in shaping people's attitudes towards conflict resolution, particular attention also is given to the socialization process. Several chapters in this volume focus on this central aspect, describing prevention programs that target youth violence.

We hope that the book will be useful not only to researchers, but also that it will facilitate conflict-resolution praxis and teaching at both undergraduate and post-graduate levels within anthropology, psychology, political studies, peace studies, and related fields. We are grateful for any suggestions or criticism that readers would like to convey to us. Please feel free to write us. We would particularly appreciate information on how the book has been applied in training and teaching situations.

We would like to gratefully acknowledge Åbo Akademi University in Vasa, Finland, and its Research Foundation in Åbo/Turku, Finland, as well as Eckerd College of St. Petersburg, Florida, for providing institutional support and financial resources to help complete this project. At Åbo Akademi University, we are particularly grateful to Johan Lindberg for his care and diligence in preparing the final manuscript for publication. We also acknowledge the numerous contributions from Sirpa Korpela and Karin Österman at all stages of this project. At Eckerd College, we wish to thank Dean of Faculty, Lloyd Chapin for his encouragement and wholehearted support. Heather Joseph capably assisted in editing chapters, and Jennifer Wisniewski helped to keep the project organized and running smoothly. At Lawrence Erlbaum Associates we are particularly grateful to Production Editor Amy Olener for so capably handling the many aspects of producing this book. We are also very grateful to Executive Editor Judith Amsel for her support and encourage-ment with this project. We warmly thank all these persons and institutions for their support and for making our editorial work more pleasant and less burdensome.

—Kaj Björkqvist
—Douglas P. Fry

Contributors

Oscar Arias   Fundacíon Arias para la Paz y el Progreso Humano, Apartado Postal 8-6410, 1000 San Jose, Costa Rica

Kaj Björkqvist   Department of Social Sciences, Åbo Akademi University, FIN-65100, Vasa, Finland

H. B. Kimberley Cook   Department of Anthropology, University of California at Los Angeles, Los Angeles, CA 90024, USA

Leonard D. Eron   Institute for Social Research, University of Michigan, Ann Arbor, MI 48106, USA

Ivo K. Feierabend   Department of Political Science, San Diego State University, San Diego, CA 92182, USA

Adam Fraczek   Institute of Psychology, Polish Academy of Sciences, Warsaw, Poland

C. Brooks Fry   United Growth Research Organizations, 4200 S. Shepherd, Houston, TX 77098, USA

Douglas P. Fry   Anthropology Department, Eckerd College, St. Petersburg, FL 33733, USA, and Department of Social Sciences, Åbo Akademi University, FIN-65100, Vasa, Finland

Johan Galtung   The Spark M. Matsunaga Institute for Peace, University of Hawaii, Honolulu, Hawaii, 96822 USA, and Universität Witten/Herdecke, D-58448 Witten, Germany

Ilsa M. Glazer   Department of Behavioral Sciences, Kingsborough Community College, City University of New York, Brooklyn, NY, 11235, USA

Nancy G. Guerra   Department of Psychology, University of Illinois at Chicago, Chicago, IL 60612, USA

Jan Hjärpe   Section of Islamology, University of Lund, Teologiska institutionen, S-223 62 Lund, Sweden

C. Richard Hofstetter   Department of Political Science, San Diego State University, San Diego, CA 92812, USA

Douglas Hollan   Department of Anthropology, University of California at Los Angeles, Los Angeles, CA 90024, USA

L. Rowell Huesmann   Institute for Social Research, University of Michigan, Ann Arbor, MI 48106, USA

Martina Klicperová   Institute of Psychology, Czech Academy of Sciences, 11000 Prague 1, Czech Republic

Kirsti M. J. Lagerspetz   Department of Psychology, Turku University, FIN-20500, Turku, Finland

Simha F. Landau   Hebrew University, Institute of Criminology, PO Box 24100, Mount Scopus, Jerusalem 91905, Israel

M. Melissa McCormick   Department of Anthropology, University of Arizona, Tucson, AZ 85721, USA

Mary K. Meyer   Department of Political Science, Eckerd College, St. Petersburg, FL 33733, USA

Carolyn Nordstrom   Department of Peace and Conflict Studies, 347 Campbell Hall, University of California, Berkeley, CA 94720, USA

Ernest G. Olson   Department of Anthropology and Religion, Wells College, Aurora, NY 13026, USA

Dan Olweus   Department of Psychosocial Sciences, University of Bergen, Bergen 5007, Norway

Karin Österman   Department of Social Sciences, Åbo Akademi University, FIN-65100, Vasa, Finland

Concetta Pastorelli   Department of Psychology, University of Rome, La Sapienza, Rome, Italy

Clayton A. Robarchek   Department of Anthropology, Wichita State University, Wichita, KS 67208, USA

John Paul Scott   Department of Psychology, Bowling Green State University, Bowling Green, OH 43402, USA

Patrick H. Tolan   Department of Psychology, University of Illinois at Chicago, Chicago, IL 60612, USA

Richard Van Acker   Department of Psychology, University of Illinois at Chicago, Chicago, IL 60612, USA

Elie Wiesel   Boston University, 745 Commonwealth Avenue, Boston, MA 02215, USA

Part I

Introduction
and Theoretical Considerations

Chapters in this section provide complementary opening perspectives for the volume. In chapter 1, Fry and Björkqvist present three primary themes, manifestations of which run through many subsequent chapters. Fry and Björkqvist elaborate upon the themes that 1) a diversity of possible approaches to conflict exist, and thus a variety of alternatives to violence also exist, 2) conflict and conflict resolution are cultural phenomena, and 3) general cross-cultural conflict principles may be identified and applied. They next briefly describe the plan of the book.

In chapter 2, Fry and Fry at first examine two conflict models (i.e., Black, 1993; Rubin, Pruitt & Kim, 1994) that they suggest may facilitate cross-cultural comparisons and the development of nomothetic conflict theory. They review the four conflict strategies advanced by Rubin et al. (1994): contending, problem solving, avoidance, and yielding. This strategic model can be used in the analysis of conflict within a given culture and in making comparisons regarding the prevalence of particular strategies in different cultures. Fry and Fry also see Rubin et al.'s (1994) definition of conflict—"perceived divergence of interests"—as being useful across cultural settings. The second theoretical work discussed by Fry and Fry is Black's (1993) model of social control. Black provides a holistic classification of conflict and its management according to form and style. Black also provides a series of testable propositions—for example, a model relating third-party roles to social distance and level of authoritativeness. References to both Rubin et al.'s (1994) and Black's (1993) conflict models occur throughout this volume (see especially chapters by Klicperová et al. and Landau, but also Cook, McCormick, Meyer, and Olson).

In the second part of their chapter, Fry and Fry begin to address the book's "alternatives to violence" theme. They focus their discussion on four topical areas

1

relevant to reducing violence: human flexibility and the conflict-resolution options this permits, socialization and resocialization potentials, new and redesigned systems and institutions for conflict resolution, and the importance of world views and attitudes towards conflict.

In chapter 3, Björkqvist continues the introductory process by reviewing various conceptualizations of aggression, violence, and conflict. Björkqvist emphasizes that whereas anger may be a universal human emotion, it does not always lead to aggression. Likewise, feelings of frustration do not invariably result in aggression. Furthermore, aggression is certainly not a drive analogous to drives for sex, hunger, or thirst. Overall, Björkqvist emphasizes that many different options exist for dealing with anger, frustration, and conflict besides resorting to aggression.

Björkqvist notes that many scientists, in fact, the majority of authors writing on this subject suggest it is incorrect to regard warfare as an inevitable consequence of human nature; it is a popular myth, which easily becomes self-fulfilling. He makes reference to the Seville Statement on Violence, a 1986 declaration by a group of scientists from different disciplines, and subsequently endorsed by numerous scientific organizations, that warfare cannot be attributed to violent genes, a violent brain, and so on.

REFERENCES

Black, D. (1993). *The social structure of right and wrong.* San Diego: Academic.
Rubin, J. Z., Pruitt, D. G., & Kim, S. H. (1994). *Social conflict: Escalation, stalemate and settlement* (2nd ed.). New York: McGraw-Hill.

1

Introduction:
Conflict-Resolution Themes

Douglas P. Fry
Eckerd College

Kaj Björkqvist
Åbo Akademi University

This chapter provides an overall introduction to the book. The book has three overarching themes. In the first part of the chapter, each theme is introduced and the underlying rationale discussed. The themes are, 1) alternatives to violence exist, 2) conflict and conflict resolution are cultural phenomena, and 3) cross-cultural conflict principles can be identified and applied. In the second part of the chapter, the plan of the book is presented.

—The Editors

The three major themes of the book that were mentioned in the preface now receive some elaboration. We propose that one reason for making the first theme explicit—that alternatives to violence exist—is because of the prevalence of beliefs in Western culture that human nature is violent and that warfare is inevitable (Adams & Bosch, 1987; Fry & Welch, 1992; also see chapter 3, this volume). If such beliefs were true, we would expect to find violence and warfare in all cultures, but cross-cultural comparisons show that this is not the case. First, people in some societies live their lives nonviolently (cf. Dentan, 1968; Fabbro, 1978; Howell & Willis, 1989; Montagu, 1978; Sponsel & Gregor, 1994; also see chapters 5 and 6, this volume). Cultures with little physical aggression can be found throughout the globe and include the Buid of the Philippines, the Chewong of Malaysia, the Copper Eskimo of Canada, the Hutterites of Canada and the United States, the Mbuti of central Africa, the Piaroa of Amazonia, the Semai of Malaysia, the Siriono of

Bolivia, the Tikopia of the western Pacific, the Toraja of Indonesia, the Veddahs of Sri Lanka, the Yames of Orched Island near Taiwan, and certain Zapotec communities of Mexico, among others. Second, warfare is *not* practiced by all cultures, being absent among numerous peoples including, for example, the Andaman Islanders, Arunta, Arapesh, Birhor, Buid, Hadza, !Kung, Mission Indians, Punan, Semai, Semang, Todas, Yahgan, and various other societies (Lesser, 1967; Montagu, 1978, 1994, p. xii). It is also noteworthy that in 1948, Costa Rica abolished its military forces as a bold step away from the institution of war (see chapters 14 and 15, this volume). Thus, humans do not always and everywhere engage in warfare.

The cross-cultural variation in levels and forms of violence as well as the demonstrated ability of humans to form new institutions and to give up old ones suggest that human nature and social systems are flexible. Warfare is not inevitable, and conflicts do not everywhere and always erupt in violence (see chapters 2 and 3, this volume). There are various ways of handling conflict, such as through nonviolent protest, democratic elections, symbolic strikes, boycotts, appeal to courts or arbitration boards, grievance hearings, direct bipartisan negotiation, mediator-assisted negotiation, discussion and problem solving with or without the assistance of a conciliator or mediator, family and marriage counseling, psychotherapy, and so on.

A second theme reflected throughout this volume is that conflict resolution is a cultural phenomenon. Ross (1993, p. 19) coined the term *culture of conflict*, which reflects "a society's relevant norms, practices, and institutions" regarding conflict, which provides a framework for people's perception of conflict. Scripts that persons may follow for conflict resolution are accordingly defined within a given culture of conflict. Similarly, Avruch (1991, p. 11) talks of the culture of conflict resolution, emphasizing that conflicts and their resolution are "cultural events" (also see Lederach, 1991). This idea of conflict resolution as a cultural phenomenon could be illustrated for any culture, but here we consider examples from cultures that value peacefulness in interpersonal relations. Dentan (1968) wrote of the Semai of Malaysia: "They seem to have worked out ways of handling human violence that technologically more 'advanced' people might envy." Robarchek (1990, p. 67), who also studied the Semai, explained that in that culture, "People come to evaluate themselves largely in terms of these cultural values which thus become incorporated as components of individual self-images, developed and maintained by the continuing feedback of daily interaction.... Ideals of generosity, friendliness, and nonaggressiveness, largely realized in the behavior of most people, constitute central components of individuals' self-images as well" (p. 68). Likewise, studies on the Xingu of Amazonia illustrate how psychological images related to violence and peacefulness are dependent upon cultural beliefs. Gregor (1990, 1994) discussed how the Xingu image of what is "good" is linked to peacefulness psychoculturally, in terms of which emotions and actions are valued as appropriate and which are not. "The good man is circumscribed in his behavior, he avoids confrontations, and he rarely shows anger" (Gregor, 1990, p. 110).

Many chapters in this volume (e.g., 4, 7, 8, 12, 16, and 19) also illustrate the influences of culture on conflict resolution processes. Some chapters (e.g., 2, 5, 6,

8, 18, and 19, this volume) specifically describe how conflict beliefs, attitudes, and scripts of behavior are internalized by individuals within particular cultural settings and strengthened through culturally-based norms and institutions (also see Briggs, 1994; Fry, 1992, 1993, 1994). Other chapters focus on political culture in relation to conflict resolution (e.g., 9, 15, and 16, this volume) or examine historical and ethnic dimensions of culture vis-à-vis conflict resolution (e.g., 4, 10, 11, and 13, this volume).

An important implication of this second theme—with its emphasis on cultural influences—is that one should exercise caution when attempting to apply conflict-resolution techniques across cultural settings. Avruch (1991, p. 2), for example, related the frustration of a conflict-resolution workshop attendee with processes such as "producing manuals for resolving conflicts in easy steps" that are insensitive to cultural differences. Lederach (1991, p. 184) recommended that conflict resolvers, attempting to mediate within a culture different from their own, need to be both flexible and sensitive to avoid acting like the proverbial bull in a china shop: "Personal experience suggests we should recognize that our premises and assumptions about conflict process are not necessarily shared by those who we are attempting to help, and that we may, inadvertently, break a lot of china in our attempts to find the aisles."

With this caution in mind, we nonetheless propose the third theme: Through studying conflict resolution from different cultural settings, it will be possible to enhance the repertoire of alternatives to violence and discover general conflict-resolution principles. The idea is *not* to construct a manual with conflict-resolution steps, but rather to expand the number of options to consider in approaching conflict, and to search for general principles that may contribute to conflict-resolution models and theories. Thus, while we are cautious about pulling conflict-resolution "tidbits" from a specific cultural caldron within which they acquire meaning as part of the cultural whole, if conflict-resolution theory and praxis are going to move forward, we suggest that paying particular attention to recurring cultural patterns and isolating underlying principles are essential (e.g., Ross, 1993).

This book is organized into six topical sections, each with a short section introduction wherein the editors offer integrative comments and highlight particular issues related to the section. In Part I, the three introductory chapters raise theoretical issues related to conflict and its resolution, review models and typologies, and introduce issues to be addressed in the book. In Part II, Cultural Influences on Conflict Resolution, five chapters consider cultural phenomena including nonviolence, world view, formal and informal social control, patterns of avoidance, redundancy of conflict-management mechanisms, social networks and community influences on conflict-resolution. Societies considered in this section include the Semai of Malaysia, the Toraja of Indonesia, native Margariteño Islanders of Venezuela, Tongan Islanders of the South Pacific; furthermore, Eastern and Western cosmologies of conflict are considered as well.

The five chapters in Part III, The Challenge of Resolving Ethnic Conflict, continue the investigation of cultural phenomena vis-à-vis conflict, but more particularly they share a focus on ethnic relations and intergroup conflict. Case studies and analyses are drawn from Sri Lanka, Mozambique, Northern Ireland, the Middle East, and African Americans and Jews of New York. Chapters in Part IV, Conflict Resolution as an Alternative to War, discuss political aspects of conflict and its resolution. In the first of three chapters, Oscar Arias, former President of Costa Rica and recipient of the Nobel Peace Prize for his leading role in bringing peace to Central America, shares his perspectives on this peace process. The other two chapters in this section examine cooperation, nonviolence, and democracy as aspects of political culture that lead toward peace, by presenting data and analyses on Latin America and the Czechoslovakian "Velvet Revolution."

The three chapters in Part V, Socialization for Conflict Resolution, consider developmental and socialization influences on conflict behavior, and present findings from Finland, Italy, Israel, Norway, Poland, and the United States. One chapter examines sex differences and developmental patterns, whereas the other two chapters focus on preventing and mitigating aggression among youth. The sixth and concluding section of the book contains a conversation with Nobel Peace Prize laureate Elie Wiesel on conflict-resolution and related issues facing humanity today. A concluding chapter by the editors considers some theoretical and practical implications of the research reported in this volume.

We hope the reader will find this volume rife with insights about the nature of conflict-resolution processes, some of which may be applied creatively in a variety of social settings to reduce violence. In the concluding chapter, we will return to this issue and consider the following questions: What lessons can we extract from the various chapters for reducing violence? What do these chapters suggest in terms of more general conflict resolution principles?

REFERENCES

Adams, D., & Bosch, S. (1987). The myth that war is intrinsic to human nature discourages action for peace by young people. In J. M. Ramirez, R. A. Hinde, & J. Groebel (Eds.), *Essays on violence. Series on psychobiology* (Vol. 3, pp. 121–137). Sevilla: Universidad de Sevilla.

Avruch, K. (1991). Introduction: Culture and conflict-resolution. In K. Avruch, P. W. Black, & J. A. Scimecca (Eds.), *Conflict resolution: Cross cultural perspectives* (pp. 1–17). Westport, CT: Greenwood.

Briggs, J. L. (1994). "Why don't you kill your baby brother?": The dynamics of peace in Canadian Inuit camps. In L. E. Sponsel & T. Gregor (Eds.), *The anthropology of peace and nonviolence* (pp. 155–181). Boulder, CO: Lynne Rienner.

Dentan, R. K. (1968). *Semai: A nonviolent people of Malaya.* New York: Holt, Rinehart, & Winston.

Fabbro, D. (1978). Peaceful societies: An introduction. *Journal of Peace Research, 15,* 67–83.

Fry, D. P. (1992). "Respect for the rights of others is peace": Learning aggression versus non-aggression among the Zapotec. *American Anthropologist, 94,* 621–639.

Fry, D. P. (1993). The intergenerational transmission of disciplinary practices and approaches to conflict. *Human Organization, 52,* 176–185.

Fry, D. P. (1994). Maintaining social tranquillity: Internal and external loci of aggression control. In L. E. Sponsel & T. Gregor (Eds.), *The anthropology of peace and nonviolence* (pp. 133–154). Boulder, CO: Lynne Rienner.

Fry, D. P., & Welch, J. N. (1992, December). *Beliefs about human nature and conflict: Implications for peace education*. Paper presented at the meetings of the American Anthropological Association, San Francisco, CA.

Gregor, T. (1990). Uneasy peace: Intertribal relations in Brazil's Upper Xingu. In J. Haas (Ed.), *The anthropology of war* (pp. 105–124). New York: Cambridge University Press.

Gregor, T. (1994). Symbols and rituals of peace in Brazil's Upper Xingu. In L. E. Sponsel & T. Gregor (Eds.), *The anthropology of peace and nonviolence* (pp. 241–257). Boulder, CO: Lynne Rienner.

Howell, S., & Willis, R. (1989). *Societies at peace: Anthropological perspectives*. New York: Routledge.

Lederach, J. P. (1991). Of nets, nails, and problems: The folk language of conflict-resolution in a Central American setting. In K. Avruch, P. W. Black, & J. A. Scimecca (Eds.), *Conflict resolution: Cross-cultural perspectives* (pp. 165–186). Westport, CT: Greenwood.

Lesser, A. (1967). War and the state. In M. Fried, M. Harris, & R. Murphy (Eds.), *War: The anthropology of armed conflict and aggression*. New York: Natural History Press.

Montagu, A. (1978). *Learning non-aggression: The experiences of non-literate societies*. New York: Oxford University Press.

Montagu, A. (1994). Foreword. In L. E. Sponsel & T. Gregor (Eds.), *The anthropology of peace and nonviolence* (pp. ix–xiv). Boulder, CO: Lynne Rienner.

Robarchek, C. A. (1990). Motivations and material causes: On the explanation of conflict and war. In J. Haas (Ed.), *The anthropology of war* (pp. 56–76). New York: Cambridge University Press.

Ross, M. H. (1993). *The management of conflict*. New Haven: Yale University Press.

Sponsel, L. E., & Gregor, T. (Eds.). (1994). *The anthropology of peace and nonviolence*. Boulder, CO: Lynne Rienner.

2

Culture and Conflict-Resolution Models: Exploring Alternatives to Violence

Douglas P. Fry
Eckerd College

C. Brooks Fry
Growth Research Organizations

An implication of conflict being a cultural phenomenon is that culturally specific ways of perceiving and responding to conflict can remain invisible, as unquestioned social assumptions, to the members of any given culture. Definitions of conflict as perceived divergence of interests and of aggression as the infliction of harm are discussed in the first part of this chapter. Several conflict management models are briefly reviewed, and it is suggested that such models are useful for allowing predictions about conflict management to be made across cultural circumstances. The second part of the chapter focuses on four propositions relevant to reducing violence: 1) the flexibility of human behavior and institutions permits various conflict options; 2) socialization and resocialization processes have implications for teaching and rewarding nonviolent conflict options instead of aggression, especially among youth; 3) social systems and institutions that allow for conflict prevention, management, and resolution can be greatly enhanced at virtually every social level; and 4) attitudes, beliefs, and world views that lead toward less damaging and more effective means of dealing with conflict can be augmented in place of belief systems and ethos that bolster the use of aggression.
—The Editors

In the first part of this chapter, we highlight several matters particularly relevant to a comprehensive, cultural perspective on conflict resolution. We consider definitions, strategies, and typologies. Next, we begin the exploration that continues throughout the book, of how to deal with conflict in ways that are far less destructive and often more effective than violence. We consider the relevance of the flexibility of human nature and social institutions; socialization and resocialization processes; the development of alternative conflict resolution systems and institutions; and the importance of norms, attitudes, and values that are supportive of positive, effective alternatives to violence.

CULTURE AND MODELS

As discussed in chapter 1, human conflict and conflict resolution are cultural phenomena. The ways that conflicts are perceived and handled reflect a culturally shared set of attitudes and beliefs. In some societies the emphasis is on punishing wrongdoers, but in many cultures, conflict management hinges upon repairing strained or broken relationships (e.g., Just, 1991; Lederach, 1991; Nader, 1969; Shook & Ke'ala Kwan, 1991; White, 1991). Some cultures have formal mechanisms for handling conflict, such as courts or arbitration boards, whereas other cultures rely on informal mechanisms, such as teasing, gossip, exclusion, witchcraft, and so on (Black, 1993; Fry, 1992a, 1994; Hollan, 1988; White, 1991, p. 188; chapters 7 and 8, this volume).

An implication of conflict being a cultural phenomenon is that the culturally typical ways of perceiving and responding to conflict remain in some ways invisible to the members of any given society as unquestioned assumptions within their social universe. Furthermore, options for dealing with conflict, which lie outside a person's cultural repertoire, tend to remain unconsidered. Exploring cross-cultural diversity in how conflicts are handled opens up new possibilities.

To date, many anthropological investigations of conflict resolution have looked within particular cultures and have emphasized the culturally specific nature of conflict resolution processes (Avruch & Black, 1991; Avruch, Black, & Scimecca, 1991). On the other hand, many nonanthropological conflict-resolution sources have tended to focus on the modern complex societies of the West, and they sometimes convey an implicit assumption that conflict-resolution models and techniques are very generally applicable (e.g., Fisher & Ury, 1981; Katz & Lawyer 1985; also see Scimecca, 1991, for examples). One of the central issues of this book involves balancing and integrating the obvious importance of cultural influence with the search for more general patterns and models of conflict, a process that may move our understanding of conflict resolution forward, analytically and practically.

Rubin, Pruitt, and Kim (1994, p. 5) provided a clear definition of conflict that can be applied widely across cultural settings: "conflict means perceived divergence of interest, or a belief that parties' current aspirations cannot be achieved simultaneously." By focusing on perceived divergence of interests, Rubin et al. (1994) suggested that some conflicts can be resolved when the parties realize—perhaps with the help of a third party—that their perceptions of divergent interests are erroneous.

One type of (mis)perception occurs when disputants assume that something of importance to them is also of great importance to the other party. Once uncovered and corrected, erroneous assumptions can lead to mutually satisfactory ways of resolving a conflict, as illustrated by President Jimmy Carter's mediation leading to the Camp David Accords of 1978 between Israel and Egypt:

> Carter's initial efforts to mediate a settlement, proposing a compromise in which each nation would retain half of the Sinai, proved completely unacceptable to both sides. President Carter and his staff persisted, eventually discovering that the seemingly irreconcilable positions of Israel and Egypt reflected underlying interests that were not incompatible at all. Israel's underlying interest was *security*; Israel wanted to be certain that its borders would be safe against land or air attack from Egypt. Egypt, in turn, was primarily interested in *sovereignty*—regaining rule over a piece of land that had been part of Egypt as far back as biblical times. (Rubin et al., 1994, p. 2)

Besides illustrating the importance of not assuming that disputing parties share the same underlying interests or motivations, this example is instructive in several other regards. First, Carter recounted how real progress was made after Begin and Sadat were given the opportunity to interact informally (Carter, 1982). Second, the fact that Carter invited the disputants to Camp David in Maryland illustrates the utility of picking a neutral location for mediations, and the fact that he kept Begin and Sadat isolated from the pressures and influences of constituencies and the press shows his use of site closedness—two mediation "tricks" discussed by Rubin et al. (1994, pp. 204–205).

Because divergent interests among individuals, or among groups of individuals, are natural consequences of sociality (interdependence), conflict can be considered an inevitable feature of social life. However, conflict can be dealt with in a variety of ways: denying its very existence, negotiating a mutually desirable solution (or problem solving), compromising, threatening verbally, attacking physically, appealing to a third party, and so on. Thus *conflict* is not synonymous with *aggression*, which, whether verbal or physical, can be defined as inflicting harm or causing pain (physical, psychological, and/or social) to another person (see Björkqvist & Niemelä, 1992, p. 4).

Rubin et al. (1994) advocated viewing conflict in terms of general strategies (each consisting of a variety of more narrow tactics) which vary in terms of outcomes and perceived feasibility for the parties involved. The strategies include *contending* (high concern for one's own outcomes and low concern for other's outcomes), *problem solving* (high concern for both one's own and other's outcomes), *yielding* (low concern for one's own outcomes and high concern for other's outcomes), and *avoiding* (low concern for both one's own and other's outcomes).

This strategic model is generally applicable. Cross-culturally, much conflict behavior can be classified as fitting one or more of these strategies. Furthermore, some cultures tend to favor particular strategies. For example, the Yanomami (also spelled Yanomamö) people (Chagnon, 1992; Lizot, 1994) engage in much contending (with culturally specific tactics, including verbal and physical threatening, exchange of insults, shifting alliance formation for defense and offense, club fights, ax fights, spear fights, ambushes, and raids). The Semai (see chapter 5, this volume) and native Hawaiians within the family context (see Shook & Ke'ala Kwan, 1991) favor problem solving as a strategy, making extensive use of third parties, as occurs in their culturally specific conflict-resolution events, *Becharaa'* and *Ho'oponopono*, respectively. The Toraja (see chapter 6, this volume) and the Irish of South Armagh (see chapter 10, this volume) make heavy use of avoidance (and at times yielding), again in culturally specific ways.

Thinking in terms of strategies, it becomes clear that problem solving comes closest to conflict resolution, because contending, which encompasses low concern for the other party's outcomes, involves the butting of heads (including physical and verbal aggression), and avoidance and yielding (both capable of preventing violence and the escalation of conflict) do not involve finding a solution that reconciles interests or needs. With problem solving, both sides may achieve favorable results, may prevent future conflict, and may maintain their relationship. Thus problem solving actually resolves conflict.

Rubin et al. (1994, pp. 168–173) went on to highlight three kinds of problem solving: 1) compromises, 2) choosing a procedure for deciding who will win, and 3) integrative solutions. They maintained that "integrative solutions are almost always the most desirable. They tend to last longer and to contribute more to the relationship between the parties and the welfare of the broader community than do compromises and agreements about how to choose the winner" (p. 173). The Camp David Accords illustrated an integrative solution, because they responded to the interests of both parties, something the proposed compromise—splitting the territory—did not accomplish.

Black (1993) also advanced the search for cross-cultural regularities and principles. Black, a sociologist who uses a substantial number of anthropological, historical, and judicial examples in his work, proposed a five-part typology of conflict management, which partly overlaps the four strategies of Rubin et al. (1994). Simha Landau (chapter 12, this volume) applies Black's conflict management typology to Israeli society, Martina Klicperová et al. (chapter 16, this volume) explore some of Black's propositions in relation to the Czech and Slovak Republics, and Black himself provides various ethnographic illustrations to support the broad cross-cultural applicability of his model.

The utility of models such as Rubin et al.'s (1994) and Black's (1993) is that they are nomothetic, or generally applicable, permitting accurate predictions to be made across a wide variety of conditions, and thus they advance understanding of conflict management processes generally, across socio-cultural circumstances. Consider Black's observations that certain third-party roles have rough equivalents in various cultures. "Our typology classifies third parties along two dimensions: the *nature* [italics added] of their intervention (whether partisan of not) and the *degree* [italics added] of their intervention" (Black, 1993, p. 97). Nonpartisan third-party roles include (in order of increasing authoritativeness) friendly peacemaker, mediator, arbitrator, judge, and repressive peacemaker. For instance, the third-party role of arbitrator—a person who will issue a decision that should be considered binding but who lacks any power to enforce compliance with the decision—can be found in various cultures. Black (1993) discussed the relationship of these third parties (settlement agents) to the disputing principals and proposed the general rules: "[1] The settlement agent and the principals form an isosceles triangle of relational distance, with the settlement agent at the apex … [2] The authoritativeness of settlement behavior is a direct function of the relational distance between the settlement agent and the principals … [and] of the relative status of the third party" (Black, 1993, pp. 15–17). Thus, any third party should be approximately equally distant, in social terms, from the disputants, and although a friendly peacemaker is of the same social level as the disputants and may serve only to distract or temporarily separate them, mediators, arbitrators, and judges are increasingly higher in social rank and correspondingly exert increasing control over the outcome of a conflict. A repressive peacemaker, however, has the most authoritative position and treats fighting itself "as offensive and punishable, regardless of why it occurs" (Black, 1993, p. 117). Although it is important to keep in mind that Black's typology consists of "ideal types" and that his predictions are statistical, not absolute, his efforts demonstrate that it is possible to find patterns of conflict behavior that occur in various cultural settings. This observation moves us away from the point of view that every aspect of a conflict is unique to the given culture in which it occurs. Overall, Rubin et al. (1994) and Black (1993) provided useful approaches, because these authors remained sensitive to culture while proposing more generally applicable conflict-management models. Both works also facilitate thinking conceptually about paths away from violence towards less damaging and more beneficial alternatives for managing conflict.

In the remainder of this chapter, we discuss four critical areas for reducing violence. First, a consideration of conflict processes leads to a clear conclusion that human beings and their social institutions are extremely flexible. This foundation-level observation is a necessary precursor to proposing that alternatives to violence are in fact possible. Second, we suggest that special attention should be paid to how people learn to express conflict, how socialization within a culture of conflict occurs, and how individuals who practice violence can relearn alternative paths that are both personally and socially less destructive. Third, we explore social systems and institutions that can be established to handle conflicts more equitably and at lower costs than through reliance on violence. Finally, we consider the area of cultural attitudes, beliefs, and world views in relation to alternatives to violence.

HUMAN FLEXIBILITY AND THE POTENTIAL FOR CHANGE

Sometimes human aggressiveness is assumed to stem from a violent "animal nature." However, as de Waal (1989, 1995) emphasized, the fact that besides engaging in aggression, many species of primates also are skilled at reconciling and maintaining peaceful social relationships, challenges stereotypical images of animal ferocity. Likewise, Sponsel (1994, p. 7) concluded from a review of the literature that "recent field studies of nonhuman primate behavior have revealed that nonviolence predominates over violence." To mention an example of a species very closely related to humans, pygmy chimpanzees respond to tension in their social group, by "making love, not war," or, in other words, by engaging in sexual behavior instead of aggression. Primatologist de Waal (1995, p. 83) wrote, "The species is best characterized as female-centered and egalitarian and as one that substitutes sex for aggression." Primatologist Kano (1986/1992, p. viii) explained that, ". . . by frequent use of quasi-sexual behavior during interactions, they conceal the operation of rank and associate with one another very adeptly. They prove that individuals can coexist without relying on competition and dominant-subordinate rank." Overall, the fact that various species of primates are skilled at limiting aggression argues against attributing human violence to an instinctively aggressive "animal nature."

A similarly uncritically accepted notion is that war is an inevitable result of an aggressive "human nature," a belief held by a substantial percentage of Westerners (Adams & Bosch, 1987; Fry & Welch, 1992; Wahlstrom, 1985). It follows that a first step in considering alternatives to violence should be to reevaluate the image of "human nature" as innately or immutably violent. Fry and Welch (1992) reported that a one-semester college course resulted in a change in attitudes and beliefs about the inevitability of war. The college course, which explored variation in human aggressiveness and peacefulness and the diversity of conflict-resolution methods across cultures, resulted in a marked reduction in the number of students who, after completing the course, perceived "war as an intrinsic part of human nature" (64% to 21%), or that "wars are inevitable because human beings are naturally aggressive creatures" (40% to 13%). When surveyed before and again after the course about whether "humans are capable of abolishing war," the change in opinion was in the opposite direction (56% to 75%). These findings suggest simultaneously that a substantial number of people may not even consider alternatives to war and violence as being within the realm of possibility, but also that such attitudes about "human nature" and warfare can be changed.

It is also sometimes assumed that human social institutions are inflexible, thus precluding the possibility of finding alternatives to violence. But history and anthropology provide innumerable instances of major social change, including examples of cultures supplanting violent practices or institutions with less violent ones, sometimes on their own and at other times when influenced by outside forces. Greenberg (1989) recounted how a Chatino Indian community, located in the southern highlands of Mexico and previously fraught with violent murders and maimings, in a movement initiated by the women and later supported by the male authorities, banned alcohol consumption—a major social change—and drastically reduced the bloodshed. On a less dramatic but nonetheless important scale, the Scandinavian countries, wishing to reduce family violence and also to reinforce clearly the ideal that hitting others is inappropriate, outlawed spanking and physical punishment of children by any person under any circumstance (Gelles & Straus, 1988). Another example of a social change leading away from violence is provided by the abolition of the army in Costa Rica. President Oscar Arias (chapter 14, this volume) writes, " ... the underlying spirit of peace live[s] on to this day in a country that has proven the seemingly utopian hypothesis that a small, poor, demilitarized country can survive amidst mighty and wealthy neighbors."

On occasion violence has been reduced via the type of third-party intervention that Black (1993, pp. 116–117) labeled repressive peacemaking, as occurred when colonial powers imposed peace on warring indigenous peoples. Interestingly, in the case of the Mendi of New Guinea, when forced to abandon warfare by the government, rival clans shifted to a nonviolent, ritualistic form of competition by striving to outdo each other in throwing the most elaborate feasts. Following years of planning, each rival clan in turn throws expensive and elaborate cassowary-bird feasts for the other. "The cassowary contest now provides replacement for interclan warfare. . . . As long as each clan has displayed the maximum generosity, both clans win" (Coast Community College, 1995). Traditionally, competing chiefs on the Trobriand Islands sought to enhance their prestige by hosting nights of dancing, at which times fighting could break out. Colonial missionaries attempted to substitute the British game of cricket for the sexually provocative dances. "The Trobrianders made cricket their own by adding battle dress and battle magic and by incorporating erotic dancing into the festivities" (Haviland, 1996, p. 434; also see Weiner, 1977). Thus, for both the Mendi and the Trobrianders, although the pressure to cease hostilities came from outside, the ritual elaborations and manifestations of the new peace represent a creative blend of cultural characteristics (Coast Community College, 1994, 1995).

PREVENTION: LEARNING CONFLICT RESOLUTION INSTEAD OF VIOLENCE

Socialization and social learning processes are crucial for shaping behaviors and represent a second important area relevant to reducing violence across social levels. Through socialization within their culture, individuals acquire views as to what the world is like, adopt a particular set of values, and gain an understanding of the cultural meaning of events and actions (see Briggs, 1994; Gregor, 1994). In any culture, socialization involves modeling and imitation, reinforcement and punishment, cognition and reflection (see chapter 18, this volume). Attitudes and ideas about conflict and how to deal with it, as well as patterns of behavior, begin early in life and tend to persist into adulthood. For example, in longitudinal studies, Eron and Huesmann (1984) found that individuals who were aggressive at 8 years of age also tended to be aggressive at age 30; the same intraindividual consistency was true regarding prosocial orientations toward conflict and social relations generally.

Parents play important roles in the development of their children's attitudes and behavior about conflict. Parents, from their adult perspectives, are aware of community interests as well as their own. The young child is not yet aware but can be taught from an early age not only to recognize and respect the rights of others but also to experience the importance of working with others toward common goals. The young child must have opportunity for differentiation as an individual, including the early ego development reflected by the child in phases such as "let *me* do it," or, with great pride as tasks are mastered, "*I* can do it myself." Subsequently, as the child matures, there must be opportunities to identify with community interests and to make a shift to include "what *we* can do together" as community members.

This realization opens the door to new possibilities, including the creation of nonviolent conflict resolution systems and institutions.

In addition to specific childhood experiences, the emotional climate in which the child grows is important in determining the adult's world view, attitudes, and behavior. A warm, friendly, supportive climate contrasts with a cold, hostile, frightening one. The former is apt to produce adults able to work easily together in solving problems and resolving conflicts. The latter climate can have lasting effects by contributing to an adult's view of the world as a dangerous place filled with hostility. In such circumstances, some adults become so defensive and suspicious that they can hardly conceive of resolving conflicts by any means but violence. Others may just give up and express feelings of helplessness. In either case, conflicts generally are not handled in a productive manner; they are not resolved.

A comparison of two Zapotec communities from Mexico illustrates the importance of social environments on the development of conflict styles (see Fry, 1988, 1992b, 1993, 1994). San Andrés and La Paz are pseudonyms for two neighboring communities that are similar in many respects. However, San Andrés is more aggressive than La Paz, with higher homicide and assault rates, more wife-beating, and a greater use of physical punishment on children. Additionally, the community images and conflict ideologies differ substantially: The people of La Paz perceive themselves as tranquil and respectful, whereas the citizens of San Andrés more ambiguously complain about jealous, aggressive, troublemakers in their basically good community (Fry, 1994).

Thus the social climates differ between these two communities. Children in La Paz observe adults shunning violence and treating each other respectfully. These La Paz youngsters only rarely witness physical aggression or receive beatings, because the adults consider the spoken word to be an effective and appropriate way to train children. One La Paz father expressed, "One must explain to the child with love, with patience, so that little by little the child understands you" (Fry, 1993, p. 180). In San Andrés, by contrast, typically several homicides occur as the child is growing up, and all the children in the community hear the details of such violence recounted by their elders. The youngsters in San Andrés also see fist fights, wife beatings, and disciplinary switchings regularly, and they learn that it is sometimes acceptable in the social climate of their community to hit other persons. Systematic behavioral observations revealed that by the 3-to-8 year age range, children from La Paz engaged in statistically significantly less aggression and play aggression than did their age mates in San Andrés (Fry, 1988, 1992b). Thus, the contrasting community patterns of dealing with conflict were already being adopted by young children in these very different learning climates.

The broader significance is that socialization provides a powerful means to prevent violence from becoming internalized during an individual's development. It is eminently possible and sensible to encourage the learning of prosocial orientations and to discourage aggressive, antisocial responses to conflict initially, before they become habitual (for further discussion see Fry, 1993). Additionally, resocialization away from violent responses is also possible in some cases. For example, Guerra and Slaby (1990) were able to increase the social problem-solving skills and decrease aggressive attitudes and behaviors among adolescents incarcerated for aggressive offenses through a 12-session cognitive intervention program, and Gelles and Straus (1988) reported that during a follow-up study, about half the parents who had participated in a 21-week counseling program for child abuse remained violence-free. Other examples of socialization and/or resocialization as a means to prevent or reduce aggression are provided in chapters 18 and 19. Clearly, the benefits of making appropriate investments of financial and social resources for children and adolescents in order to prevent aggressive attitudes and behaviors from becoming established are immense.

Although violence can be direct and brutal, it also can be *structural*, as Galtung (1969) pointed out, and just as brutal, inflicted by inequitable social institutions that contribute to poverty, hunger, and disease. Along a similar line, Sponsel (1994, p. 4) noted that security should be reconsidered in more encompassing terms: "Also among the threats to national, international, and global security are injustice, racism, poverty, malnutrition, illiteracy, and environmental problems." Population growth is certainly high on the list, for as Ashley Montagu (personal communication, March 1996) recently expressed, "If we don't solve the overpopulation problem, we can forget about all the others." Overcrowding of the planet is inevitable if population trends continue, bringing both real and perceived shortages of many vital resources. New conflicts will be engendered and numerous old ones will be intensified (cf. Homer-Dixon, Boutwell, & Rathjens, 1993). In light of these considerations, the necessity of developing more holistic and preventive orientations toward conflict cannot be overemphasized.

ALTERNATIVE SYSTEMS AND INSTITUTIONS

A third area relevant to reducing violence involves creating new institutions, applying old institutions at new social levels and in new ways, and redesigning systems for handling conflict. Most nations today accept the use of military force. However, alternative strategies, systems, and institutions for dealing with conflict could be developed and enhanced (cf. Johansen, 1984). Some flavor of the variety of conflict resolution options that are available is apparent from Scimecca's (1991, pp. 29–30) listing of Alternative Dispute Resolution processes currently being utilized in the USA: adjudication, arbitration, court-annexed arbitration, conciliation, facilitation, med-arb (mediation-arbitration), mediation, minitrial, negotiation, and use of ombudspersons.

Ury, Brett, and Goldberg (1988) demonstrated how systems for dealing with conflict can be redesigned and improved. They presented a tripartite model of conflict options: 1) power contests, 2) rights contests, and 3) interest-based approaches.

> Our basic proposition is that, in general, it is less costly and more rewarding to focus on interests than to focus on rights, which in turn is less costly and more rewarding than to focus on power. The straightforward prescription that follows is to encourage

the parties to resolve disputes by reconciling their interests wherever it is possible and, where it is not, to use low-cost methods to determine rights and power. (Ury et al., 1988, p. 169)

One of the strengths of this approach to dispute resolution is that it illustrates the sequence of 1) studying and analyzing existing conflict resolution systems, 2) designing a (culturally appropriate) alternative set of options for resolving disputes tailored for specific settings, and 3) implementing and fine-tuning approaches associated with bringing about change toward a better conflict resolution system.

In terms of creating new institutions or redesigning conflict systems, such endeavors can range from instituting a peer mediation program in a school, thus providing a new mechanism for students to settle their differences without coming to blows (cf. McCormick, 1988), to the more elaborate redesigning of a grievance procedure such as undertaken by Ury et al. (1988) in a coal mine plagued by disputes, to the establishment of a new levels of governance as illustrated by the European Commission, European Parliament, and the European Court of Justice, which now provide totally new political, legislative, and legal mechanisms for resolving conflicts at a regional level. Disputes between member nations and violations of Union laws may be brought to the attention of the European Commission, and if not settled at that point, can be referred to the European Court of Justice, which is currently hearing 60 to 80 cases a year. A member of the European Parliament recently expressed that, with the development of the Union, warfare *among member countries* "has become unthinkable. Peace is therefore the primary achievement of the process of European integration" (Bertens, 1994, p. 2).

Ury et al. (1988, p. 172) quite explicitly suggested the utility of conflict system redesign at the international level:

> An effective dispute resolution system offers a way to accomplish the essential functions of violence and war, but at a significantly lower cost. The ultimate challenge is to devise workable dispute resolution systems not only for families and organizations, but also for relations among nations. In an increasingly interdependent and insecure world, our survival depends on finding a better means of resolving our differences than resorting to the ultimate power contest—nuclear war.

Renner (1993), for instance, provided some specific examples of proposals to improve the conflict prevention and conflict resolution system of the United Nations through redesign. To briefly mention a few ideas, a UN early-warning office could be established specifically to monitor potential conflicts. Hot-spot and early-warning reports from around the globe could allow UN mediation and arbitration services to be employed before conflicts have a chance to escalate. Another change could be to provide the United Nations with a satellite information capacity: "By confirming or denying alleged border violations, troop movements, or illicit flows of weapons, or by providing warnings against surprise attack, it could help build confidence between opposing parties" (Renner, 1993, p. 40). Additionally, the United Nations could make much greater use of conflict-resolution techniques: "routine, low-key efforts could help to defuse tensions and resolve disputes at an earlier stage, long before violent conflict is imminent" (Renner, 1993, p. 42). Greater funding of the United Nations and specifically of its conflict prevention, resolution, and peacekeeping activities might seem to be warranted, especially in light of the huge discrepancy between world military expenditures and the UN peacekeeping assessments, a ratio of 1,877 to 1 in 1991 (Renner, 1993, p. 50). In summary, the overall point of this section is that numerous opportunities across a multitude of social levels exist for instituting new conflict prevention and conflict-resolution procedures and, in some cases, for totally redesigning dispute-resolution systems.

THE IMPORTANCE OF WORLD VIEW

A fourth way of reducing violence involves the fostering of norms, attitudes, and values—an ethos—that support nonviolent conflict resolution. Anthropological studies repeatedly demonstrate the potent impact of world view, belief system, and values on patterns of peacefulness–aggressiveness within a culture (e.g., Briggs, 1994; Fry, 1992b; Gregor, 1994; Just, 1991; Robarchek, 1980, 1994; Ross, 1993). Whether we are talking about a city neighborhood, an indigenous community, a country, or the international community, the culture of conflict in each case involves a world view with norms, attitudes, and values—reflecting different levels of uniformity and consistency. The international community, for example, can be viewed as having certain shared views, expectations, norms, and institutions (see chapters 9 and 15).

One assumption currently widespread in the international community is that warfare is permissible. Galtung's (1990, pp. 291–292) idea of *cultural violence*, defined as the aspects of culture that legitimize violence, is relevant to the acceptance of warfare by today's people and leaders: "Cultural violence makes direct and structural violence look, even feel, right—or at least not wrong. ... The study of cultural violence highlights the way in which the act of direct violence and the fact of structural violence are legitimized and thus rendered acceptable in society." However, a world view of "cultural nonviolence," or perhaps more positively, "cultural peacefulness," is also possible—many cultures already have such ethos—and, we suggest, fostering such views represents a fourth important path away from violence. It is certainly possible to imagine an international community where warfare is no longer considered a viable option and where conflicts are resolved through other types of institutions (Fry, 1985; Johansen, 1984; Ury et al., 1988). President Harry Truman once observed: "When Kansas and Colorado have a quarrel over water in the Arkansas River, they don't call out the National Guard in each state and go to war over it. They bring suit in the Supreme Court of the United States and abide by the decision. There isn't a reason in the world why we cannot do that internationally" (Ferencz & Keyes, 1991, p. 22).

John B. Calhoun had a long and extraordinarily productive life, much of which he spent at the National Institute of Mental Health where he worked as its most famous expert on the effects of crowding on mammalian populations. Calhoun

(1962) reported severe disruption of animal social behavior under crowded conditions, and he soberly contemplated the possible implications of his research for humanity living on an overpopulated planet. At the time of his death in 1995, Calhoun was working diligently to foster what he called a *compassionate revolution*—fundamental nonviolent changes in our relationships with one another and with the natural world. In essence, Calhoun emphasized the necessity of new attitudes and values in counteracting violence and for solving other problems in the world.

In April 1991, a group of distinguished world leaders—Ali Alatas, Benazir Bhutto, Gro Harlem Brundtland, Fernando Henrique Cardoso, Jimmy Carter, Václav Havel, Julius Nyerere, Jan Pronk, Maurice Strong, and many others—met in Stockholm, Sweden and drafted a report called "Common Responsibility in the 1990s." The report made a number of specific proposals in the areas of peace, development, environment, human rights, population, and global governance. Significantly, the document reflects a new global world view, which emphasizes interdependence and the necessity of cooperation. For example:

> Cooperation on issues that require countries to act in accordance not only with national interest but also according to global norms will demand a system that more clearly defines rights and obligations of nations. When agreed upon, such rights and obligations must be respected. Norms must gradually acquire the status of law. . . . The reality of the human neighborhood requires us urgently to seek a compact on establishing a strengthened system of global governance. (Alatas et al., 1991, pp. 36, 37)

President Truman's call for law, John Calhoun's call for compassion, and the Stockholm group's call for cooperation and respect of norms all share a concern with fostering new values and attitudes for humanity's common well-being, if not survival. It is important not to underestimate the potential of enhancing and reinforcing such world views that favor nonviolent approaches to conflict as powerful and important mechanisms for contributing to violence reduction at various social levels.

The Stockholm group (Alatas et al., 1991) invoked the image of the world as a neighborhood, with neighbors cooperating, respecting each other, and following common norms and laws. The group proposed that because the fates of the people of the earth are interdependently linked, the serious common problems facing humanity can and should be addressed by the nation-neighbors working in concert for the common good and they furthermore stress that greater global governance will facilitate this endeavor.

Additionally, such imagery and attitudes are important because they offer hope. Many people today feel hopeless and helpless when confronted with the major problems of the world, including violence in its direct and structural forms. It is vitally important to counteract the hopelessness and to emphasize constructive roles, actions, and possibilities for resolving some of the current problems in our communities and the world. It also is important to provide alternative images of futures unencumbered by violence in the streets and by the "war system," that is, futures in which attitudes and institutions allow conflicts to be resolved without violence and war (Johansen, 1984; Renner, 1993; Ury et al., 1988). Holding a vision of a more positive future in which multiple alternatives to violence allow for less destructive resolution of conflicts may be an important motivator for working toward the realization of such a vision. As Noam Chomsky (1992, p. 64) pointed out, harboring pessimistic assumptions will lead to their realization, whereas maintaining the hope necessary to "commit onself to the struggle" may contribute to achieving a better world. That is each person's choice.

REFERENCES

Adams, D., & Bosch, S. (1987). The myth that war is intrinsic to human nature discourages action for peace by young people. In J. M. Ramirez, R. A. Hinde, & J. Groebel (Eds.), *Essays on violence. Series on psychobiology* (Vol. 3, pp. 121–137). Sevilla: Universidad de Sevilla.

Alatas, A., Azócar, P. A., Bhutto, B., Brandt, W., Brundtland, G. H., Solís, M. C., Cardoso, F. H., Carlsson, I., Carter, J., Chidzero, B., Planchart, R. F., Geremek, B., Al-Hamad, A., ul Haq, M., Havel, V., Heath, E., Iglesias, E., Lee, H-K., Lewis, S., Manley, M., Martynov, V., Mbeki, T., McNamara, R., Morse, B., Nyerere, J., Ndriaye, B., Okita, S., Pronk, J., Ramphal, S., Sadik, N., Salim, S., Sengupta, A., Shevardnadze, E., Sorsa, K., Strong, M., Urquhart, B. (1991). *Common responsibility in the 1990s: The Stockholm initiative on global security and governance.* Stockholm: Prime Minister's Office.

Avruch, K., & Black, P. W. (1991). The culture question and conflict resolution. *Peace and Change, 16*, 22–45.

Avruch, K., Black, P. W., & Scimecca, J. A. (Eds.). (1991). *Conflict resolution: Cross-cultural perspectives.* Westport, CT: Greenwood Press.

Bertens, J.-W. (1994, January). *The European Movement: Dreams and realities.* Paper presented at the seminar The EC after 1992: The United States of Europe? Maastricht, The Netherlands.

Björkqvist, K., & Niemelä, P. (1992). New trends in the study of female aggression. In K. Björkqvist & P. Niemelä (Eds.), *Of mice and women: Aspects of female aggression* (pp. 3–16). San Diego: Academic.

Black, D. (1993). *The social structure of right and wrong.* San Diego: Academic.

Briggs, J. L. (1994). "Why don't you kill your baby brother?": The dynamics of peace in Canadian Inuit camps. In L. E. Sponsel & T. Gregor (Eds.), *The anthropology of peace and nonviolence* (pp. 155–181). Boulder, CO: Lynne Rienner.

Calhoun, J. B. (1962). Population density and social pathology. *Scientific American, 206*, 139–146.

Carter, J. (1982). *Keeping faith: Memoirs of a president.* New York: Bantam.

Chagnon, N. A. (1992). *Yanomamö.* Fort Worth, TX: Harcourt Brace Jovanovich.

Chomsky, N. (1992). *Deterring democracy.* London: Vintage Books.

Coast Community College (1994). *Faces of culture—Cricket the Trobriand way: A case study in culture change* [Film]. Fountain Valley, CA: Coast Community College District.

Coast Community College (1995). *Faces of culture—Kinship and descent groups, part 1* [Film]. Fountain Valley, CA: Coast Community College District.

Eron, L., & Huesmann, R. L. (1984). The relation of prosocial behavior to the development of aggression and psychopathology. *Aggressive Behavior, 10*, 201–211.

Ferencz, B. B., & Keyes, K., Jr. (1991). *Planethood.* Coos Bay, OR: Love Line Books.

Fisher, R., & Ury, W. L. (1981). *Getting to yes.* Boston, MA: Houghton Mifflin.

Fry, D. P. (1985). Utilizing human capacities for survival in the nuclear age. *Bulletin of Peace Proposals, 16*, 159–166.

Fry, D. P. (1988). Intercommunity differences in aggression among Zapotec children. *Child Development, 59*, 1008–1019.

Fry, D. P. (1992a). Female aggression among the Zapotec of Oaxaca, Mexico. In K. Björkqvist &
P. Niemelä (Eds.), *Of mice and women: Aspects of female aggression* (pp. 187–199). San Diego:
Academic Press.

Fry, D. P. (1992b). "Respect for the rights of others is peace": Learning aggression versus
non-aggression among the Zapotec. *American Anthropologist, 94,* 621–639.

Fry, D. P. (1993). The intergenerational transmission of disciplinary practices and approaches to
conflict. *Human Organization, 52,* 176–185.

Fry, D. P. (1994). Maintaining social tranquility: Internal and external loci of aggression control.
In L. E. Sponsel & T. Gregor (Eds.), *The anthropology of peace and nonviolence* (pp. 133–154).
Boulder, CO: Lynne Rienner.

Fry, D. P., & Welch, J. N. (1992, December). *Beliefs about human nature and conflict: Implications for
peace education.* Paper presented at the meetings of the American Anthropological Association,
San Francisco, CA.

Galtung, J. (1969). Violence, peace and peace research. *Journal of Peace Research, 6,* 167–191.

Galtung, J. (1990). Cultural violence. *Journal of Peace Research, 27,* 291–305.

Gelles, R. J., & Straus, M. (1988). *Intimate violence.* New York: Simon & Schuster.

Greenberg, J. (1989). *Blood ties: Life and violence in rural Mexico.* Tucson, AZ: University of Arizona
Press.

Gregor, T. (1994). Symbols and rituals of peace in Brazil's Upper Xingu. In L. E. Sponsel & T.
Gregor (Eds.), *The anthropology of peace and nonviolence* (pp. 241–257). Boulder, CO: Lynne
Rienner.

Guerra, N. G., & Slaby, R. G. (1990). Cognitive mediators of aggression in adolescent offenders:
2) Intervention. *Developmental Psychology, 26,* 269–277.

Haviland, W. A. (1996). *Cultural anthropology* (8th ed.). Fort Worth: Harcourt Brace.

Hollan, D. (1988). Staying "cool" in Toraja: Informal strategies for the management of anger and
hostility in a nonviolent society. *Ethos, 16,* 52–72.

Homer-Dixon, T. F., Boutwell, J. H., & Rathjens, G. W. (1993). Environmental change and violent
conflict. *Scientific American, 268*(2), 38–45.

Johansen, R. C. (1984). Toward an alternative security system. In B. H. Weston (Ed.), *Toward
nuclear disarmament and global security: A search for alternatives* (pp. 569–603). Boulder, CO:
Westview.

Just, P. (1991). Conflict resolution and moral community among the Dou Donggo. In K. Avruch,
P. W. Black, & J. A. Scimecca (Eds.), *Conflict resolution: Cross-cultural perspectives* (pp.
107–143). Westport, CT: Greenwood.

Kano, T. (1992). *The last ape: Pygmy chimpanzee behavior and ecology* (E. O. Vineberg, Trans.).
Stanford, CA: Stanford University Press. (Original work published 1986)

Katz, N., & Lawyer, J. (1985). *Communication and conflict resolution skills.* Dubuque, IA: Kendall.

Lederach, J. P. (1991). Of nets, nails, and problems: The folk language of conflict resolution in a
Central American setting. In K. Avruch, P. W. Black, & J. A. Scimecca (Eds.), *Conflict
resolution: Cross-cultural perspectives* (pp. 165–186). Westport, CT: Greenwood.

Lizot, J. (1994). Words in the night: The ceremonial dialogue—One expression of peaceful
relations among the Yanomami. In L. E. Sponsel & T. Gregor (Eds.), *The anthropology of peace
and nonviolence* (pp. 213–240). Boulder, CO: Lynne Rienner.

McCormick, M. M. (1988). Mediation in the schools: An evaluation of the Wakefield pilot
peer-mediation program in Tucson, Arizona. Chicago, IL: American Bar Association.

Nader, L. (1969). Styles of court procedure: To make the balance. In L. Nader (Ed.), *Law and
culture in society* (pp. 69–91). Chicago, IL: Aldine.

Renner, M. (1993). *Critical juncture: The future of peacekeeping* (Worldwatch Paper 114). Washington DC: Worldwatch Institute.

Robarchek, C. A. (1980). The image of nonviolence: World view of the Semai Senoi. *Federated
Museums Journal, 25,* 103–117.

Robarchek, C. A. (1994). Ghosts and witches: The psychocultural dynamics of Semai peacefulness. In L. E. Sponsel & T. Gregor (Eds.), *The anthropology of peace and nonviolence* (pp. 183–196). Boulder, CO: Lynne Rienner.

Ross, M. H. (1993). *The management of conflict.* New Haven: Yale University Press.

Rubin, J. Z., Pruitt, D. G., & Kim, S. H. (1994). *Social conflict: Escalation, stalemate and settlement* (2nd ed.). New York: McGraw-Hill.

Shook, E. V., & Ke'ala Kwan, L. (1991). *Ho'oponopono*: Straightening family relationships in Hawaii. In K. Avruch, P. W. Black, & J. A. Scimecca (Eds.), *Conflict resolution: Cross-cultural perspectives* (pp. 213–229). Westport, CT: Greenwood.

Scimecca, J. A. (1991). Conflict resolution in the United States: The emergence of a profession? In K. Avruch, P. W. Black, & J. A. Scimecca (Eds.), *Conflict resolution: Cross-cultural perspectives,* (pp. 19–39). Westport, CT: Greenwood.

Sponsel, L. E. (1994). The mutual relevance of anthropology and peace studies. In L. E. Sponsel & T. Gregor (Eds.), *The anthropology of peace and nonviolence* (pp. 1–36). Boulder, CO: Lynne Rienner.

Ury, W. L., Brett, J. M., & Goldberg, S. B. (1988). *Getting disputes resolved: Designing systems to cut the costs of conflict.* San Francisco, CA: Jossey-Bass.

de Waal, F. (1989). *Peacemaking among primates.* Cambridge: Harvard University Press.

de Waal, F. (1995). Bonobo sex and society. *Scientific American, 272,* 82–88.

Wahlstrom, R. (1985, September). *On the psychological premises for peace education.* Paper presented at the Third European Conference of the International Society for Research on Aggression, Parma, Italy.

Weiner, A. B. (1977). Trobriand Cricket: An Ingenious Response to Colonialism—Review. *American Anthropologist, 79,* 506–507.

White, G. M. (1991). Rhetoric, reality, and resolving conflicts: Disentangling in a Solomon Islands society. In K. Avruch, P. W. Black, & J. A. Scimecca (Eds.), *Conflict resolution: Cross-cultural perspectives* (pp. 187–212). Westport, CT: Greenwood.

3

The Inevitability of Conflict But Not of Violence: Theoretical Considerations on Conflict and Aggression

Kaj Björkqvist

Åbo Akademi University

This chapter describes sources of conflict and aggression from a theoretical point of view. Three main theories on the origin of aggression are analyzed: 1) instinct (Trieb) theory, 2) the frustration-aggression hypothesis, and 3) social learning theory. It is concluded that aggression is not an innate drive functioning in accordance with the reservoir model, like hunger or sex, but aggression may serve as a means to fulfill other drives, whether innate or learned. Scripts for how to behave in conflict situations are learned, and they are to a great extent dependent on culture. Anger, which is a natural human emotion, may serve as an invigorating factor, encouraging the choice of aggressive scripts. Whereas conflict constitutes an inevitable part of social life, violence can be avoided, and alternative scripts employed.

—The Editors

In this chapter, I discuss theories about interpersonal conflict and aggression. I argue that anger, frustration, and conflict constitute inevitable ingredients of everyday social interaction; likewise, they are familiar intrapsychic dynamic forces within each individual. Conflicts do not, however, necessarily have to lead to acts of violence.

THE INEVITABILITY OF CONFLICT

Conflict can be defined as "a struggle over values and claims to scarce status, power, and resources, a struggle in which the aims of opponents are to neutralize, injure, or eliminate their rivals" (Coser, 1956, p. 8).

There are two basically different views on the necessity, or inevitability, of conflict. According to one view, conflict is an aberration in society, a kind of social pathology (Parsons, 1951; Smelser, 1962). Conflicts can be eliminated by giving all people involved what they need. Conflict is, in accordance with this view, always dysfunctional and does not facilitate evolution or improvement, neither of society as a whole nor of relations between individuals. Conflict is not an inevitable ingredient of human life.

According to the other point of view, conflicts are inevitable by-products of human interaction (Coser, 1956). Conflicts are consequences of the impossibility of always giving all people involved what they want.

Desire and needs are not identical, and the fact that people cannot get all they want does not automatically and in all cases imply that they do not get what they need. Rubin, Pruitt, and Kim (1994, p. 5) accordingly described conflict in more careful terms, as "perceived divergence of interest, or a belief that the parties' current aspirations cannot be achieved simultaneously."

Coser (1956) is of the opinion that conflict, although inevitable, is not inherently pathological or always necessarily dysfunctional. On a short-term basis, a conflict may seem dysfunctional, but on a long-term basis, it may be functional and lead to improvement of a society in question. Lyons (1993) also suggested that conflict often can be a constructive force in social life. The issue of functionality, though, is epistemologically problematic, and based on post hoc analysis.

Levi-Strauss (1958) suggested that conflicts of different kinds are latent in every culture, and the reason why norms are formed is to prevent latent and potential conflicts. Norms are ritualized ways of handling conflict. Norms with respect to clothing may serve as an example: For instance, by concealing genitals, sexual excitation caused by visual stimulation is reduced, and sexual conflict to a great extent is avoided.

There are norms for how to dress in a large variety of societal roles, a fact facilitating the preservation of these roles. Human speech also is highly ritualized and regulated by norms; in fact, every aspect of communication and social life has norms of its own. Individuals who do not follow norms are regarded as deviant and, if central and important norms are violated, the individual in question may be punished. Every society has rules of etiquette, the neglect of which leads to sanctions. Preliterate people have systems of social control, although they do not perhaps have a written law.

Levi-Strauss' view may be compared to Freud's (1930/1948) opinion on norms and culture, presented in his book *Das Unbehagen in der Kultur* [Civilization and its Discontents]: According to Freud, the internalization of norms into an intrapsychic superego is the result of the clash between the pleasure-principle and the reality-principle. Humans cannot get everything they want. Taken as a whole, culture facilitates human well-being, but culture also puts limitations on the individual.

The position taken in this chapter is that conflicts really are inevitable. However, they should not in all cases be regarded as dysfunctional, or as a kind of social pathology. Conflicts are of many different types, some functional, some dysfunctional. Some conflicts are harmful, but, in some cases, conflicts may improve society and social relations on a long-term basis.

AGGRESSION AND ANGER

Violence and aggression are related concepts, often used synonymously in everyday language; they are not, however, identical but rather partly overlapping concepts, violence being only one form of aggression. The emotion of anger also is often mistakenly used as a synonym of aggression. Aggression is an act, not an inner state. The emotion of anger is often (but not always) a precursor of aggression.

Buss (1961, p. 1) defined *aggression* as "a response that delivers noxious stimuli to another organism." That definition does not exclude harm delivered to another person or organism unintentionally. If Buss' definition is taken literally, hitting and injuring another person accidentally by car would be an aggressive act.

Authors of a behaviorist orientation have tried to avoid references to inner states or intentions, but they use instead terms such as goal-direction. Dollard, Doob, Miller, Mowrer, and Sears (1939, p. 7) defined aggression as "an act whose goal-response is injury to an organism (or organism-surrogate)." Baron (1977, p. 7) defined aggression as "any form of behavior directed toward the goal of harming or injuring another living being who is motivated to avoid such treatment."

Aggression here is defined as an intentional act, carried out with the purpose of causing physical or mental pain to another individual or organism (see also Björkqvist & Niemelä, 1992). In order to be regarded as painful, the act must be of a kind that the object is motivated to avoid. If the perpetrator does not succeed in his or her intentions, and no injury occurs, the act may still be regarded as aggressive.

There is experimental evidence (Holm, 1985; Björkqvist, Lindström, Pehrsson, 1989) that people pay attention to at least the following four factors when they attribute aggressiveness to an act: 1) its intentionality, 2) the extent of injury or harm, 3) the reason (e.g., offensive attack vs. defense), and 4) the method.

While aggression is a kind of behavior or an act, aggressiveness is the inclination to intentionally behave in a harmful way. One may distinguish between situationally determined 'state aggressiveness' and the more profound 'trait aggressiveness,' that is, the inclination to behave aggressively in a variety of situations, a personality trait).

It is noteworthy that intentional harmful behavior may be carried out without any feeling of anger whatsoever, so to say, in cold blood. It is common practice to differentiate between *emotionally determined aggression*, originating from anger, and *instrumental aggression*. In the latter case, the aggressive behavior is only an instrument for the accomplishment of a specific goal. Feshbach (1964), who was the first to make the distinction between these two, used the label *hostile aggression* for the emotionally determined category, whereas Fraczek (1989) referred to it as *emotogenic aggression*. These two types of aggression do not necessarily exclude one another, and aggressive acts are, indeed, in many cases, a mixture of both. But, as

Lagerspetz (1984) suggested, the most common emotion of soldiers in war is not anger, but fear. Anger is not a prerequisite for aggression.

Accordingly, it is important to keep in mind that anger and aggression are conceptually different. This distinction is of special importance when we discuss whether violence is an inevitable outcome of conflict. Although anger may lead to aggressive behavior, it does not necessarily do so in every case. Anger is a natural, invigorating emotion, biologically geared from the limbic system, especially from the hypothalamus and the amygdala (Herbert, 1989); it is an emotion everyone has experienced and will experience, perhaps on a daily basis. The well-known cross-cultural study on nonverbal expressions of emotions by Ekman and Friesen (1971) suggest that the emotion of anger is similarly displayed in different cultures in an almost universal fashion. How we deal with our anger, however, whether we will utilize its force for aggressive or constructive purposes, is learned.

THE ORIGIN OF AGGRESSION

The history of psychology has witnessed three main theories about the origin of aggression: 1) instinct theory, claiming that aggression is an innate drive, 2) the frustration–aggression hypothesis, and 3) the social learning theory of aggression. I discuss their advantages—and problems—one by one.

Instinct Theory

The most well-known proponents of the theory (Sigmund Freud, and Konrad Lorenz) have written in German, and the so called instinct theory, accordingly, should rather be labeled the *Trieb*-theory, because there is a vast difference between the German *Trieb* and the English instinct (German: *Instinkt*). When Freud's work was translated into English, the translators wrongly chose the word instinct instead of drive, which would have been the etymologically correct equivalent. This mistake has caused enormous confusion within the field of psychology of motivation, and the damage cannot be undone.

The closest way to describe what *Trieb* really means is that it implies an innate (Latin *in natus*: present at birth) drive, functioning in accordance with the so called reservoir model. The drive is triggered by internal rather than external stimuli, examples being the hunger, thirst, and sexual drives. The internal pressure plays a more central and important role than external stimulation, and it determines the strength of the drive, although external stimuli may contribute. The reservoir model suggests that in the same way as a reservoir slowly fills with water, increasing the pressure in the tank, drive strength also continuously increases over time, if the need is not fulfilled. The longer the time since last fulfillment, the greater the pressure.

If the theory were correct and aggression really is a *Trieb* in the suggested sense, then humans would feel an ever-increasing drive toward being aggressive, also without external frustration. The pressure would sooner or later force each one of us to carry out acts of aggression.

Freud originally stated that there existed only one basic drive in humans, the libido or Eros, from which other motivation is derived (Freud, 1920/1940). Later, after experiencing the horrors of World War I, he came to the conclusion that there also must exist within man an opposite, destructive drive, which he labeled *Thanatos* after the Greek god of death (Freud, 1930/1948). The English-language literature has labeled this drive the death instinct.

Freud was involved in correspondence with Albert Einstein, in which they discussed whether this proposed destructive drive really existed, and if it did, would this drive explain why humans so easily get involved in warfare (Einstein & Freud, 1933/1972). Einstein denied the existence of Thanatos, but Freud held a more pessimistic view. According to him, humans have indeed an innate drive toward destruction, and therefore, warfare cannot be avoided.

A circumstance little known or at least seldom described in the literature is that Freud was of the opinion that the death *Trieb*, Thanatos, primarily is self-destructive, directed inwards toward people themselves, and that outward aggression only is a channeled derivation from it. Eros and Thanatos symbolized to him the ongoing struggle between the wish for life and the wish for death, within each individual.

Psychoanalysts after Freud found the idea of an innate self-destructive drive difficult to reconcile and Hartmann, Kris, and Loewenstein (1949) suggested that there is, indeed, a drive toward destruction within humans, but the primary direction of this drive is outward aggression, not inward self-destruction. This viewpoint has been commonly accepted within psychoanalysis ever since. That is, the notion of an innate aggressive drive stems, in a strict sense, from Hartmann, Kris, and Loewenstein, not from Freud.

Ethologist Konrad Lorenz also suggested the existence of an innate, aggressive drive in his book *On Aggression* (1966). The exact translation of the German original name *Das Sogenannte Böse* (Lorenz, 1963) would be "The So-Called Evil," revealing Lorenz's viewpoint that aggression is not necessarily bad. It is obvious from Lorenz's presentation that he thought this drive to function in accordance with the previously mentioned reservoir model. Montagu (1976, p. 92) describes it as a "hydraulic model." Lorenz (1966) suggested that the best way for humankind to avoid violence is to find vicarious outlets for this drive, such as the viewing of aggressive sports—a kind of catharsis hypothesis (Feschbach, 1955). The serious problem of violence among soccer fans—"soccer hooliganism"—is a real-life refutation of this hypothesis, as are the findings of increased aggressiveness after violent film viewing (e.g., Goranson, 1970; Huesmann & Eron, 1986).

The instinct, or *Trieb* theory, should thus be regarded as refuted: The need to aggress is not an innate drive comparable to hunger, thirst, or sex, functioning in accordance with the reservoir model. If that were the case, everyone of us would feel, without external stimuli or frustration, an ever-increasing drive to become aggressive, perhaps a need to go out and hit someone about once a week, in order to have the drive fulfilled. This is certainly not the case.

There is, however, at least one circumstance of biological nature that may have a strong tendency to lead men and women into interpersonal conflict: the natural emotion of anger, experienced when one is frustrated. The ability to get angry has probably served as an invigorating mediator enhancing the tendency towards aggressive behavior.

Subhuman primates show both territorial and hierarchical behavior (Mason & Mendoza, 1993). Humans display territorial and hierarchical patterns of behavior, too, but whether these reflect innate drives or learned behavior is a matter of dispute (Knauft, 1994). Aggression is often useful and sometimes even necessary in the defense of one's territory. In prehistoric times, individuals who were not able to learn aggressive behavior may not have been able to survive and propagate.

Mammals living in social groups have hierarchies or "pecking orders" (Tinbergen, 1951). The studies by Goodall (1991) on chimpanzees living in the wild present lively descriptions of violence between chimpanzees, as a consequence of hierarchical disputes. Hierarchical orders may be noted also among humans. These social hierarchies are to a great extent sex-specific, males forming hierarchies of their own, females of their own (Björkqvist & Niemelä, 1992). Individuals of the same sex also have a tendency to compete over mating partners. When the hierarchy within a group is known and accepted, there is little overt aggression: When the order is disputed, aggression increases.

The conclusion derived is that aggression is not an innate drive in itself, but it may serve as a means to fulfill other drives, whether innate or learned. Aggression may also have been necessary to attain vital resources in periods and geographical areas where resources have been scarce. The emotion of anger serves as an energizing power, rendering violent solutions of conflicts more likely than nonviolent ones (but still not inevitable).

The Frustration–Aggression Hypothesis

The second (chronologically speaking) influential theory about the origin of aggression is the frustration–aggression hypothesis, presented in the work *Frustration and Aggression* by Dollard, Doob, Miller, Mowrer, and Sears (1939). According to this hypothesis, the source of aggression is always a frustration of some kind, whether a recent, situationally relevant frustration or a previous one (e.g., stemming from the childhood). In the latter case, one could speak of bottled-up frustrations, leading to an aggressive personality, a tendency to behave aggressively in a variety of situations.

The original version of the hypothesis, as presented by Dollard, et al. (1939), stated that frustration always caused aggression, and that aggressive behavior would never appear without previous frustration (i.e., there is a direct, necessary connection between the two).

This argument has several problems. The first difficulty is epistemological: Inductive inferences about causal relationships, like the one between frustration and aggression, are impossible to prove (Popper, 1959).

Second, frustration may well lead to other forms of behavior than aggression, for instance depression. Or, frustrations may inspire the individual to constructive problem-solving. Frustration often has other consequences than aggression.

Only two years after the publication of *Frustration and Aggression*, one of its authors, Neal Miller wrote an article (1941) in which he revised his opinion. According to his revised version of the hypothesis, the connection between frustration and aggression is not necessary but likely. Frustrations may have consequences other than aggression.

Fraczek (1989) has suggested that frustrations are not a necessary prerequisite of aggression, and individuals may be aggressive out of pure habit. He coined the term *habitual aggression*, to describe this pattern of behavior. He did not, however, mention habitual aggression in connection with the frustration–aggression hypothesis, but the existence of habitual aggression would as such imply a refutation of the frustration-aggression hypothesis, even in its revised version (Miller, 1941).

It is, however, possible that aggression may be caused by frustration, but also by habituation; and, frustration likewise may have consequences other than aggression, as suggested by Miller (1941). In that case, a second, rather diluted, revision of the frustration–aggression hypothesis—including multiple causes of aggression, and multiple effects of frustration—might be considered acceptable. This version was presented in an article by Björkqvist (1990).

Figure 3.1 presents the frustration–aggression hypothesis, covering the modification suggested by Miller (1941), as well as the modification presented by Björkqvist (1990).

In 1989, I asked Neal Miller whether the interpretation of Miller's (1941) article just presented was correct. Miller's answer was "yes," but that he now also would

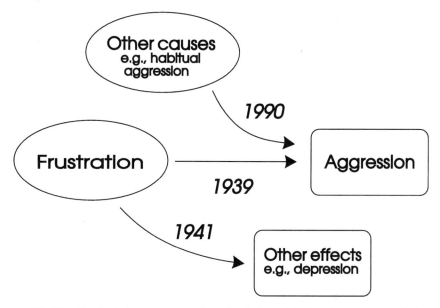

FIG. 3.1. The frustration–aggression hypothesis. The original version was suggested by Dollard et al. (1939), the suggested additional causal path in the revised version was suggested by Miller (1941), and the "diluted version" was suggested by Björkqvist (1990).

be ready to accept that other causes of aggression than previous frustration might exist (N. Miller, personal communication, June, 1989).

Social Learning Theory

The third main theory on the origin of aggressive behavior, social learning theory, dominated psychological thinking during the 1960s and 1970s, but it seems now to be giving way to more cognitively oriented hypotheses. According to it, aggression is not an innate drive, but it is learned. The main proponent of this theory has been Albert Bandura (e.g., Bandura, 1973). The theory has focused mainly on the issue of how aggression is learned, and especially on observational learning. The learning of aggression occurs by conditioning. The conditioning may be direct or vicarious; it is direct when the individual learns that aggression pays, by a kind of trial-and-error strategy, or through instrumental conditioning. Note that the principle of trial-and-error described by the associationist Thorndike (1906) is in fact identical with the principle of instrumental conditioning as proposed by the behaviorist Skinner (1938). Social learning theory suggests that learning from models should be regarded as *vicarious conditioning*, (i.e., learning occurs by watching models attaining their goals through aggressive means). If the model succeeds, it has the effect of a positive vicarious reinforcement on the viewer.

The concept of vicarious conditioning appeared the first time in the book *Social Learning and Imitation* by Miller and Dollard (1941), who attempted to explain all kinds of learning, also the difficult issue of learning from models, in behaviorist terms as kinds of conditioning.

I basically agree with Bandura's theory, the only serious criticism being that he was not able to distance himself enough from behaviorist learning theory. In the same vain as Miller and Dollard (1941), he presented imitation as if learning from models occurs only if the model is successful, ie., rewarded (Bandura, 1973). It is not certain whether he really was of this opinion, but this is the impression the reader gets.

I have suggested in other articles (Björkqvist & Österman, 1992; Björkqvist, in press) that the learning of aggression from models cannot be explained in terms of vicarious conditioning only. At a minimum, the following four factors are important: 1) the degree of similarity between the model situation and the actual situation, 2) the degree of identification between actor and model, 3) the success or failure of the model (vicarious conditioning), and 4) the amount of exposure to the model situation.

Heavy exposure to an aggressive model (e.g., a father) who is unsuccessful and does not reach his goals by aggressive behavior may as such be an influence strong enough to cause imitation, if the child has no other scripts of behavior (Schank & Abelson, 1977) to assimilate. Recent authors within aggression research (eg., Huesmann & Eron, 1986; Björkqvist & Österman, 1992; Björkqvist, in press) suggested that cognitive theory is better able to explain the learning of aggression than traditional, behaviorist-oriented social learning theory.

SCIENTISTS SPEAK OUT

The belief that aggression is an innate drive and that human beings are inevitably disposed to warfare is so widespread that scientists repeatedly have found it necessary to try to dispel and uproot this idea from humankind at large. As Bateson (1989, p. 47) put it: "The prophecy that, in time, humans are bound to fight each other is liable to be self-fulfilling."

Anthropologist Margaret Mead (1940) wrote, on the brink of the World War II, an essay titled "Warfare is Only an Invention, Not a Biological Necessity." Montagu (1976), in his book *The Nature of Human Aggression*, also spoke strongly against the belief that warfare is inevitable. *Aggression and War: Their Biological and Social Bases* by Groebel and Hinde (1989) is a tune in the same key.

Lagerspetz (1984) suggested that aggressiveness is not the most important factor leading to human warfare, as far as human nature and personality traits are concerned. Far more important are obedience and suggestibility; important prerequisites are also idealism, sociality, and, in fact, altruism, even to the point of sacrificing oneself for the benefit of others.

THE SEVILLE STATEMENT ON VIOLENCE

In May 1986, 20 scholars from different countries, representing a variety of disciplines—psychology, neuroscience, biology—gathered in Seville, Spain, in order to draft what has become known as the "Seville Statement on Violence." In it, they challenged a number of alleged biological findings that have been used as a justification for violence and warfare. In the opening paragraph, the scientists state that they consider it their responsibility to address these alleged findings because they have contributed to an unnecessary atmosphere of pessimism in our time.

Central paragraphs of the Seville Statement begin with the words: "It is scientifically incorrect ... ", and then continue with the presentation of arguments against, according to the signatories, common misconceptions in regard to humankind's alleged predisposition for warfare.

In the statement, it is pointed out that it is scientifically incorrect to claim that war or any other violent behavior is genetically programmed into our human nature. Genes provide only a developmental potential, which can be actualized in conjunction with the ecological and social environment. Except for rare pathologies, genes do not produce individuals predisposed to violence. It is also scientifically incorrect to claim that war is caused by "instinct," or any such motivation.

Likewise, it is according to the signatories, scientifically incorrect to claim that humans have a "violent brain," and that we have inherited a tendency to make war from our animal ancestors. Although fighting is widespread within the different animal species, only few cases of destructive intraspecies group violence have been reported.

A disturbing circumstance, of which the signatories perhaps were not aware at that time, is that Jane Goodall (1991), who spent years studying groups of chimpanzees living in the wild, reported warlike conflicts between groups of chimpanzees, including systematic ambush, ending in killings of members of the rival group.

Warfare is, according to the statement, a peculiar human phenomenon that does not occur in other animals. The fact that warfare is frequent among humans, the statement suggests, indicates that war is a product of human culture: Language, tools, and technology have made warfare possible. Warfare is, however, not inevitable; there are cultures that have not engaged in warfare, whereas other have had wars frequently. Further, there are cultures which have engaged in warfare frequently during certain periods, although they have been living in peace with their neighbors at other times (The Seville Statement on Violence, 1986/1989).

People used to justify slavery and sexist domination by claiming that they were biological and inevitable. These claims were found to be untrue, slavery was ended, and the world community is working to stop racial and sexist domination. In the same fashion, the signatories of the Seville Statement suggest, the world is now fooling itself by believing that war and violence cannot be ended because they constitute a part of our biological makeup.

The Seville Statement was endorsed by a number of nongovernmental organizations, among them United Nations' Educational, Scientific, and Cultural Organization (UNESCO). An impressive number of scientific organizations also have endorsed the statement, among them, the American Psychological Association (APA), the American Anthropological Association (AAA), and the International Society for Research on Aggression (ISRA). The initiative to draft the Seville Statement was, in fact, made by individual ISRA members.

The validity of the Seville Statement has not gone unquestioned, and, within ISRA, there were debates about whether the society should endorse the statement or not.

When the Council of Representatives of the APA voted to endorse the Seville Statement in 1987, the Board of Scientific Affairs emphasized that, in their opinion, it is not a question of a scientific statement on the issue of specific inherited behavioral traits. Rather, it is a social statement designed to eliminate unfounded stereotypic thinking on the inevitability of war.

CONCLUSIONS

In summary, aggression is not an innate drive (or instinct) per se, functioning in accordance with the reservoir model, like drives to satisfy hunger, thirst, and sex. Throughout human evolutionary history, interpersonal aggression may have had, however, a facilitating and mediating role in the fulfillment of other drives, whether these are innate or learned, such as territorial and hierarchical drives, and struggles for getting access to mating partners. Aggressive behavior has certainly played an evolutionary role for survival, especially when resources have been scarce. Although scripts of aggressive behavior are learned, not innate—nobody knows how to fight without training or modeling—it may be argued that the ability to learn aggression has been useful for survival, and natural selection for the ability to get angry when vital interests are threatened may have occurred.

The emotion of anger is often a predecessor of aggressive behavior, with anger serving as an invigorating factor, making aggressive behavior more likely. Anger should definitely not be regarded as unnatural; it is an emotion as natural as any other. Anger, however, does not have to lead to violence. There is not proof of the existence of any biological factor making violent solutions of conflicts inevitable. It is especially important to keep in mind that forms of aggressive behavior are learned, not innate. While every child has innate programs for laughing, crying, crawling, and walking, there is no innate programming for clenching fists, beating, kicking, or shooting others. These patterns or scripts of behavior are learned, especially by watching aggressive models. This learning is more likely to occur in a society acceptive of and, even more likely, in one glorifying aggression. If modern warfare is a consequence of human culture rather than of human nature, perhaps culture is also the best cure against it. As the Seville Statement put it, the species that invented warfare should also be capable of inventing peace. What is needed, above all, is a change in the general attitude towards violence.

REFERENCES

Bandura, A. (1973). *Aggression: A social learning analysis*. Englewood Cliffs, NJ: Prentice-Hall.

Baron, R. A. (1977). *Human Aggression*. New York: Plenum.

Bateson, P. (1989). Is aggression instinctive? In J. Groebel & R. Hinde (Eds.), *Aggression and war: Their biological and social bases* (pp. 35–47). New York: Cambridge University Press.

Björkqvist, K. (in press). Learning of aggression from models: From a social learning towards a cognitive theory of modeling. In S. Feshbach & J. Zagrodzka (Eds.), *Human aggression: Biological and social roots*. New York: Plenum.

Björkqvist, K. (1990). Om aggressionens ursprung: Teoretiska synpunkter [On the origin of aggression: Theoretical considerations]. *Nordisk psykologi, 42*, 233–249.

Björkqvist, K., Lindström, M., Pehrsson, M. (1989, June). *Four dimensions determining the attribution of aggression to behavior. Sex differences regarding the acceptance of instrumental and emotional aggression*. Presented at the 5th European Conference of the International Society of Research on Aggression, Szombathely, Hungary.

Björkqvist, K., & Niemelä, P. (1992). New trends in the study of female aggression. In K. Björkqvist & P. Niemelä (Eds.), *Of mice and women: Aspects of female aggression* (pp. 3–16). San Diego, CA: Academic Press.

Björkqvist, K., & Österman, K. (1992). Parental influence on children's self-estimated aggressiveness. *Aggressive Behavior, 18*, 411–423.

Buss, A. H. (1961). *The psychology of aggression*. New York: Wiley.

Coser, L. (1956). *The functions of social conflict*. New York: Free Press.

Dollard, J., Doob, L. W., Miller, N. E., Mowrer, O. H., & Sears, R. R. (1939). *Frustration and aggression*. New Haven, CT: Yale University Press.

Einstein, A. & Freud, S. (1972). *Warum Krieg?* [Why war?]. Zürich, Switzerland: Diogenes. (Original work published 1930)

Ekman, P. & Friesen, W. V. (1971). Constants across cultures in the face and emotion. *Journal of Personality and Social Psychology, 17*, 124–129.

Feschbach, S. (1955). The drive-reducing function of fantasy behavior. *Journal of Abnormal and Social Psychology, 50*, 3–12.

Feshbach, S. (1964). The function of aggression and the regulation of aggressive drive. *Psychological Review, 71*, 257–272.

Fraczek, A. (1989, November). Lecture at the Polish-Finnish Symposium on Aggression, Jablonna, Poland.

Freud, S. (1940). *Gesammelte Werke* [Collected works] (Vol. 13). London, England: Imago. (Original work published 1920)

Freud, S. (1948). *Gesammelte Werke* [Collected works] (Vol. 14). London: Imago. (Original work published 1930)

Goodall, J. (1991). *Through a window: 30 years with the chimpanzees of Gombe.* Boston, MA: Houghton Mifflin.

Goranson, R. E. (1970). Media violence and aggressive behavior: A review of experimental research. In L. Berkowitz (Ed.), *Advances in experimental social psychology* (pp. 1–31). New York: Academic.

Groebel, J., & Hinde, R. (Eds.). (1989). *Aggression and war: Their biological and social bases.* New York: Cambridge University Press.

Hartmann, H., Kris, E., & Loewenstein, R. (1949). Notes on the theory of aggression *Psychoanalytic Study of the Child, 3,* 9–36.

Herbert, J. (1989). The physiology of aggression. In J. Groebel & R. Hinde (Eds.), *Aggression and war: Their biological and social bases* (pp. 58–71). New York: Cambridge University Press.

Holm, O. (1985). *Four determinants of perceived aggression and a fourstep attribution model.* Umeå, Sweden: Umeå University Press.

Huesmann, R. L., & Eron, L. (Eds.). (1986). *Television and the aggressive child: A cross-national comparison.* Hillsdale, NJ: Lawrence Erlbaum Associates.

Knauft, B. M. (1994). Culture and cooperation in human evolution. In L. E. Sponsel & T. Gregor (Eds.), *The anthropology of peace and nonviolence* (pp. 37–67). Boulder, CO: Lynne-Rienner.

Lagerspetz, K. M. J. (1984). Psychology and its frontiers. In K. M. J. Lagerspetz & P. Niemi (Eds.), *Psychology in the 1990's* (pp. 23–44). Amsterdam: North-Holland.

Levi-Strauss, C. (1958). *Anthropologie structurale* [Structural Anthropology]. Paris: Plon.

Lorenz, K. (1963). *Das Sogenannte Böse. Zur Naturgeschichte der Aggression* [The so-called evil: On aggression]. Vienna, Austria: Borotha Schoeler-Verlag.

Lorenz, K. (1966). *On Aggression.* New York: Harcourt, Brace & World.

Lyons, D. M. (1993). Conflict as a constructive force in social life. In W. A. Mason & S. P. Mendoza (Eds.), *Primate social conflict* (pp. 387–408). Albany, NY: State University of New York Press.

Mason, W. A., & Mendoza, S. P. (Eds.). (1993). *Primate social conflict.* Albany, NY: State University of New York Press.

Mead, M. (1940). Warfare is only an invention—not a biological necessity. *Asia, XL,* 402–405.

Miller, N. E. (1941). The frustration–aggression hypothesis. *Psychological Review, 48,* 337–342.

Miller, N. E., & Dollard, J. (1941). *Social learning and imitation.* New Haven, CT: Yale University Press.

Montagu, A. (1976). *The nature of human aggression.* New York: Oxford University Press.

Parsons, T. (1951). *The social system.* New York: Free Press.

Popper, K. (1959). *The logic of scientific discoveries.* London, England: Hutchinson.

Rubin, J. Z., Pruitt, D. G., & Kim, S. H. (1994). *Social conflict: Escalation, stalemate, and settlement.* New York: McGraw-Hill.

Schank, R., & Abelson, R. (1977). *Scripts, plans, goals and understanding: an enquiry into human knowledge.* Hillsdale, NJ: Lawrence Erlbaum Associates.

Seville Statement on Violence. (1989). Reprinted in J. Groebel, J. Hinde, & R. Hinde (Eds.), *Aggression and war: Their biological and social bases* (pp. xxiii–xvi). New York: Cambridge University Press. (Original work published 1986)

Skinner, B. F. (1938). *The behavior of organisms.* New York: Appleton.

Smelser, N. (1962). *Theory of collective behavior.* New York: Free Press.

Thorndike, E. L. (1906). *Animal intelligence.* Psychological Monographs, 1, No. 8.

Tinbergen, N. (1951). *The study of instinct.* Oxford, England: Clarendon Press.

Part II

Cultural Influences
and Conflict Resolution

The chapters in this section appear together because of their common, explicit focus on culture and hence their direct relevance to the theme of "conflict resolution as a cultural phenomenon." The chapters also speak to a variety of more specific issues including: 1) community or group-centered versus individual-centered conflict resolution, 2) nonviolent world views, attitudes, and norms, 3) redundancy of social controls, and 4) informal conflict resolution mechanisms.

In his chapter, Galtung takes a macroscopic view of culture by comparing and contrasting the two major cultural views of East and West toward conflict. We see an example of how cultural world view drastically influences a person's culture of conflict—Ross' (1993, p. 19) term for "a society's relevant norms, practices, and institutions" related to conflict. Galtung invokes a knot–net metaphor for viewing conflict, calling to our attention the implications of focusing either on the knots (individuals) or the net (the social relationships). The tendency to perceive conflict resolution in terms of mending damaged or torn relationships—as opposed to the typically Western focus on individuals—is a point that other chapters in this section also illustrate. Black's (1993) discussion of four conflict styles—conciliatory, therapeutic, penal, and compensatory—is relevant and illustrated here. The focus on repairing the net of relationships, which Galtung notes is representative of the East, corresponds to Black's conciliatory style of conflict management, whereas the focus on the knot—the individual—which Galtung describes as representative of the West, can involve various elements of therapeutic, penal, and compensatory conflict styles. In the therapeutic style, the individual is "treated;" in the penal style, the individual is punished for committing some act; and in the compensatory style, the individual determined to be at fault pays restitution for damaged or stolen property.

As emphasized in the chapter by Fry and Fry, cultural attitudes, values, and world views can be harnessed either to augment or to reduce violence. One alternative to violence involves the psychocultural development and maintenance of nonviolent beliefs, attitudes, and values—an ethos—such as occurs among the Semai and the Toraja peoples. Chapters by Robarchek and Hollan consider psychocultural systems that promote the internalization by individuals of nonviolent means of dealing with conflict. Additionally, Robarchek emphasizes how interdependency and nurturance towards others are central aspects of the Semai world view. In terms of Black's (1993) four styles, the Semai culture of conflict clearly stresses the conciliatory style, and to some degree a therapeutic style, over penal and compensatory elements. The paramount importance of reaffirming relationships within the social group and of dealing with emotions during Semai conflict resolution are noted by Robarchek in his chapter and elsewhere when he enumerates the foci of the dispute resolution process as encompassing: "the resolution of the issues in a dispute, the restatement and reaffirmation of the paramount values of the group, the reintegration of the disputants into the group, the reduction of anxiety over dependency strivings, and the abreaction of emotion and consequent reduction of the threat and fear elicited by strong emotions" (Robarchek, 1979, p. 122). In his chapter, Robarchek extracts from his work with the Semai a more general social principle for reducing violence: View conflict as a group concern and employ community-focused, not just individual-focused, mechanisms to deal with it.

Like the Semai, the Toraja also attempt to minimize violence within their culture. Again, as for the Semai, we see examples of a community involved in conflict management. Hollan emphasizes that violence is prevented in Toraja culture through a redundant, or overlapping, set of social controls. He also explains that not all conflicts are resolved; rather, many conflicts are simply avoided. Both Black (1993) and Rubin et al. (1994) discuss avoidance as a major approach to conflict, and McCormick, in her chapter in Part III, also demonstrates how the Northern Irish practice a great deal of avoidance.

Cook takes a different slant from most chapters in this volume by emphasizing positive aspects of conflict among the native Margariteño Islanders of Venezuela. Conflict certainly can have positive aspects (cf. Rubin et al., 1994, pp. 7–8), and at the same time, as Nader (1991) points out, an emphasis on social harmony can mask social injustice and exploitation—forms of structural violence, to invoke Galtung's (1969) concept. Cook sees conflict and its resolution as a dynamic, ongoing process. Her analysis parallels both Robarchek's and Hollan's (and Galtung's for the East), because it emphasizes the importance of community, discussed by her in terms of social networks.

In cultures everywhere, much conflict finds expression through a multitude of informal channels and mechanisms, many of which are nonviolent and some of which effectively deal with disputes. In the final chapter in this section, Olson provides an interesting example of informal social control on the Islands of Tonga. Olson contrasts the peaceful kava-drinking circle with alcohol-drinking events in which fighting can erupt. Olson's description and analysis of the kava circle shows how elders and other community members reinforce community values and how through the use of humor and joking, inappropriate behavior can be criticized, sometimes resulting in the reduction of conflict or the solution of a social problem, as the wayward individual conforms to group expectations and community norms. In conclusion, all chapters in this section uniformly focus on culture. More specifically, chapters provide illustrations of the continuum of informal to formal conflict-resolution mechanisms, discuss the belief systems and social mechanisms, such as redundancy, through which nonviolence is fostered and maintained, and offer insights about conflict resolution as a community or group-centered process.

REFERENCES

Black, D. (1993). *The social structure of right and wrong.* San Diego: Academic.
Galtung, J. (1969). Violence, peace and peace research. *Journal of Peace Research, 6,* 167–191.
Nader, L. (1991). Harmony models and the construction of law. In Avruch, K., Black, P. W., & Scimecca, J. A. (Eds.), *Conflict resolution: Cross-cultural perspectives* (pp. 41–59). Westport, CT: Greenwood.
Robarchek, C. A. (1979). Conflict, emotion, and abreaction: Resolution of conflict among the Semai Senoi. *Ethos, 7,* 105–123.
Ross, M. H. (1993). *The management of conflict.* New Haven: Yale University Press.
Rubin, J. Z., Pruitt, D. G., & Kim, S. H. (1994). *Social conflict: Escalation, stalemate and settlement* (2nd ed.). New York: McGraw-Hill.

4

Conflict Life Cycles in Occident and Orient[1]

Johan Galtung
Universität i Tromsö

Johan Galtung has written extensively in the fields of peace research and conflict studies, and he has repeatedly advanced these fields with his innovative perspectives, reflected, for instance, in his formulation of the concepts of structural violence (1969) and cultural violence (1990). In this chapter, Galtung explores the world views or cosmologies of the Eastern and Western megacivilizations in relation to conflict. He points out how conflicts are individualized in the West and viewed socially–collectively in the East, and how different time cosmologies in the West and East result in contrasting views of conflict. The chapter concludes with a consideration of how these divergent cosmologies are related to international conflicts. As examples, Galtung applies the cosmological precepts of East and West to derive alternative interpretations of the Vietnam and Gulf wars.
—The Editors

DEEP CULTURE, TIME COSMOLOGY, AND SOCIAL COSMOLOGY

We have a conflict formation; we are looking for a conflict transformation: between these lie conflict dynamics, the life-cycle of a conflict. The term itself directs attention to such figures of thought as birth/genesis, maturation/dynamics, death/resolution or dissolution. But, these terms may also be highly misleading, or at least culturally biased.

The deep culture or cosmology[2] of a civilization obviously conditions not only the perception of conflict life cycles but also the actual behavior in conflict, with a major

---

[1]Reprinted by permission of Sage Publications Ltd. from J. Galtung, *Peace by Peaceful Means*, Copyright 1996 by Sage Publications, Ltd.

[2]By this is meant the collectively shared but usually unstated, to the point of being subconsciously held, assumptions in a culture about what is natural and normal; it represents how things simply *are*.

bearing on conflict transformation. The level of knowledge of this factor, by participants or outsiders, will also affect the outcome. That level is not necessarily higher among insiders than among outsiders to the civilization, because cosmology by definition is rooted in the collective subconscious, not in the individual conscious. For any student of human conflict, this type of knowledge is essential.[3]

Two civilizations—the hard Occident and the Buddhist civilizations—are explored for their image of conflict life cycles. Christianity (with Judaism and Islam) and Buddhism are actually mega-civilizations defining Occident and Orient respectively. Ideas about how these basic religions view conflict should be a useful guide (cf. Conze, 1959; Galtung, 1993).

Using the conceptualization of time as a point of departure, some insights come readily. If Christian time is bounded with a beginning (genesis) and an end (apocalypsis-catharsis), then we would also expect the view of a conflict life cycle to be encased by finite time. A conflict would be seen as having a clear beginning, a birth or genesis, and a clear ending after a crisis, as an apolcalypsis or catharsis. The cosmology will impose itself, demanding corresponding behavior and attitudes.

By contrast, Buddhist time is infinite. For all practical purposes there is no beginning and no end, although there is the transcendence of *nirvana*, a transformation to other unknown and unknowable types of existence. Conflict would be seen as interminable, with no beginning and no end, flowing from eternity to eternity like an infinite river, possibly with a delta somewhere infinitely far out where the energies accumulated in that river pour into the ocean and take on other forms. The conflict is transformed, preferably to a higher (i.e., less violent) level, but not extinguished.[4] Time cosmology will be imposed on the conceptualization of conflict, demanding this image of the process, expecting actors and commentators to feel, behave, talk, and write accordingly, imposing neither beginning nor end.

Then, add to time cosmology an element of social cosmology: individual versus collective/social. Using the knot–net metaphor (cf. Panikkar, 1982); which is more real, the knots or the net? To the Christian soul, being individual, social reality will have to be conceived as comprised of individual knots and not of social nets. For Mahayana Buddhism, individual connectedness is what is reality; although separable and eternal, individual souls are an illusion. For Buddhism, nets are real; knots are not.

Again, this will affect the way conflict is viewed. Whereas Christianity would individualize conflicts, even to the point of seeing conflict as originating in one

---

[3] Thus, when two persons in conflict meet to negotiate, we are dealing with (at least) four levels: 1) the *persona*, the masks they show each other; 2) the consciously held but not necessarily revealed *strategies*; 3) the *individual subconscious* of both parties; and 4) the *collective subconscious*, which may or may not be similar depending on whether they come from the same culture. A conflict theory based on only levels one and two is rather naive.

[4] An example: In multinational states, conflicts between national groups do not disappear with federation, but some separation and autonomy *may* facilitate less violent approaches, with the center of the federation as ultimate decision maker. However, that decision making will often be quite vertical, meaning that it could also be an exercise in structural violence. Consequently, confederation, with a very weak center, might be a transformation away from structural conflict, meaning to a higher level. Needless to say, this is a delicate balance.

individual, who, through the conflict, may affect the lives of Others, Buddhism would see conflict as arising within a collectivity of significant Others. This collectivity does not necessarily have to be synchronic. The net is what matters, sidewards and diachronically backwards and forwards, relating to sentient life in present, past, and future. Reality is unbounded in social space as well as in time.

Christianity will not deny individual connectedness in the sense that the acts of one person can affect the life of Others. But the ethical unit of account is the individual endowed with the capacity to will—hence not merely behaving, but acting. An individual is an actor. For Buddhism the ethical unit of account is collective, denying neither individual existence nor capacity to will. But responsibility does not lie with individuals alone.

To return to the river metaphor: The Buddhist conflict river flows from eternity to eternity, now quick, now slow, with eddies curling back on themselves, sometimes in cycles, sometimes in giant waterfalls, sometimes uphill, sometimes down, with tributaries and forking paths. It is analogous to *samsara*, the birth–rebirth cycle. What could be a corresponding Christian water metaphor? Would an appropriate analogy be a geyser, arising out of troubled waters underneath, rising to a climax, possibly released as evaporation, dwindling, disappearing, or spreading, moving others to a cataclysm?

Individualized conflict in finite time versus collectivized conflict in infinite time are very different points of departure for conflict theory and conflict praxis. The first image lends itself epistemologically to Occidental atomism, nomothetic (generalizing) conflictology, with destructive theory formation, possibly based on a typology of actors. The second image lends itself to the dialectics of Oriental holism with ideographic conflictology, there being one connected humankind, or lifekind.

CHRISTIAN AND BUDDHIST TIME
AND CONFLICT COSMOLOGY

With this general conceptualization we can now turn to more concrete images of conflict transformation. Both civilizations have strong views on disharmony. Both of them see harmony as coming to the person who follows the precepts, be they the Ten Commandments of Christianity or the Noble Eight-Fold Path in Buddhism.[5] Conflicts (disharmony) come to the person who strays away from the Law—the Law of God in Christianity and the Law of *karma* in Buddhism. God is omnipresent, omniscient, and omnipotent, caused by nothing but Himself and holding individuals accountable. Likewise, the *karma* is an omnipresent dialectic between an ethical determinism, making human beings accountable to themselves (whatever you say and do sooner or later comes back to you), and allowing the possibility of improving one's *karma* through acts of volition, the individual will.

The Law comes to human beings by being received, not only in the sense of being heard and understood, but in the sense of being internalized as binding. What Moses and the Christ did for Judeo-Christianity, the Buddha did for Buddhism; the Law

---

[5]This is comprised of right understanding, right thought, right speech, right action, right livelihood, right effort, right mindfulness, right concentration.

being above all of them, applying also to them. What they both did was to spell out the Law, as articles of faith and commandments, 3 and 10 in Christianity (and 5 in the pillars of Islam); 4 and 8 in Buddhism. With these the moral base or benchmark has been laid. Infraction leads to disharmony. Thereby conflicts arise, possibly with others, for sure with the Law, and thus with themselves. In Christianity, conflicts arise with God and Christ; in Buddhism both individual and shared bad *karma* are created.

Any infraction will be detected. The moral value of an act is registered by an omniscient God; its merit/demerit will be deposited in the omnipresent *karma*. God adjudicates, as salvation or damnation. The *karma* improves or deteriorates. What then?

From this point on, similarities between the two traditions break down, and two different flowcharts must be established. There are similarities, but also conspicuous dissimilarities. Thus, there is similarity between the Christian wish to improve one's standing with God if a sin has been committed and the Buddhist wish to improve the *karma* after demeritorious acts. There is similarity in the view that the individual alone may be incapable and needs help from God (Christianity) or from Others (Buddhism), but also this in itself already represents dissimilarity between the approaches, with profound bearing on how conflict life cycles are conceptualized.

The Christian process is a complex chain of sin, submission to God, confession of the sin committed, repentance, penitence, atonement, and possible forgiveness (by God). The final decision rests with God, and Him alone; His will is the Law; He alone decides by an act of grace between salvation and damnation.

Basic to this approach is its pervasive verticality. The sin committed against God's Law and His Son: "Inasmuch as ye have done it unto one of the least of my brethren, ye have done it unto me" (Matthew 25:40; also see Matthew 25:45). One's relation to God has to be repaired, whereas the victim is secondary. The moral content of an act lies in its relation to God, because His is the Law. With that relation restored, the sin is canceled and the person starts with a clean slate. The person is, in a religious sense, born again.

Christianity distinguishes between *peccatum* and *peccator*, the sin and the sinner, condemning the former, and offering a way out for the latter. This assures finiteness in time and individualization in space. The conflict process starts with an act of sin by a fallible human actor and ends with an act of grace by the infallible God. All of the focus is on the sinner, the one who infracted the Law; the rest is context. The stage is then set for a possible repetition of the sequence, or no more sin, or for the final, the mortal sin, the point of no return.

The Buddhist process introduces a very different sequence. If there is no God, no heaven, no hell, no eternal salvation or damnation, no eternal and separable soul, then any demerit is not relative to God nor to oneself, but to the net of significant Others. Only in that community can the demerit be canceled. One way would be through action dialogue, undoing the evil and restoring relationships through merits. Another would start with a verbal dialogue, identifying why and how that bad collective *karma* developed and how it can be improved toward ever higher levels; then going ahead and doing this.

Basic to this paradigm is its pervasive horizontality. The demerit of an act lies in what it does to other forms of sentient life. The act cannot be undone, but that relation can be changed. The significant Others do not have to be alive as identifiable individuals today; the relation of demerit may also be to life already dead or not yet (re)born. In other words, there is no way of individualizing the relation. The relation, bad or god, is in the collectivity, and there it will remain, from eternity and to eternity. A nonfinite time perspective is guaranteed through responsibility, not only for acts committed in the past, but for all acts of merit and demerit affecting the *karma*, regardless of when and where. Only by assuming full responsibility for the merits and demerits of that collectivity is the illusion of individual separateness and permanence eliminated.

Karma is a very holistic concept transcending individual life spans in time and space. At the same time it is also very dialectic, the demerit introducing a contradiction in *karma* to be superseded through dialogues with words and action; through meritorious acts. If this is the general way of viewing the human condition, then it makes little sense to separate conflicts from each other, bracketing them in time and space. To label one part of this *holon* guilty and the other not guilty makes no more sense than to label the right hand guilty and left hand not guilty in a crime of two-handed strangulation. As merit and demerit is shared, its distribution on individuals becomes a metaphysical question. Any merit is (partly) due to inspiration from significant Others anyhow; so is any demerit, because they should have prevented the individual from straying. What is not metaphysical is the willingness to do something about it, each part of the *holon* making contributions to navigate the collective self, with parts dying and being reborn, through the complex topology of the Buddhist River of Life.

Christianity offers eternal life, in salvation or damnation, but in practice it is concerned with finite life between biological birth and death. Buddhism offers no *resurrection in carnis*; this biological life stops with the death of the body. In practice however, it conceives of life as an eternal flow of energy from eternity to eternity, lived with less suffering and more bliss to Self and Others, the better the interconnectedness sidewards, backwards, and forwards. For the Christian there is no appeal because there is no second life; the split second of one's existence here on earth determines eternity. For the Buddhist, eternity itself is the time perspective for improving the *karma*, life being an interconnected chain of opportunities to do so. Nothing is final; there are always opportunities to improve the *karma*.

Comparing the two views that are presented here in somewhat overdrawn fashion, one cannot help feeling that whereas Christianity makes guilt too dichotomous, Buddhism draws no line, preferring the joint search for causes of bad *karma*. Where Christianity is too asymmetric, Buddhism is too symmetric. And whereas Christianity is cruel in its insistence that this highly finite life determines eternal afterlife, Buddhism is too gentle in giving us unlimited time to improve our *karma*. Along both dimensions, moderated positions could be designed, and an eclectic compromise might be preferable. But we are not free to design our civilizations. The fact is that these two perspectives on conflict life cycles exist: one as an infinite number of finite life cycles between birth, as an individual act of sin, and redemption, through a divine act of grace, and the other as a finite number of infinite life cycles, starting nowhere and anywhere, with ups and downs, ultimately ending in the ever-flowing ocean of eternity.

SECULAR VERSIONS
OF CHRISTIAN AND BUDDHIST PERSPECTIVES

So much for Christian and Buddhist perspectives, both religious in the sense of relinking with *that out there*, with God, or with *karma*. One of them demands that we bend to the will of God, the other that we bend *karma* to our desire for enlightenment (*sartori*). But how many, and who, believe in the reality of the Law of God and the Law of *karma* today? There are processes of secularization in the Christian and Buddhist civilizations, and the processes sap both perspectives of much of their content. Nevertheless, in line with general cosmology theory, we would expect most of the form of these perspectives, such finite-atomistic versus infinite-holistic, to survive content variation.

The Occidental secular perspective is known as the Western legal tradition, meaning that which the Roman, German, and English legal traditions have in common. Transcendental references are found, but they are ritualistic. Basically, the ultimate sources of Law are in the successors to God, as the Prime Mover, meaning the constituent legal act by King or Assembly, self-constituted as their own causes and sources for domestic law, and the United Nations for international law. Recipients are successor Kings, Assemblies, General Assemblies, and producers of lesser laws, defining more or less explicitly the prescribed, the permitted, and the proscribed. An act detected and registered as proscribed is a transgression; the actor is then adjudicated in accordance with the laws of due process. The verdict remains equally dichotomous: guilty or not guilty. Then comes a sentence, today in terms of money (fines) or time (prison), which may be adjusted to make the guilty–not guilty dichotomy less sharp. Heavy punishment may be alleviated through an act of grace. Afterward the slate is clean again, in theory, at least after a period of probation.

The verticality is still there. The sin, now called a *crime* is seen as committed upwards, against King-State-People. The victim recedes into oblivion. Penitence, now called *punishment*, is only external, inflicted from the outside to the outside of the evil-doer—to the purse or the body. For a time, the complex spiritual process induced by Christian teachings was kept alive inside prisons; now it is for all practical purposes defunct. Now, convicted criminals pay and do time. Only recently has there been a trend to sentence law-breakers to work for the community and to compensate the victim.

We would expect something similar in the secularized versions of Buddhism, only with less emphasis on the written law and the "whodunit" than in the West, and with more emphasis on some type of reconciliation. But rather than the search for causes by going into oneself, meditating on the wrong done, and then a patient dialogue with the offended Other, this process is perhaps also increasingly left to a third party—in Japan often to the proverbial police in the police "box." The task of verbalization, and the search for diagnosis, prognosis, and therapy, is left to others who then become conflict processors. Lay or professional, there is less self-reliance and as a consequence less maturation in the conflict parties themselves, nor is there improvement of their *karma*, only a smoothing of relations. The goal is outer, not inner change. The metaphysical, spiritual underpinning of Buddhist conflict processes is waning.

The basic conceptual structure may still remain at the deeper level, as less of a tendency to see conflict as starting with one act and ending with another, and less of a tendency to see conflict as rooted in one actor and not in a relationship. But the conflict conceptualization is becoming verticalized, and not only in Japan, with its long feudal tradition opposed to the ideal "temple and the tank" (village temple and well, for soothing the soul and body) autonomous village of classical Buddhism. As a consequence we would expect law, lawyers, and litigation to be on the increase in the Buddhist part of the world as the Buddhist perspective becomes secularized.

Is there a middle way, a position between the spiritualism of the past—often very obscurantist—and contemporary conflict transformation processes, often steered by cynical outsiders who demand no inner, personal effort at all, only, possibly, a consultation fee? In the West there is the gentler Christianity of a softer Occident; in the Orient a possible revival of Buddhist patterns of conflict processing. Buddhist spiritualism may also prove more acceptable to Westerners whose God has died than to a Christianity with a God very much alive to Easterners.

SOME IMPLICATIONS AT THE INTERNATIONAL LEVEL

To explore international-level implications of how conflicts are conceptualized, let us compare the Vietnam War and the Gulf War, both with the United States as a major party. There was a major difference between the two wars. In the Vietnam War, the U.S. conviction that North Vietnam was guilty of some crime progressively eroded, and the United States was more inclined to doubt its own righteousness. By contrast, in the Gulf War the United States and Bush were convinced of their own righteousness and the guilt of Iraq and Hussein. As possibly the most Christian country in the world, the United States would be expected to conceive of both wars as beginning with sins—transgressions by the other side. Whether top-level decision makers really believe this matters less, as long as the conflict discourse takes place within that mind set. "Casting the first stone" is a metaphor that captures the Christian approach, usually not tempered by the warning against doing so in a glass house. "You may hit yourself," as a Buddhist would be quick to point out, "and we are both parts of the web of life; you in me, I in you."

As a background to the comparison, let us take a brief glance at two cases from World War II made to fit the Western script: United States–Japan and United States–Germany. There were transgressions defining the beginning: Pearl Harbor on December 7, 1941 and the attack on Poland on September 1, 1939. There were acts defining the end: the capitulation signed in Rheims on May 8, 1945 and in

Tokyo Bay on September 2, 1945. With the evil acts so well defined, identifying the authors of those evil acts was an easy matter.

Verticality was imposed on the situation, not only through capitulation and surrender of arms as obvious acts of submission, but through tribunals (the Nürnberg and the Far East Tribunals being the most famous) extracting something close to confessions, individualizing the conflict with the concept of war criminals who committed crimes against humanity. The structure of occupier–occupied served to institutionalize the verticality. Reparations were only one form of punishment, another being marginalization from the world by denying United Nations membership.

Because the crimes of the Axis Powers were unspeakable, proof of basic change was called for afterward. The opportunity came with the Berlin blockade of 1948–1949 and the Korean War of 1950–1953, eagerly seized upon by the two occupied countries to prove that they had indeed embraced the cause of the occupiers, particularly the United States—not difficult because their anti-Communist credentials were impeccable. The Allies, particularly the United States, used this occasion to exercise the divine privilege of grace, bestowing peace on them (but no formal peace treaty with Germany), restoring them to international normalcy (1951 for Japan, 1954 for Germany, 1955 for Austria). General acceptance of the process, no doubt derived from following the Western script so well, with the Japanese quickly learning what to do.

The Vietnam War witnessed none of this. The United States did not win, so there could be no sequence initiated by Vietnamese acts of submission. However, the Vietnamese did not win either, so they could not extract submissiveness, even capitulation from the United States to be followed by Washington tribunals for premeditated crimes against humanity committed by such U.S. war-makers as Lyndon Johnson, Robert McNamara, Richard Nixon, and Henry Kissinger.

There is still a general uncertainty as to how to interpret the post-Vietnam War situation. Given the two scripts and the role of Buddhism as part of the Vietnamese *san fa* (three teachings, with Confucianism and nationalism), what is to be anticipated?

We would expect the Vietnamese to be less concerned with confessions of guilt as long as the other side does not insist on being nonguilty and very much concerned with entering a dialogue to explore what went wrong and how relations could be improved. No doubt a dialogue of that kind would be conducted in secular terms by the Vietnamese, as by the other three Mahayana Buddhist countries (China, Korea, and Japan), the Buddhist aspect being in the deep structure, not the surface. There may be reference to inscrutable Oriental wisdom—inscrutable only to those who fail to scrutinize. All this would be done with no expression of rancor if the rule herein described is adhered to, with smiles (although it should be remembered that the semantics, syntax, and pragmatics of smiles in the Orient are non-Western). The basic ingredients remain the same: much inner dialogue (also known as meditation) within and much outer dialogue between.

How does this look to the U.S. side? First, the United States might see pleas for dialogues as signs of economic despair, but refuse to engage in them lest these be used for propaganda purposes, fearing harsh words. The absence of a you-are-guilty finger-pointing at the United States would, in a dichotomous zero-sum discourse, be seen as a sign that the Vietnamese have turned around, no longer seeing the United States as guilty and themselves as not guilty. The thousands of refugees would be seen as confirming the shortcomings in socialist Vietnam. From this it does not follow that the United States was right, but neither does it follow that the Vietnamese were right. The subtle smiles may be taken as signs of forgiveness for possible U.S. wrongs. In essence, each party interprets the same phenomenon within its own framework, remaining a far apart as ever.

The Gulf War was less ambiguous, at least so far. There was a clear beginning in the act of aggression committed when Iraq occupied Kuwait on August 2, 1990. The ideal end would have been not only withdrawal from Kuwait and capitulation by some Iraqi military forces, but capitulation of the Ba'ath regime with a Baghdad tribunal for Saddam Hussein and some others, for crimes against humanity, followed by the rest of the Germany–Japan routine. A sense of completion of the Christian conflict life cycle *Gestalt* would have ensued. The book could be closed. The temptation must have been enormous.

Let us then introduce a Buddhist perspective on the Gulf conflict. In that perspective, August 2, 1990 and January 17, 1991 are still there; so are the twelve Security Council resolutions in general and Resolution 678 in particular (with its "with all necessary means" language). But the conflict formation now extends sideward, backward, and forward, relating to other actors and parties, to past history and future consequences—a much more complex view than the simplicity of international law applied (correctly) to the Iraqi transgression. That backward perspective has also been used by Germany (Versailles as act of aggression) and Japan (Western economic sanctions as acts of aggression), but in an exculpatory, nonholistic manner, picking what served their own guilt budget.

The closest Western approximation to Buddhist conflict transformation would be a multilateral conference with all system parties around the table, with all issues on the table, and with time to articulate and process the conflicts in the system, preceded by meditation, and without preconditions. Holistic and dialectic, mature, but very rarely practiced during conflict.

REFERENCES

Conze, E. (1959). *Buddhist scriptures*. London: Penguin.
Galtung, J. (1993). *Buddhism: A quest for unity and peace.* Colombo: Sarvodaya Publishing Services.
Galtung, J. (1969). Violence, peace, and peace research. *Journal of Peace Research*, 6, 167–191.
Galtung, J. (1990). Cultural violence. *Journal of Peace Research*, 27, 291–305.
Panikkar, R. (1982). La notion des droits de l'homme, est-elle un concept occidental? [Is the concept of human rights a Western concept?] *Diogenes, 120,* 87–115.

5

A Community of Interests: Semai Conflict Resolution

Clayton A. Robarchek
Wichita State University

In this chapter, Robarchek describes the becharaa', a conflict-resolution process used by the Semai Senoi people of Malaysia. The Semai are one of the most nonviolent cultures in existence. The author first provides a description of the Semai world view, noting the key values of nurturance, dependency, and nonviolence. An analysis is then presented of how the community headman, disputants accompanied by their kin, and any other interested community members meet to resolve conflicts through the becharaa' process, and how this procedure deals with both emotional and social-relational aspects of conflict. Robarchek concludes by considering implications for reducing violence in modern, complex societies. He suggests that attempts could be made to restore the psychological salience of local communities, which support the development of individual identities, in order to promote prosocial behavior among members, via enhancing meaningful reference groups (relationships) and communicating shared prosocial expectations of behavior.

—The Editors

My objective is to describe and analyze a process of conflict-resolution utilized by a group of Malaysian Aborigines, the Semai Senoi, one of the least violent societies known to anthropology. I also explore implications that are possibly relevant to our own urban societies. As we shall see, the Semai process is closely tied to cultural assumptions and values and to the structure and content of social relations. It is unlikely, therefore, that this process simply could be transplanted to a complex urban industrial society such as our own. It does not necessarily follow, however, that the Semai approach to conflict is merely an interesting but ultimately irrelevant bit of ethnographic trivia. To the contrary, understanding how and why this process works in Semai society may illuminate some of the reasons why conflict so often eventuates in violence in our own society.

The chapter is based on ethnographic research conducted by my wife and myself among the Semai in 1973–1974 and 1979–1980. The analysis is also informed, at least implicitly, by research that we conducted in 1987 and 1992–1993 among the Waorani of Ecuadorian Amazonia. That society was, until quite recently, the most violent known to anthropology, with a homicide rate of more than 60%. Although this paper does not explicitly deal with the Waorani case, the analysis is informed by the inevitable comparisons and contrasts that highlighted the striking differences between these two societies.

ETHNOGRAPHIC OVERVIEW

There are around 15,000 Semai living in small hamlets scattered along the deeply dissected and heavily forested mountainous spine of the Malay Peninsula. They and a number of smaller groups, all linguistically related, are the aboriginal occupants of the peninsula, probably descended from the Hoabihnian peoples who populated mainland Southeast Asia some 12,000 years ago. In the past two millennia, they have been displaced by technologically more advanced peoples, especially Malays from Sumatra and, like many of their cultural and linguistic relatives throughout the region, they are now largely confined to the mountainous interior, which is largely unsuitable for padi rice agriculture.

Each band is a politically autonomous unit occupying a traditional territory, usually a small river valley or a segment of a larger one. Traditionally, residence groups seldom numbered more than 100. Social organization is highly egalitarian. Each band has a headman, usually (but not always) a member of the kindred that claims descent from a founding resident of the band territory. The headman is the classic "first among equals," who exercises some moral authority as spokesman for the group but who wields no institutional power beyond his own powers of persuasion. The society is gender-egalitarian as well. The ideal social personalities of men and women are essentially the same, and there is no rigid gender role dichotomy. Although most headmen are men, a few are women.

The traditional subsistence economy was based on swidden gardening, hunting, fishing and gathering. The rainforest soils are low in fertility and new areas of forest must be felled each year for gardens. When all the arable land in the vicinity of a settlement has been exhausted, the band moves to a new location, leaving the previous gardens to be reclaimed by the forest. After a fallow period of 30 to 40 years, the process can be repeated. This was the system that was in operation during our first fieldwork in the early 1970s, but it is now rapidly being transformed, largely as a consequence of government policies, into a peasant economy based on commodity production and wage labor.

THE CULTURAL CONSTRUCTION OF SEMAI REALITY

Every cultural system is in part a culturally constructed reality. What follows is a very brief synopsis of Semai world view and values, of Semai experiential reality as it is culturally constituted. (Methodological issues associated with the derivation of such abstractions have been discussed at length elsewhere, e.g., Robarchek, 1986, and will not be addressed here).

The Semai look at the world as a hostile and dangerous place filled with innumerable dangers, human and nonhuman, known and unknown, nearly all of which are entirely beyond human control. There is a fundamental division in the human world into *hii'* and *mai*: we and they, kin and nonkin, band members and outsiders. Within the first of each pair of categories, one finds nurturance and security; among the second, danger and death.

This conception of the human world is mirrored in the nonmaterial world in the dichotomy of *gunik* and *mara'*. *Gunik* are protective "spirit" kin, who can be called upon to aid their human kin in resisting the attacks of *mara'*, the malevolent "spirits" associated with various aspects of the natural world—wind, thunder, waterfalls, hilltops, trees, boulders, and so on. *Mara'* besiege the human community, attacking human beings because it is their nature to do so, bringing injury, illness and death. People must be constantly on guard to avoid precipitating attacks by these forces, and nearly every activity, from gardening to children's play, is hedged with taboos and rituals to aid in warding off these ubiquitous dangers.

The only real defense, however, is provided by the community and its *gunik*, "spirits" who were once *mara'* but who have come to humans in dreams and asked to join the dreamer's family. Henceforth, the *gunik* calls the dreamer "mother" or "father" and is called "child" by its new parent, "sibling" by his or her other children, and so on, ramifying throughout the kindred. A *gunik* teaches its parent a song, and this song can be sung at a three-night "sing" to summon the spirit to aid its human kin in warding off or curing the attack of malevolent *mara'*.

THE STRUCTURE AND CONTENT OF SOCIAL RELATIONS

In such a world, surrounded by implacable malevolence and danger, nurturance and security are to be found only within the company of kindred and community. In time of trouble, they will be called upon for support and assistance; in time of sickness, they will summon their spirit kin to drive away the attacking mara'. Without them, individual survival is impossible, and anything that calls into question or threatens to disrupt these relations of dependence and nurturance within the community is intensely threatening to individuals.

This is reflected in the two core values of nurturance (the giving of material or emotional support) and affiliation (the maintenance of harmonious interpersonal relations). Good and bad are defined primarily in terms of behaviors associated with these values, with goodness defined positively in terms of nurturance (helping, giving, sharing, feeding, and so on) and badness in terms of behaviors disruptive of affiliation (getting angry, quarreling, and fighting). Good people are generous and nurturant; bad people are aggressive and violent. These values come to constitute central components of a Semai ego ideal, and individuals are judged against these standards by their neighbors and by themselves. Conflict, then, is intensely threatening because it calls into question both individual self-image and the integrity of the group, the only refuge in an otherwise hostile world.

In response to an oral sentence-completion test item: "more than anything else, he/she is afraid of . . . ," the most common response—more common than "*mara*'," "tigers," and "death" combined—was "a conflict." People go to great lengths to avoid conflict and will usually tolerate annoyances and sacrifice personal interests rather than precipitate an open confrontation.

THE *BECHARAA'*: A FORMALIZED CONFLICT-RESOLUTION PROCESS

Occasionally, however, feelings are too intense or issues too important or intractable, and conflict cannot be avoided. In such cases, it is the responsibility of anyone in the community who is aware of the conflict to bring it to the attention of the headman, who will convene a *becharaa'*, a formal assembly to resolve the dispute. From its onset, a dispute between individuals thus becomes the concern and responsibility of the entire community.

The headman summons the principals and their kindreds for a full debate and discussion of the matter. Although kindreds are obligated to support their members in disputes, this does not divide and polarize the community. Descent is bilateral and band endogamy is common; thus the opposing kindreds virtually always overlap to a significant degree. This means that some people will be members of both kindreds, and that members of one kindred will have members of *their* kindreds in the other group. A person who embroils himself in a dispute thus strains relations not only with his opponent's kin, but with his own as well, and he can expect to be reprimanded by them if he is found to have been at fault in any way.

The *becharaa'* usually begins in the late afternoon. The principals and their kindreds, along with interested spectators, assemble at the headman's house where they sit discussing recent events, hunting, gardening—anything but the dispute that has brought them together. At some point, an elder member of one of the kindreds begins a long monologue in which he reaffirms the interdependence of the community and the dependence of each upon the others for his or her very survival. He recalls past incidents of aid given and received, and he stresses the need for maintaining unity and harmony within the community. Several others follow with similar declamations, all emphasizing that the current conflict is an aberration, and that it must be resolved so that the natural state of amity can be restored.

At some point, one of the principals begins to state his case. Attempting to put his own actions in the best possible light, he explains why he acted as he did and why his opponents' actions were wrong. He may offer several different, even contradictory, explanations for his actions. The other principal then states his case. He may address the points raised by his adversary, or he may ignore them completely and take an entirely different tack. At times, both parties may be speaking simultaneously, not arguing directly, but each directing his remarks to the assembly.

One by one, relatives of the principals argue their kinsmen's cases, often questioning them to bring out particular points. Other interested parties may also offer their observations and opinions. Although the issues at stake may be of vital concern—infidelity, divorce, land claims, fruit tree ownership, and so on—little anger or other emotion is displayed. The emphasis is on the clarity, forcefulness and persuasiveness of the arguments, and a good debater is respected and admired.

This discussion may go on for several hours or, more likely, continuously for several days and nights. The headman's household provides food, and participants catch a few hours sleep on the floor from time to time, then arise to rejoin the discussion. All the events leading up to the conflict are examined and reexamined from every conceivable perspective in a kind of marathon encounter group. Every possible explanation is offered, every imaginable motive introduced, every conceivable mitigating circumstance examined. Unresolved offenses and slights going back many years may be dredged up and reexamined.

In the course of all this, arguments are rebutted and assertions are answered, although not systematically, until finally a point is reached where there is simply nothing left to say. In fact, a proper *becharaa'* cannot end until no one has anything left to say. When that point is reached at last, the headman is called forward to deliver his judgment. Although his contribution is presented as a judgment, he in fact gives voice to the implicit consensus that has emerged during the discussion. After all the charges and countercharges have been examined, there remains a residue of indefensible acts, which have, by this time, been recognized and thoroughly discussed. The headman lectures one or both parties on their guilt in the matter, instructs them in proper behavior—in the courses of action that they should have pursued—and directs them not to repeat these offenses or to ever raise this dispute again. He may also assess a fine or impose damages (both usually small sums) against either or both.

The elders of each of the two kindreds then lecture their own kinsman in the same vein and, in long monologues, they and the headman again reaffirm the interdependence of the community and the necessity of maintaining unity and harmony within it. With that, the affair is deemed closed forever and, because all have had the opportunity to have their say, the community is admonished never to raise the matter again. Elsewhere I provide descriptions and analyses of specific *becharaa'* (Robarchek 1979, 1990).

PSYCHOSOCIAL DYNAMICS
OF SEMAI CONFLICT AND RESOLUTION

The *becharaa'* is only one component in a well-integrated system operating on psychological, social, and cultural levels, one that is quite consciously oriented toward sustaining peaceful social relations. Nonetheless, it is an important component, and understanding how and why it works has broader relevance for us.

Human conflict has three universal components: affective, substantive, and social, and the *becharaa'* successfully addresses all three. The affective component of a conflict—the emotions generated by it—often presents the most intractable problems. Rage, anger, jealousy, grief, envy, and so on, are often the primary experiential facts of a conflict situation. These powerful emotions can present the most formidable barriers to the restoration of social relations and, until these are resolved, it may be impossible to adequately address the others.

The extended discussion by all interested parties and from all conceivable perspectives, facilitates a kind of emotional catharsis, the process that Freud called *abreaction* and that more behavioristically inclined psychologists refer to as *desensitization* (see Robarchek, 1979 for a detailed discussion of the psychodynamics of the *becharaa'*). The feelings generated by the conflict are repeatedly elicited anew and finally dissipated through the repeated recalling and reexperiencing of the events that precipitated them. The principals and their supporters tell their stories over and over, symbolically reexperiencing the precipitating incidents until they no longer have the capacity to elicit an emotional response in anyone. The Semai stress that a *becharaa'* should end only when no one feels the need to say anything more.

This dissipation of the emotional content of the dispute facilitates the resolution of the substantive and social components of the matter. In a small-scale face-to-face society such as this one, the brute facts of the matter are seldom in question, so the extended discussion concentrates on exploring, in exasperating and seemingly infinite detail, all the motives and actions of all the parties. In the process the issues are clarified and each party's fault in the matter is examined. The headman can then give voice to the community consensus that has been achieved concerning the substantive issues that precipitated the dispute. All parties are then ready to accept the new state of affairs that has been legitimated by the formal resolution process.

With the anger or other strong feelings exhausted and the substantive issues resolved, a personal reconciliation of the disputants can be effected and normal social relations among the former antagonists and their kindreds can be resumed.

Since there exists no superordinate control (Whiting, 1950) in Semai society, participants in the *becharaa'* must want to abide by the community's decision, and must want to behave in accordance with the group consensus. This is accomplished in two ways: first, by eliminating much of the motivational power of the conflict through the dissipation of its emotional content; and second, by making reintegration into the group contingent upon acceptance of its will. A person who refuses to accept the group's consensus, as voiced in the headman's lecture, risks alienation both from the band as a whole and from his or her own kindred, the last source of security in an otherwise unremittingly hostile world. The *becharaa'* works because of the central place that the group holds in the psychological economy of individuals; it works because the group, and, therefore, its evaluations and objectives, matters to individuals.

IMPLICATIONS FOR COMPLEX SOCIETIES: THE INDISPENSABILITY OF COMMUNITY

Conflict in human societies is universal and unavoidable. We are social beings, but we also have individual self-interests. Social living thus inevitably generates jealousy, envy, rivalry, gossip, pettiness, evaded obligations, and so on. In most societies, social, cultural, and psychological constraints operate to moderate such conflicts and, in most cases, to restore normal social relations. With no countervailing force to restrain self-interest and to promote moderation, compromise and conciliation, however, conflicts and the emotions that they engender can spiral into acts of violence. This was precisely what we found among the Waorani, where even minor conflicts, propelled by unrestrained individual self-interest, often escalated into homicidal violence.

The growing problem of violence in complex societies is often treated as a problem of social control, but, in reality, our emphasis is almost entirely on the *control* aspect, with little or none on the *social* component. A great many people in our societies, especially young people, have no primary reference group to provide a sense of identity, to inculcate positive societal values, and to act to promote and reinforce behavior consistent with those values. They lack any positive group, either kin or community, whose interests take precedence over their own.

This is a primary reason why small communities are generally much less troubled by violence and other antisocial behavior than large ones: They are still communities. Networks of long-term relationships communicate a consistent set of expectations and monitor members' behavior for compliance. Regardless of their own inclinations, people are expected to conform to the community's norms. In small, face-to-face societies, the hand of community social control, through gossip, shaming, and ridicule, can be heavy if the individuals do not conform. As with the Semai, however, community control is effective only because the community has some psychological salience, because individuals define themselves in terms of it, locate their identities within it and, willingly or not, put its demands and expectations ahead of their own impulses.

An intense and acrimonious political debate currently rages over the question of what to do about violence in our society, and much of the controversy centers on the possibility of reforming those who exhibit violent behavior. Given that concern, it is not surprising that much of the discussion has focused on the individual offender and the likelihood of his successful rehabilitation. Our research among the Semai (and the Waorani; see Robarchek & Robarchek, 1992, 1996) suggests, however, that conformity to social norms—the willingness to give society's interests precedence over one's own wishes and impulses—is largely rooted in individuals' relationship to the community. But urbanization and increasing mobility have diminished or eliminated the psychological salience of the face-to-face community in the lives of most people, and urban planning and often ill-conceived social engineering have done the same in the urban neighborhood. The result has been increasing isolation, disinvolvement and normlessness. Lacking other meaningful reference groups, young people have created their own, and urban gangs are one result.

If our objective is to reorient behavior toward social goals, we must find ways to reconstitute individual identities. One way is to restore the psychological salience of local communities so that individuals locate their identities within them and put the community's demands and expectations ahead of their own impulses. Although this may seem like little more than a utopian yearning for a return to a more noble past, there are, in fact, successful models available to us. Groups such as Alcoholics Anonymous (AA), the Black Muslims, and the Native American Church, all demonstrate the reorientation of individual identities within reconstituted communities. (See Dentan 1992, 1994, for a discussion of the dynamics of AA and other such intentional groups and of their orientations to peacefulness.) Finally, we can take a lesson from the gangs themselves: They provide a reference group that defines and gives form to individual identities, even though the values they uphold and promote are seldom those of the wider society.

ACKNOWLEDGMENTS

Support for the comparative study of violence, for field research among the Waorani, and for data analysis was provided by research grants from the Harry Frank Guggenheim Foundation. Support for a second field project among the Waorani was provided by a research grant from The United States Institute of Peace.

REFERENCES

Dentan, R. K. (1992). The rise, maintenance and destruction of a peaceful polity: A preliminary essay in political ecology. In J. Silverberg & J. P. Gray (Eds.), *Aggression and peacefulness in humans and other primates* (pp. 214–270). New York: Oxford University Press.

Dentan, R. K. (1994). Surrendered men: Peaceable enclaves in the post-enlightenment west. In L. Sponsel & T. Gregor (Eds.), *The anthropology of peace and nonviolence* (pp. 69–108). Boulder, CO: Lynne Reinner.

Robarchek, C. A. (1979). Conflict, emotion and abreaction: Resolution of conflict among the Semai Senoi. *Ethos, 7,* 104–123.

Robarchek, C. A. (1986). Helplessness, fearfulness and peacefulness: The emotional and motivational context of Semai social relations. *Anthropological Quarterly, 58,* 177–183.

Robarchek, C. A. (1990). Motivations and material causes: On the explanation of conflict and war. In J. Haas (Ed.), *The Anthropology of War* (pp. 56–76). Cambridge, England: Cambridge University Press.

Robarchek, C. A., & Robarchek, C. J. (1992). Cultures of war and peace: A comparative study of Waorani and Semai. In J. Silverberg & J. P. Gray (Eds.), *Aggression and peacefulness in humans and other primates* (pp. 189–213). New York: Oxford University Press.

Robarchek, C. A., & Robarchek, C. J. (1996). Waging peace: The psychological and sociocultural dynamics of positive peace, society proceedings. In A. W. Wolfe & H. Yang, (Eds.), *Anthropological Contributions to Conflict Resolution* (pp. 64è). Athens, GA: University of Georgia Press.

Whiting, B. (1950). Paiute sorcery. *Viking Publications in Anthropology, 15.*

6

Conflict Avoidance and Resolution Among the Toraja of South Sulawesi, Indonesia

Douglas Hollan
University of California, Los Angeles

The Toraja people of Indonesia manage to prevent many conflicts from becoming violent. In this chapter, Hollan notes that the Toraja make heavy use of avoidance. He also explains how the Toraja maintain the peace through a complex and overlapping set of intra- and interpersonal controls of emotions and conduct. This redundancy of checks on conflict and aggression is particularly effective, as, for example, individuals simply avoid adversaries, limit their expressions of anger, share and recount the culturally accepted attitudes about the tragic consequences of aggressive acts, and when a dispute cannot be ignored, submit to a mediation process conducted by a village elder, who tends to be more concerned with restoring social harmony than with individual rights or punishing a disputant.

—The Editors

In this chapter, I discuss conflict avoidance and resolution among the Toraja of South Sulawesi, Indonesia. I examine the sources and types of conflicts Toraja villagers most typically contend with and I discuss the ways in which they attempt to avoid or to resolve such conflicts. Throughout the chapter I emphasize that the successful avoidance or resolution of conflict (by the Toraja and others) usually involves a number of redundant controls on thoughts, emotions, and behaviors. To illustrate this point, I demonstrate how the resolution or avoidance of conflict in Toraja involves the interaction of both interpersonal and intrapersonal controls.

CONFLICT RESOLUTION IN ANTHROPOLOGICAL PERSPECTIVE

Many contemporary anthropologists argue that, because human conflicts are always deeply rooted in local moral economies and local ways of conceptualizing fairness, justice, and human nature, attempts to avoid or to resolve conflicts—if they are to be successful—must draw upon these same locally constructed views of human value and behavior (see, for example, Avruch, Black, & Scimecca, 1991; Watson-Gegeo & White, 1990). Further, some anthropologists noted that peace and conflict, aggression and nonaggression are extremely complex forms of behaviors that are shaped and structured not by a single variable or determinant but by sets of cultural and psychological controls that are mutually reinforcing and redundant (Bateson, 1972; Fry, 1994; Hollan, 1988; Levy, 1978). To understand historically significant patterns of peace and conflict from an anthropological perspective requires, then, that we situate such patterns in their appropriate cultural context and that we look for redundant influences on thought, emotion, and behavior.

THE TORAJA

The Toraja number approximately 350,000 and live in the interior, mountainous regions of South Sulawesi, Indonesia. They are primarily wet-rice farmers who also cultivate small gardens of sweet potatoes, cassava, and assorted vegetables. Kinship is traced bilaterally and Toraja society is stratified into three primary groups: those of noble descent, commoners, and dependents. Although ranking in this hierarchy is theoretically ascribed at birth, status and prestige may be enhanced by conspicuous and generous slaughtering of livestock at community feasts (see Volkman, 1985).

A majority of the Toraja are now Christian, although some middle-aged and older villagers remain adherents of the traditional religion, *Alukta*, which is based on the veneration and propitiation of various spirits, gods, and deceased ancestral figures.

The Toraja are a strongly sociocentric people. Like many other Austronesian language groups, they place a high value on affiliation and harmony within the community and criticize self-serving, boasting behavior. Most forms of overt anger and aggression are feared and are actively (and successfully) discouraged, but as I have noted elsewhere (Hollan 1988, 1992; Hollan & Wellenkamp, 1994), this does not preclude significant levels of interpersonal hostility that find indirect expression through gossip, patterns of avoidance, and fears of magical poisoning and trickery.

PATTERNS OF CONFLICT

Interethnic and Intervillage Conflict

Historically, the Toraja were a diverse group. In contrast to the lowland Islamic kingdoms of the Bugis and Makassar, the Toraja area of Sulawesi remained politically decentralized prior to the arrival of the Dutch in 1906, with nobles competing for control of various local areas. Intervillage warfare occurred intermittently, and headhunting was practiced both to avenge a death and to obtain heads that were needed for the funerals of high status persons. With the exception of a brief period of unification in the 17th century, political allegiance rarely extended beyond the village or hamlet. Even today, local ties remain an important part of the social and political landscape.

Before the last quarter of the 19th century, Toraja contact with the outside world was limited to sporadic encounters with the lowland Bugis and Makassar. Some of these contacts were peaceful, involving trade and intermarriage among elites and the payment of tribute from highlanders to lowlanders, but others were decidedly hostile, as the Toraja defended themselves against attack and invasion.

Contacts with outsiders became more extensive in the closing decades of the 19th century as lowlanders, spurred by changes in international markets, became more interested in obtaining Toraja coffee and slaves. Trade alliances were established in which lowlanders provided Toraja nobles with firearms in exchange for help in acquiring desired goods. One of the consequences of these increasing contacts with the outside world was heightened political instability, as Toraja nobles used their newly acquired weapons to raid one another for slaves and coffee and to confiscate both land and livestock (Bigalke, 1981).

The political situation in the highlands remained volatile until the Dutch arrived in 1906. In addition to outlawing the slave trade, the Dutch killed or imprisoned many of the most powerful Toraja nobles and froze land holdings. The Dutch retained control of the Toraja highlands until 1942, when the Japanese occupied the area during World War II. Although the Dutch returned to power for a brief period of time after 1945, they eventually relinquished control to Indonesia nationalists in 1949. Toraja and the province of South Sulawesi eventually became integrated into the new Indonesian national state based in Jakarta, but not before a number of lowland groups had arisen to fight for local control (Harvey, 1974, 1977). These groups remained active in and around the Toraja highlands, disrupting commerce and travel, until the central government finally gained control in 1965. Since then, the Toraja highlands have remained peaceful and efforts have been made to build roads, schools, and health clinics and to develop international tourism (see Adams, 1988; Volkman, 1985)

Intravillage and Intrafamilial Conflict

Since pacification, most conflict in Toraja involving openly angry or aggressive behavior occurs among fellow villagers or family members within a village or hamlet. Although conflict of this nature seems limited relative to U.S. standards (Hollan & Wellenkamp, 1994, p. 112), it is possible to identify occasions when such behavior is most likely to occur. One such occasion is the division of meat at rituals, when cuts of sacrificed livestock are distributed to participants according to their relative status and prestige (see Volkman, 1985). Because even the most fair-minded, well-intentioned meat divider cannot simultaneously satisfy the status aspirations of all of those in the community, it is inevitable that some people will be dissatisfied and feel shamed by their allotment. In this special context, the open expression of anger is considered acceptable, although any anger expressed during a meat division should not be carried over into daily life.

Because the expression of anger during meat divisions is anticipated and relatively controlled—it occurs only in the context of a ritual and often is theatrical and purposeful—it is considered a normal problem. More disturbing to villagers, but equally expected, are openly angry responses to other incidents in which one feels publicly shamed, such as when one's spouse has committed adultery or when sexual matters are discussed in front of close relatives of the opposite gender (Hollan & Wellenkamp, 1994, pp. 114–115). Conflict is also likely to arise when one feels that a spouse has failed to fulfill important household responsibilities (Hollan & Wellenkamp, 1996) or when one feels tricked or deceived by fellow villagers. Much of the daily concern about being tricked and deceived has to do with sharing and exchanging resources and services. People fear that others either will make illegitimate requests of them—that they will ask for something when there is no genuine need—or that they will borrow something and never return or repay it. Villagers also fear that when they make a legitimate request of others, they may be turned down by fellow residents who falsely claim that they do not have the resources to fulfill the request (Hollan & Wellenkamp, 1994, pp. 155–157).

By far the most serious and potentially violent conflicts that occur in Toraja appear to be the culmination of protracted disputes over limited resources, especially land. Waterson (1981, pp. 342, 366–371) reported that a large percentage of formal civil suits have to do with disputes over land, and my own court research corroborates her findings. This in itself suggests the volatile nature of such disputes since, generally speaking, Toraja villagers would prefer to settle their disagreements at the village or district level. A large percentage of criminal cases also has to do with disputes over land. Of the single murder and eleven assaults recorded for all Toraja in 1982, the murder and a majority of the assaults involved land disputes.

THE AVOIDANCE AND/OR RESOLUTION OF CONFLICT

Those behaviors which a given culture emphasizes, which are salient, controlled by dominant values, necessary for its particular socio-environmental adaptations—are *necessarily produced and controlled by a redundant set of influences.* All stable systems use redundant sets of controls to maintain essential variables. (Levy, 1978, p. 231, italics in original)

The Toraja, like some other Malaysian and Indonesian groups, seem relatively successful at limiting the types of intravillage conflict just described, and this success can be linked to the exigencies of life in small, face-to-face, farming communities (Hollan & Wellenkamp, 1994, pp. 217–219) and to a number of other social and cultural factors, including:

the commitment to and internalization of religious and cultural values that stress social harmony, cooperation, patience, and acceptance (C. Geertz, 1960; Bonokamsi,

1972); the role of complex patterns of etiquette and respectful behavior that have the effect of preventing or defusing potentially disruptive conflicts (C. Geertz, 1960; H. Geertz, 1961); childrearing and enculturative practices that lead to behavioral patterns of passive withdrawal or fearful avoidance, and fear of intense emotional arousal, rather than to patterns of active assertion and aggression (Bateson & Mead, 1942; H. Geertz, 1961; Dentan, 1978; Robarchek, 1977); illness beliefs that link the experience and/or expression of disturbing emotions to serious physical ailments (H. Geertz); and the importance of dissociative mechanisms in splitting anger off from conscious awareness and limiting outwardly aggressive acts to circumscribed, well-controlled ritual or illness contexts (Bateson & Mead, 1942; Connor, 1979; Suryani, 1984; Lee, 1981; Hollan, 1984). (Hollan, 1988, pp. 52–53)

I next discuss some of these social and cultural factors and then examine the intrapersonal emotion work such factors both promote and rely upon for their effectiveness. It is the combination, and mutually reinforcing influences, of these different levels of control that account for the relatively successful minimization of conflict in Toraja villages.

Interpersonal Controls

Bateson (1972, pp. 108–112) noted the tendency of many societies to develop patterns of cumulative interaction in which the actions of one individual or group become the stimuli for a counteraction on the part of some other individual or group. Such schismogenic patterns may be either symmetrical, in which the actions of an individual or group promote similar actions from some other individual or group (e.g., in cases of competition and rivalry), or complementary, in which the actions of an individual or group promote dissimilar, though mutually appropriate, actions on the part of some of other individual or group (e.g., in cases of dominance–submission, succoring–dependence, exhibitionism–spectatorship, and the like.) Bateson also observed that schismogenic patterns may become vicious cycles that lead to continued and escalating conflict unless they are defused and controlled.

The Toraja have developed a number of social and cultural practices that have the effect, intended or unintended, of limiting or diffusing potentially schismogenic interactions:

Cross-Cutting Values

Although status within the Toraja social hierarchy is theoretically ascribed at birth, it is currently possible for individuals to significantly enhance their status and prestige through the conspicuous and generous slaughter of livestock at community feasts (Volkman, 1985). As Geertz and Geertz said of the Balinese, "What matters to a [Toraja] man—or to a woman—is public repute: the social deference it brings, the sumptuary rights it confers, the self-esteem it engenders, the cultural assertion it makes possible" (1975, p. 163). Although status competition leads to the conflictual nature of the meat division already described and tends toward a pattern of runaway symmetrical schismogenesis, it is undercut and limited by an equally strong value placed on sharing, reciprocity, and mutual aid (Hollan & Wellenkamp, 1994, pp. 46–48). Most Toraja villagers are acutely aware that they cannot afford to push their own interests and status position too far without at the same time jeopardizing their ability to solicit others' aid and support in time of need. This cross-cutting of values, needs, allegiances, and roles has the (largely unintended) consequence of insuring that competitive rivalry over status is held within reason-able limits.

Institutionalization of Nonschismogenic Patterns of Interaction

Practices that directly diffuse potentially schismogenic interactions include:

Patterns of Avoidance.   As in Bali (Bateson, 1972, p. 113), Toraja villagers generally prefer to avoid the people with whom they are in conflict rather than to confront them directly. These patterns of avoidance are widespread and are evident, among other times, both during and after the division of meat at feasts, in the aftermath of disputes between household members, and among those who are involved in reciprocity disputes (Hollan & Wellenkamp, 1994, pp. 203–205). Although avoidance may do little, if anything, to diffuse hostility among disputants (cf. Bateson, 1972, p. 113), it does impede conflicts from moving in the direction of confrontation and climax.

The Limitation of Open Displays of Angry or Aggressive Behavior to Specified Contexts.   As already mentioned, there are occasions when the open display of anger and aggression is anticipated, for example, during the division of meat at community feasts, during kickfights (held at the beginning of the agricultural season and in conjunction with possession rituals), and by the possessed during rituals of fertility, cleansing, and thanksgiving. However, in all these cases, it is considered highly inappropriate for the displayed anger or aggression to be carried over into everyday life or for those who are the target of the anger or aggression to bear grudges or to seek retaliation outside the specified context.

Sanctioning the Overreaction to a Breach of Conduct.   The limitation of angry, aggressive behavior to certain contexts is effective, in part, because a public and socially disruptive reaction to a breach of conduct is generally considered even more reprehensible than the original breach. Thus, for example, a person who publicly berates and humiliates someone for being a thief is criticized more than the act of theft itself (Hollan & Wellenkamp, 1994, pp. 50, 236).

The Use of Mediators Who Are More Concerned with Overall Social Welfare Than Individual Rights.   Disputes that cannot be ignored (see Patterns of Avoid-ance) are often mediated by village elders who are generally more concerned with preserving and/or reestablishing overall social harmony and welfare than with protecting individual rights or punishing wrongdoers (cf. Just, 1991), as when disgruntled spouses are urged to reconcile for the sake of children and community well-being or when divorce fines and other social sanctions are affected by ability to pay (Hollan & Wellenkamp, 1996). Although such mediation rarely resolves all the disputants' grievances, it does preclude the type of grossly unfair or unbalanced settlement that would merely fuel further conflict and dispute.

The Use of Isolated Acts of Violence or Aggression to Demonstrate Their Harmfulness

Stories of isolated and unusual acts of aggression—and their tragic consequences—are told repeatedly and preserved in public consciousness (Hollan & Wellenkamp, 1994, pp. 115–116). These tellings and retellings clearly illustrate to people how harmful and dysfunctional aggression can be.

Intrapersonal Controls

Many of the aforementioned measures depend on the ability of individuals to act in compliance with cultural norms, values, and expectations. This compliance is not achieved effortlessly but rather requires that villagers make an active, conscious effort to keep their emotions and behaviors in culturally recognized bounds. Hochschild (1979, 1983) called such effort emotion work, that she defined as "the [deliberate and conscious] act of trying to change in degree or quality an emotion or feeling" (Hochschild, 1979, p. 561). That is, it is the active effort to evoke, shape, or suppress certain feelings. According to Hochschild, the concept of "emotion work" fills a conceptual gap which exists between the approach of Freud, on the one hand, and that of Erving Goffman, on the other. Freud concentrates on what one might also call emotion work, but it is work that is performed unconsciously and involuntarily through defense mechanisms, such as repression. Goffman, on the other hand, in his work on impression management (1959), concentrates on the management of one's outward behavior. He implied that managing one's behavioral displays (including displays of emotion) is accomplished fairly automatically, without much conscious effort or thought. The actors in Goffman's accounts "actively manage outer impressions, but they do not actively manage inner feelings" (Hochschild, 1979, p. 557).

The Toraja use a number of strategies in their attempts to manage and control potentially conflict-generating emotions (Hollan & Wellenkamp, 1994, pp. 198–209; Hollan, 1992). One prevalent technique of self-directed emotion work is to remind oneself of the dangers of strong, negative emotions: that by expressing such feelings one may upset others and suffer public censure or provoke magical retaliation (Hollan & Wellenkamp, 1994, pp. 166–175); that one may experience bad fortune in life as a consequence of getting angry and quarreling with others; and that by even experiencing negative emotions, one leaves oneself vulnerable to serious physical or mental illness.

A second common strategy is to consciously suppress or avoid troubling thoughts or feelings such as disappointment, envy, or anger. The efficacy of this strategy became evident in the aftermath of a forest fire that had been accidentally set by two village boys. Although many villagers sustained losses from the fire, people in general declined to discuss the matter, saying that the deed was done and there was no point in dwelling on the losses.

A third common way of dealing with distressing events and feelings is to remind oneself that the gods and ancestors, or God, assure that people eventually get what they deserve—thus precluding the need to seek revenge or recompense oneself.

A fourth strategy involves avoiding potentially upsetting situations and trying not to expect too much from life or strive too hard. Efforts to actively limit one's desires and disappointments, and so achieve a certain detachment from the world, resemble Javanese efforts to be "not caring" (iklas) and "accepting" (terima; Geertz, 1960, p. 241). Such detachment, when it is achieved, helps individuals to disengage from schismogenic cycles of conflict and revenge.

DISCUSSION AND CONCLUSION

Like many other small scale, face-to-face farming communities in the world, the Toraja place a high value on community cooperation and interdependence, and they strongly discourage overt conflict and aggression. Although the prevalence of gossip and fears of magical poisoning and trickery indicate significant levels of interpersonal hostility, the Toraja seem remarkably successful at avoiding or resolving overt forms of conflict and aggression. As I indicate, this relatively successful management of conflict can be related to a number of ecological, sociocultural, and psychological variables.

What are the implications of the Toraja case for the wider study of human conflict and its avoidance or resolution?

1. Conflicts and their resolution are always deeply rooted in specific sociocultural and historical contexts. The types of conflicts that the Toraja typically contend with are different than those of pastoralists, for example (see Edgerton, 1971), and their successful avoidance or resolution depend upon locally construed notions of fairness, justice, and social welfare. Further, these conflicts differ in both kind and magnitude from those that were common 100 or even 50 years ago, when there was much less chance for social mobility within the village and when intervillage and interethnic conflicts were more prominent.

2. Not surprisingly, many studies of conflict resolution focus on how groups and individuals attempt to manage interpersonal and intergroup relationships that have become manifestly conflictual and problematic. Although this is certainly an important area of study, the Toraja case illustrates that it is equally important to understand how individuals and groups manage to avoid or to diffuse conflict before it becomes overt and before it requires formal recognition and mediation. Toraja use of avoidance behavior, their commitment to sharing, reciprocity, and mutual

aid that undercuts and limits status rivalry, their institutionalization of many nonschismogenic patterns of behavior, and their active management and control of potentially conflict-generating emotions all serve to prevent problematic relations from moving toward confrontation and climax. Conflict-avoidance studies would first identify the kinds of problems most likely to lead to conflict in a given group and then closely examine how and why a particular problem leads to conflict in some cases but not in others. This approach would allow researchers to more clearly elucidate the factors that are most critical to the successful avoidance or diffusion of conflict.

3. Conflict or the successful avoidance of conflict are complex surface behaviors that may be structured, both culturally and psychologically, in different ways. Aggressive behavior, for example, may be motivated out of narcissistic injury, out of fear and dread of attack, or out of attempts to preserve and maintain political or economic domination. Similarly, placidity and nonaggression may or may not involve the active suppression and control of hostility. In Toraja, overt behavior remains relatively nonconflictual despite significant levels of interpersonal mistrust and hostility. Thus, ways of avoiding or limiting conflict in Toraja must necessarily differ from those found in places like Tahiti, where interpersonal hostility is less of a social problem (Levy, 1973, 1978). Studies of conflict avoidance and resolution must account for these different ways of structuring overt forms of both aggressive and nonaggressive behavior.

4. Surface forms of historically significant conflictual or nonconflictual behavior always involve redundant controls and influences. Controls and influences on Toraja nonconflict are varied and complex and include such things as religious and cultural values, patterns of etiquette and respect, childrearing and enculturative practices, illness beliefs, and ritualized forms of dissociation and altered states of consciousness. In this chapter, I focus especially on the interaction and mutually reinforcing influences of interpersonal and intrapersonal forms of control. Interpersonal patterns of avoidance and the institutionalization of nonschismogenic patterns of interaction both promote and rely upon the development of intrapersonal forms of emotion work that suppress and control potentially conflict-generating emotional states such as envy, anger, and disappointment. Although each of these controls and influences is worthy of study in its own right, it is their combined influence that accounts for the particular form of limited and controlled conflict found in Toraja today, and it is the combined influence of such controls that should be the primary focus of studies of conflict avoidance and resolution.

REFERENCES

Adams, K. (1988). *Carving a new identity: Ethnic and artistic change in Tana Toraja, Indonesia.* Unpublished doctoral dissertation, University of Washington, Seattle.

Avruch, K., Black, R. W., & Scimecca, J. A. (Eds.). (1991). *Conflict resolution: Cross-cultural perspectives.* Westport, CT: Greenwood Press.

Bateson, G. (1972). *Bali: The value system of a steady state. In steps to an ecology of mind* (pp. 107–127). New York: Ballantine Books.

Bigalke, T. (1981). A social history of "Tana Toraja," 1870–1965. Unpublished doctoral dissertation, University of Wisconsin, Madison.

Edgerton, R. B. (1971). The individual in cultural adaptation: A study of four East African societies. Los Angeles: University of California Press.

Fry, D. P. (1994). Maintaining social tranquility: Internal and external loci of aggression control. In L. E. Sponsel & T. Gregor (Eds.), The anthropology of peace and non-violence (pp. 133–154). Boulder, CO: Lynne Rienner.

Geertz, C. (1960). The religion of Java. Chicago, IL: University of Chicago Press.

Geertz, H., & Geertz, C. (1975). Kinship in Bali. Chicago, IL: University of Chicago Press.

Goffman, E. (1959). The presentation of self in everyday life. Garden City, NY: Doubleday.

Harvey, B. S. (1974). Tradition, islam, and rebellion: South Sulawesi 1950–1965. Unpublished doctoral dissertation, Cornell University, Ithaca, NY.

Harvey, B. S. (1977). Permesta: Half a rebellion. Ithaca, NY: Cornell Modern Indonesia Project.

Hochschild, A. (1979). Emotion work, Feeling rules, and social structure. American Journal of Sociology, 85, 551–575.

Hochschild, A. (1983). The managed heart: Commercialization of human feeling. Berkeley: University of California Press.

Hollan, D. (1988). Staying "cool" in Toraja: Informal strategies for the management of anger and hostility in a nonviolent society. Ethos, 16, 52–72.

Hollan, D. (1992). Emotion work and the value of emotional equanimity among the Toraja. Ethnology, 31, 45–56.

Hollan, D. W., & Wellenkamp, J. C. (1994). Contentment and suffering: Culture and experience in Toraja. New York: Columbia University Press.

Hollan, D. W., & Wellenkamp, J. C. (1996). The thread of life: Toraja reflections on the life cycle. Honolulu: University of Hawaii Press.

Just, P. (1991). Conflict resolution and moral community among the Dou Donggo. In K. Avruch, P. W. Black, & J. A. Scimecca (Eds.), Conflict resolution: Cross-cultural perspectives (pp. 107–143). Westport, CT: Greenwood Press.

Levy, R. I. (1973). Tahitians: Mind and experience in the Society Islands. Chicago, IL: University of Chicago Press.

Levy, R. I. (1978). Tahitian gentleness and redundant controls. In A. Montagu (Ed.), Learning non-aggression (pp. 222–235). New York: Oxford University Press.

Volkman, T. (1985). Feasts of honor: Ritual and change in the Toraja highlands. Urbana, IL: Illinois University Press.

Waterson, R. (1981). The economic and social position of women in Tana Toraja. Unpublished doctoral dissertation, University of Cambridge, Cambridge, England.

Watson-Gegeo, K., & White, G. (Eds.). (1990). Disentangling: Conflict discourse in Pacific societies. Stanford, CA: Stanford University Press.

7

Conflict Resolution in Native Margariteño Society

H. B. Kimberley Cook
University of California, Los Angeles

In this chapter, Cook suggests that conflict resolution on Margarita Island, Venezuela, is an oxymoron, because conflict originates at the same time that it is resolved. In native communities on the Island, the conflict–resolution and generation process occurs via extensive use of nonviolent yet often cruel forms of informal social control such as gossip, song dueling, ostracism, and witchcraft. A formal authority structure also exists to deal with conflicts. Cook also stresses the importance of belonging to a social network, describes network fission and fusion, and analyzes the role that the social networks play in cycles of conflict resolution and recreation.

—The Editors

This chapter examines the nature of conflict resolution in a native population on the island of Margarita, Venezuela. Pruitt and Rubin (1986, p. 4) defined *conflict* as a "perceived divergence of interest." They utilized a dramaturgical model of conflict resolution that suggests that many conflicts progress through three acts or stages: escalation, stalemate, and settlement (Pruitt & Rubins, 1986, p. v). In native Margariteño society conflict is certainly a "perceived divergence of interest," and contentious tactics are heavily used, but the consequences of conflict resolution are frequently different than those suggested by Pruitt and Rubin. In native Margariteño culture, paradoxically, conflict resolution is a potent generator of conflict itself.

Doob (1991, p. ix) pointed out that sometimes in non-Western, nonindustrial societies "conflicts can be productive and 'harmony' may or may not be the ideal to be achieved." Harmony and reconciliation are not intended outcomes in the native Margariteño system of conflict resolution. In native communities on the island, conflict-resolution activities, while nonviolent, are combative and cruel (also cf. Bailey, 1991; Gilmore, 1987).

In spite of the often destructive aspects of conflict, scholars have noted the positive outcomes of conflict for societies and groups at large (Pruitt & Rubin, 1986, pp. 6–7; Gilmore, 1987). Elsewhere, I discuss the individual costs and societal benefits of conflict resolution in native Margariteño society (Cook, 1993). Here I expand on that discussion by examining the benefits that this system has for the individual.

In native Margariteño society, the term *conflict resolution* is an oxymoron. Conflict originates in activities used in its resolution. The ongoing cycle of conflict, its resolution and regeneration is embedded in a native tradition of sociocentrism that is characteristically flexible. In native communities on the island, sociocentrism is a culturally patterned response to historical and current conditions of hardship and change that have threatened native Margariteño persistence and survival (cf. Cook, 1993). The ongoing conflict generated by sociocentric networks simultaneously has a vitalizing effect on the society and the individuals who participate in it.

ETHNOGRAPHIC BACKGROUND

Margarita Island is located in the state of Nueva Esparta, approximately 20 miles off the northeastern coast of Venezuela. The island supports a large socially and economically heterogeneous population comprised of native Margariteños, Venezuelan nationals, and foreigners. Native Margariteños are mestizos of Indian, African, and Spanish descent.

I worked in economically marginal communities located in the central and western regions of the island (cf. Mata-Marin, 1976, for a discussion of marginality). Field work was conducted primarily in the town I fictitiously refer to as San Fernando.[1] During the past few decades, the island and its people have undergone intense modernization and change, (Urbano, 1981, pp. 22–65). Although affected by the changes, in San Fernando and similar communities, native Margariteños still maintain traditions related to the native system of conflict resolution that include cultural flexibility and nonviolence.

In San Fernando and in similar communities on the island, conflict is usually resolved and regenerated through nonviolent, premeditated, activities such as gossip, monologues, spying, limericks, song dueling, ostracism, and witchcraft (Cook, 1993, pp. 72–86). In some cases these informal activities prove ineffective, and formal authorities are summoned (Cook, 1993, pp. 84–85). Women play a central role in conflict-related activities (McCorkle, 1965, p. 67; Cook, 1992, pp. 149–162; 1993, pp. 63–71). Conflict centers around disputes concerning paternity, authority, and jealousy and sometimes erupts at events involving ritual aggression such as cock fighting, or during card games in which, like cock fighting gambling is involved (Cook, 1993).

---

[1]The ethnographic data were collected in December 1979 through March 1980, July through September 1981, one month in the summer of 1985, and September 1987 through May, 1988.

Some of the historical hardships that native Margariteños have had to cope with have required flexibility. These include periodic shortages of resources and employment opportunities on the island, resulting in waves of male out-migration (Alexander, 1961, pp. 555–556), extended absence of men engaged in fishing activities (Orona, 1968, p. 94), and a history of personal, sexual, and economic exploitation by money lenders (*caciques*; Orona, 1968, pp. 168–169; Cook, 1993, pp. 22–23). These historical circumstances have resulted in stressful conditions including poverty, male absence, matrifocality, polygyny, and female serial monogamy (Cook, 1993).

The current standard of living in San Fernando and other such communities is low. Houses have dirt floors and open kitchens, where food supplies often become infested with rats. Some homes lack indoor plumbing. Water is stored in large open drums that contain mosquito larvae. The residents in my sample also lacked sewage disposal services (Cook, 1993, pp. 17–18). Although the residents in San Fernando work in a variety of occupations, individuals occasionally do not have sufficient funds to cover their basic needs, such as medical expenses, food, and clothing. Native Margariteños in these communities cope with these problems through a culturally institutionalized system of sociocentrism (Cook, 1993, pp. 31–34, 41, 72–75).

SOCIOCENTRISM: THE ORIGINS OF CONFLICT

As pointed out by McCorkle (1965, p. 129), flexibility is a central feature of native Margariteño culture. For instance, membership in sociocentric networks is flexible. Membership provides native Margariteños with informal social security and is based on various combinations of social–structural, social, economic, and moral criteria (Cook, 1993, p. 32). An important theme underlying sociocentrism is the concept of family. Native Margariteño social structure is based on bilateral kinship. Although sociocentric networks vary in size and composition, they originate and expand from the primary unit of bilateral kinship systems, the ego-based network.

Family closeness is also achieved through marriage. In native Margariteño society, cousin marriage is preferred in order to "keep the blood in the family" (Cook, 1993, p. 28). Both cross and parallel cousins are chosen from within and between towns, thus geographically extending the range of family connections on the island. Margariteños also occasionally marry outsiders.

Individuals are also incorporated in sociocentric networks through social ties of adoption, friendship, and ritualized kinship (*compadrazgo*). No matter how one achieves membership, once established, one is treated with equal status as an inside member. Members of sociocentric networks are expected to participate in an economic system that requires generosity, cooperation, and exchange. Resources are passed among members according to need. Sharing goods and services is not just an ideal. According to my informants, sharing is a response to poverty that insures that no one will go without food or other essential resources (Cook, 1993, p. 23).

In order to insure mutual cooperation and sharing, members of sociocentric networks are expected to abide by values of moral authority including respect (*respeto*), decency (*sano*), and nonviolence (*tranquilo*). Orona described the native Margariteño concept of *respeto* as "respect, reverence, regard, and/or consideration" (1968, p. 65). The concepts of *sano* and *tranquilo* imply decent, nonviolent behavior. These concepts most often apply to the nature of joking or fighting activities (McCorkle, 1965, p. 64; Cook, 1993, pp. 30–31).

Remaining on the inside of sociocentric networks is tricky business. Embedded in the operation of these networks are three fundamental contradictions that generate extreme amounts of interpersonal conflict.

The first contradiction is a dichotomy between the individual and the group. Individual motivations include the maximization of personal resources without jeopardizing one's position in the group, shifting blame from one's self to others in conflict situations, and attacking and damaging one's enemies while receiving group approval for these actions. Group standards include the maintenance of a fair and even distribution of resources, the identification of cheaters, the maintenance of peaceful and harmonious relationships, and the minimization of conflict and disruption (Cook, 1993, pp. 72–73).

The second contradiction underlying the operation of sociocentrism is a strong inside–outside dichotomy. The presence of a dichotomy was first noticed by Orona in his study of native Margariteños:

> The people of Punta de Piedras are aware that they are part of a larger entity besides their island. This seems to be reflected in their feelings of centricity about their island in relation to the outside world. Strong in their minds is a "de afuera'" (from the outside) concept. Foreigners and foreign things are referred to as "*de afuera.*" In other words it is a "we" and "they" type of dichotomy. (1968, p. 334)

I suggested that the "we" versus "they" dichotomy is an inclusive element of an overarching construct of sociocentrism that is expressed redundantly at all levels of society and distinguishes between insiders and outsiders. I use these terms because the borders of the dichotomy are affected by several criteria that are selected and activated depending on differing circumstances (Cook, 1993, pp. 31–32). Sociocentric networks are based on boundaries that are ever-present, yet constantly changing.

The third contradiction in native Margariteño sociocentrism is a shifting definition of deviance. In this culture deviance can be assessed in three ways. The first definition is fairly clearly cut: An individual commits a flagrant crime that cannot be rationalized. There are simply no explanations that the accused can use to convince others that the actions had merit or benefited the group network.

Since I began fieldwork in native communities in 1979, I have observed that cases falling into this first category of deviance are rare and usually involve stealing. One such case occurred when a resident of San Fernando was arrested for stealing in another town. After being released he returned to San Fernando. People came out of their houses to stare at him, but when he attempted to speak or approach his neighbors' homes, they turned their backs to him. The ostracism was so intense that he was pressured to walk a straight line down the middle of the road as he made his way home. Following this incident he was excluded from participation in social and economic activities.

The second and most common definition of deviance involves calculation, negotiation, and an individual's reputation. In most cases when an incident occurs, people admit that a cultural standard has been broken and find some way to either justify or punish the action. This definition of deviance is often used in incidents of male fist fighting. In the cases in which men have reputations as hard workers, who are generous with their resources, and show responsibility towards their family and community, their behavior is rationalized as simple roughhousing (*repugnancia*), or decent, clean fighting. In cases where a man does not make a contribution and shows little concern or financial responsibility for those in his family and network, a simple punch on his part, is interpreted as dirty fighting, and he is punished. The third definition of deviance involves simply changing cultural rules. For the *Guayquerí* (*a native Margariteño group*), McCorkle (1965, p. 131) noted:

> *Cultural survival* (which the Guayqueries do not have), while it may be assisted by geographical and social isolation, probably mostly depends on *cultural conservatism*. While *community persistence* (which the Guayqueries do have), partly rests upon the group's *ability to adjust to changing conditions*, and may actually require discarding such cultural practices as do not help or that obstruct adjustment.

Regarding the proper behavior of women, the readjustment or elimination of rules defining deviance can be seen from both historical and current perspectives. Cultural rules of proper conduct stress the importance of the woman's place in the home, where ideally she is expected to fulfill domestic responsibilities such as child care (Cook, 1993, p. 39). But as mentioned above, historical conditions of male out-migration and the nature of fishing activities have resulted in male absence in Margarita. Historically, native Margariteño women have had to participate in male-oriented tasks involving heavy physical labor and have had to take a variety of jobs outside their homes and communities.

Historical conditions of male absence also affected rules concerning female fidelity:

> Values of morality specify that women should not be promiscuous but should remain faithful to their husbands or partners. However, the extended and sometimes permanent absences of their men realistically requires women to live solitary lives. Many women therefore choose to engage in new relationships, resulting in a pattern of female serial monogamy. (Cook, 1993, p. 40)

That rules of deviance are constantly in flux is evidenced by a discussion I had in San Fernando with three Margariteño women, a woman in her sixties and two women in their late twenties. When one of the younger women said that she had seen prostitutes working in a commercial town on the eastern side of the island, the senior woman stated: "I think that prostitution is fine. Its a business, just like cock fighting is a business. These women go to work every night just like men go to work. They have their make-up, and clothes, and things. They go do their business. They can take care of themselves and make lots of money." Whether or not my informant would actually approve of her daughter engaging in such an activity is questionable, but her ideas alone are a challenge to the traditional values of morality that dictate that a woman's place is in the home and require female fidelity. In San Fernando, no matter how *deviance* is defined, the intent is the same; individuals make decisions that are meant to economically enhance themselves and the members of their sociocentric networks.

FISSION AND FUSION: PARADOXES
AND PROBLEMS UNDERLYING CONFLICT RESOLUTION

The three categories of contradictions inherent in sociocentric networks generate a perpetual cycle of conflict. The flexible nature of sociocentrism ironically requires individuals to behave competitively and cooperatively at the same time. Social approval is based on arbitrary and shifting categories of deviance. Individuals are left in the position of competing for social approval in ways that must appear to be selfless (cf. Cook, 1993, p. 74).

Competition is acted out through battles of one-upmanship that aim at casting blame on others while avoiding shame and guilt. The competitive activities mentioned above include gossip, monologues, spying, limericks, song dueling, ostracism, and witchcraft. Although nonviolent, they are often covert, premeditated, intensely cruel, and sometimes aim at inflicting serious long-term injury on opponents. The ongoing tension they cause is reflected in the local expression characterizing the native community as a "small town, big hell" (Cook, 1993).

Battles of one-upmanship create fission and fusion that operate at various levels of society. First, within ego-based networks, fission tends to be rigid and permanent. The severity of fission is evidenced by the abrupt and often inaccurate labels ascribed to deviants such as foreigner (*extranjero*), from a different race (*raza*), or from the outside (*de afuera*). According to one informant: "The (x) family are selfish. They don't share what they have. They try to hide it. They are bad people *de afuera*. They are a different *raza*" (Cook, 1993, p. 32). When I interviewed this family, I discovered that they were fifth generation native Margariteños who had lived in a nearby town and in San Fernando for the past seven years" (Cook, 1993, p. 32).

Once an individual is ostracized from within a network, it is very difficult to gain reacceptance. If they are reincorporated, they are constantly reminded of past digressions that got them ostracized in the first place. In one case, a woman who was caught cheating on her husband has been reminded of her mistake for the past ten years by a cruel song sung in rhymed verse at seasonal events by town members.

But expulsion of an individual from one network does not necessarily exclude them from participation in the overall system. Flexibility in membership means that outcasts can form new networks, as is demonstrated by the conflict between two residents of San Fernando, María, a woman in her late twenties, and her cousin

Rosalinda, who was in her late fifties (also cf. Cook, 1993, pp. 81–83). Although both were born in Margarita, María and her children had spent some time living off the island. Rosalinda, on the other hand, had spent the last 25 years living in San Fernando, and had acquired a large network of family, *compadres*, and friends. I was never able to identify any single cause underlying the conflict, although numerous accusations were made. María suggested that her cousin was jealous because María had recently married a man that Rosalinda had intended for her daughter. Nevertheless, over the course of several months Rosalinda used her large and well-established sociocentric network against María. Through gossip, coercion, ostracism, and the withholding and denying of needed resources, Rosalinda drove her cousin out of town. Eventually, María and her husband moved to the town that her husband was from originally. In the new town, María participated as a valued new member of her husband's own large sociocentric network.

Skill and premeditation are important tools in battles of one-upmanship. In the process of winning a battle, one can lose the war. Several weeks after María moved to her husband's town, María came back to San Fernando to visit, this time accompanied by a group of her new affinal kin and friends. The visit was an uneasy one, and it was clear that María's husband and the members of his family were on María's side. What also became clear was Rosalinda's uneasiness when she realized that in the process of ostracizing an individual, she had cut herself off from a rather large network on the island. Rosalinda's situation was made further precarious by the fact that some of the members of her sociocentric network were part of María's new one. I left the field without discovering the final outcome of this case, but it was clear that Rosalinda had, to some extent, made herself into a large fish in a small pond by exerting her social influence over María at the cost of inadvertently diminishing the size of her own social network.

Although less common, fission also occurs when individuals voluntarily leave networks as is demonstrated by the case of Sandra. Sandra lives in San Fernando with her husband and his parents in a large extended family household. According to Sandra and other town members, Sandra's husband Juan was lazy, irresponsible, and possessive. While Juan did not like his wife to leave home, he occasionally went out at night to dances, leaving Sandra at home to take care of their small children. Gossip usually came back that he had been flirting with women. One night Juan joined his friends to go to a party, leaving his wife at home. As he left, she said to me: "Tonight he is out seeking his pleasure . . . he is a *marica* [a common local insult and a pejorative word for homosexual]. I am a woman and a good mother. I feel trapped in this house. In the morning I am going to go to my aunt's house." In the morning she took her children to her aunt's town for three days. During the course of my fieldwork, Sandra occasionally shifted residence when her husband's behavior became overwhelming to her.

The threat of leaving can be used to manipulate the behavior of members in one's network. In San Fernando, a powerful matriarch in her mid-sixties occasionally threatened to move in with relatives in another town when members of her family did not behave according to her wishes.

CONCLUSION

In native Margariteño society, conflict resolution functions as an explosive device. Ironically, it vitalizes the group by creating continuous instability. Within sociocentric networks interpersonal battles of one-upmanship, while often aggressive and cruel, benefit the group network by allowing for the expulsion of deviants and the inclusion of new members that make valuable contributions (for a similar yet contrasting example, cf. Gilmore, 1987).

From the macroscopic, social point of view there are potentially no permanent winners or losers in native Margariteño society. Flexibility in membership means that the cycle of fission and fusion merely shifts to different arenas, depending on the skill and motivation of the individuals involved. Fission and fusion vitalize the system and benefit individuals that participate in it. Although ostracized from one network, deviants have the opportunity to make a valuable contribution in a new one that suits them better.

It is interesting to examine Margariteño conflict in the context provided by Pruitt and Rubin (1986). They provide a convincing analysis of conflict and its resolution from a western point of view. In the Margariteño context the principles they describe have a different value and outcome. The dramaturgical model of conflict resolution utilized by Pruitt and Rubin (1986, p. v) describes many conflicts as progressing through a series of stages. This model does not explain the culturally specific use of conflict in native Margariteño society. Like Pruitt and Rubin, native Margariteños view conflict as a "perceived divergence of interest," but whereas Pruitt and Rubin (1986, pp. 7–8) viewed conflict as a problem, in Margarita it is a valuable feature built into the system. In native Margariteño culture, sociocentric networks function to provide a "perceived divergence of interest." The effect of contention is not escalation, but rather continuation.

A consistent implicit assumption of their work is that conflict is intrinsically bad. Although Pruitt and Rubin (1986, pp. 6–7) considered the alternative, they quickly moved away to the root assumption that the best thing that can happen in a situation of conflict is to resolve it: "Although it may seem paradoxical that conflict can have both harmful and beneficial consequences, this paradox is more apparent than real. What often happens is that the positive functions of conflict are swamped by the harmful consequences that derive from the use of heavy contentious tactics" (Pruitt & Rubin, 1986, p. 7). In native Margariteño society, contentious tactics are ongoing episodes that create a pattern of change and opportunity that vitalizes society and allows individuals to make social adjustments that suit them best. There are potentially no permanent winners or losers in native Margariteño society. Thus the nature of conflict resolution in native Margariteño society can be characterized by two native, coexisting expressions: "We are one big family," that lives in a "small town, big hell" (Cook, 1993).

ACKNOWLEDGMENT

This research was funded by a grant from the Organization of American States (FO4519).

REFERENCES

Alexander, C. S. (1961). Margarita Island, exporter of people. *Journal of Inter-American Studies,* 3(4), 549–557.

Bailey, F. G. (1991). *Tertius Luctans:* Idiocosm, caricature, and mask. In K. Avruch, P. W. Black, & J. A. Scimecca (Eds.), *Conflict resolution: Cross-cultural perspectives* (pp. 61–83). Westport, CT: Greenwood.

Cook, H. B. K. (1992). Matrifocality and female aggression in Margariteño society. In K. Björkqvist & P. Niemelä, (Eds.), *Of mice and women: Aspects of female aggression* (pp. 149–62). New York: Academic Press.

Cook, H. B. K. (1993). Small town, big hell: An ethnographic study of aggression in a Margariteño community. *Antropológica, Suplemento #4.* Caracas, Venezuela. Instituto Caribe De Antropología Y Sociología. Fundación La Salle De Ciencias Naturales.

Doob, L. W. (1991). Series Foreword. In K. Avruch, P. W. Black, & J. A. Scimecca (Eds.), *Conflict resolution: Cross-cultural perspectives* (pp. ix–x). Westport, CT: Greenwood Press.

Gilmore, D. D. (1987). *Aggression and community: Paradoxes of Andalusian culture.* New Haven: Yale University Press.

Mata-Marin, E. (1976). *Algunas características de la marginalidad en siete comunidades costeras del Distrito Diaz-Estado Nueva Esparta* [Some characteristics of marginality in seven coastal communities of the District Diaz-Estado Nueva Esparta]. Universidad de Oriente, Núcleo de Nueva Esparta.

McCorkle, T. (1965). *Fajardo's people: Cultural adjustment in Venezuela; and the little community in Latin American and North American contexts.* Caracas, Venezuela: Editorial Sucre.

Orona, A. R. (1968). *The social organization of the Margariteño fishermen, Venezuela.* Unpublished doctoral dissertation, University of California, Los Angeles.

Pruitt, D. G., & Rubin, J. Z. (1986). *Social conflict: Escalation, stalemate, and settlement.* New York: Random House.

Urbano Taylor, S. H. (1981). *Evolución socio-histórica del delito en el Estado Nueva Esparta.* [Sociohistorical evolution of crime in the state of Nueva Esparta]. Unpublished manuscript, Universidad de Oriente, Nucleo de Nueva Esparta. [Socio-historical evolution of crime in the state of Nueva Esparta]

8

Leaving Anger Outside the Kava Circle: A Setting for Conflict Resolution in Tonga

Ernest G. Olson
Wells College

Tonga is a Polynesian society that stresses the ideal of social harmony. As is typical in Oceania, eating and drinking together are important occasions for sustaining social relationships. The author describes and analyzes the kava drinking circle in terms of how this social event provides an informal social mechanism for airing grievances and bringing about conformity to group expectations. Humor and joking are an important part of the process. Olson notes that in contrast to the formal courtroom and alcohol-drinking situations that sometimes lead to fighting, the kava circle provides a means for the friendly and nonviolent airing of grievances and the working out of conflict through joking and good-natured talk.

—*The Editors*

Tonga, a Polynesian society in the South Pacific, offers cultural means of conflict resolution that are distinct (cf. Black, 1991). A key aspect of this distinctiveness is the emphasis placed on social harmony and the peaceful resolution of interpersonal tensions. The emphasis on social harmony is maintained despite the fact that Tongan society, as for all societies, is the site of strong currents of contention that sometimes find public expression. In the negotiation of Tongan social life, there are a number of culturally appropriate contexts and styles—within, for example, the courtroom, the church building, and village meeting hall—to express hostility and conflict without destroying public harmony. In particular, contexts involving the drinking of the indigenous substance kava reveal some key means of managing conflict in culturally appropriate ways. Kava-drinking contexts are a fruitful area for explication because they offer an alternative to the violence-prone contexts of alcohol consumption.

SOCIAL CONTROL AND VIOLENCE IN TONGA

The Kingdom of Tonga is a monarchical state that maintains an independent political and cultural identity while interacting in many ways with the rest of the world. Tongan society, missionized at the beginning of the 19th century, is today a Christian nation influenced by European (especially British) systems of law, education, and commerce. Along with such interconnections with the international sphere, there are many forces in Tongan society that foster a strong commitment to its own cultural heritage and social institutions.

Tonga, similar to other Polynesian societies (Shore, 1982; Goldman, 1970), stresses the importance of strict measures of social control. Sermons from the pulpit, pronouncements from the local court, and admonishments in the household frequently appeal to cultural ideals of interpersonal harmony. A Tongan youngster learns to show respect in responding to the wishes and needs of those who are socially superior. Even for adults, there are few contexts in which one can be openly angry and violently opposed to one's social superior. A key aspect of Tongan respectful behavior in regard to status relations is that higher status persons normally initiate interactions with lower status persons and maintain control of the verbal exchange. The importance of respectful behavior means that there are cultural restrictions on the means by which social conflict can be appropriately expressed. Violent conflict is certain to be swiftly sanctioned if it occurs in the public view where community leaders are present.

However, not all members of Tongan society are under the same degree of social monitoring. It is a common expectation that youthful males, or *talavou*, will deviate from accepted norms. Male youth are often left to more or less take care of themselves in regard to subsistence, entertainment, and social activities. *Talavou*, with fewer ties to the home than female youth, interact in peer groups that are not always carefully supervised by the adult community. Similar to the situation noted by Marshall for another society in Oceania (Marshall, 1979, p. 120), young Tongan men look for avenues to aggressively express cultural ideals of masculine bravery and bravado without being sanctioned by the community. Males, from their teenage years through their third decade of life, are the most apt to use physical violence in contexts beyond the direct gaze of the community, for example, in the outlying bush or other areas outside the village.

ALCOHOL AND VIOLENCE:
KONA AS A LICENSE FOR AGGRESSION

The ethnographic literature of Oceania emphasizes the importance of eating and drinking as forums for creating and sustaining social cohesion (Rogers, 1975). Two primary activities are found in Tonga that involve the consumption of liquid substances—alcohol, which was introduced from the West, and *kava*, which is indigenous. Activities involving the drinking of alcohol provide an insightful contrast to contexts in which there is drinking of the indigenous kava. Alcohol consumption in Tonga, as in other parts of Oceania (Marshall, 1979), is often a factor in the most serious forms and contexts of violence. The Tongan cultural understanding of alcohol is that it facilitates a disregard for social norms and brings smoldering tensions to the surface. The drinking of home-brewed beer (hopi) or commercial beer by the youth or older males is often a factor in violence; the cultural ideal of harmony is most likely to be transgressed with fights in situations where men are drinking home brew in the bush or consuming commercial beer in one of several bars or dance halls found in the closest town. Drunkenness, or kona, due to alcohol does provide a degree of license to express hostility and violence (cf. Marshall, 1979, p. 121) in that individuals are more easily forgiven for acts undertaken while under the influence of alcohol. However, alcohol-induced states of kona are viewed negatively by the community, the police, and the local courts; in fact, the courts put a priority on prosecuting cases of kona, especially those that have disrupted community harmony.

KAVA DRINKING AS SOCIAL LUBRICANT

A much less volatile and violent Tongan social context is the kava-drinking event. In Tonga, and throughout much of the Pacific, kava drinking is a key cultural phenomenon. Lebot, Merlin, and Lindstrom (1992, p. 211) in their recent cross-cultural account of kava drinking, described the multifaceted roles of kava as a "symbol of Christian atonement; kava as icon of the new state; kava as cultural fetish within developing nationalist discourse; kava as assertion of resistance and indigenous rights; kava as cash crop; kava as ethnic Valium or alcohol; kava as fulcrum of ongoing male domination and gender inequalities; kava as camouflage for developing economic equalities and class formation; kava as the shared pick-me-up of urban Pacific kava bars."

In Tonga, the drinking of kava, a liquid made from a mixture of the pounded roots of the pepper shrub *Piper methysticum* and water, is an essential ingredient of social life. Historically, kava drinking has a long tradition in Tongan religious, political, and social life; kava was central to religious ritual and largely under the domain of chiefly elites and the priests before Tonga came into contact with Europeans. The establishment of the mission and the monarchy, among other factors, allowed kava to become so much a part of the fabric of daily village life that no current description of Tongan social life is adequate without a discussion of kava drinking among the general male population.

Most evenings in the Tongan village include at least one kava party. The kava drinking party, or *faikava*, is predominantly a male activity in that it consists of males sitting cross-legged on the floor and being served the brownish liquid from a large wooden bowl supported by short legs made of the same material. Ideally, there is a female server, the *tou'a*, who sits on the floor next to the bowl and fills coconut half-shells with the liquid; each shell is then passed to the individual recipient. Each member of the circle in turn receives his own coconut shell of liquid, which he then consumes at once in a single lifting of the shell to the lips. The *faikava* is the primary context for Tongans to entertain one another while drinking kava. There are a number of different types of kava drinking events, but the most popular is found in the context of the club. There is normally a kava drinking club in every village, usually under the control of a group of men who provide the building, the bowls and shells, and the kava. The common goal for these club members is to raise funds for themselves and for numerous community projects. Particularly on Friday nights, many men of a village can be found in the local hall (usually a large tin building) participating in one of several kava circles. Tongan males feel it ideal that each circle should include a female server who, in addition to sitting beside the kava bowl and overseeing the serving of the kava, actively participates in verbal exchange within the circle. There is some tendency to drink among friends but in most cases a circle will be somewhat diverse by age and social position.

Kava drinking in Tonga is a male dominated activity that embodies the most social of events as participants relax and enjoy the company of those gathered in the circle around a kava bowl. Tongan social life requires that individuals act in consort with other people; group activity is very much a part of everyday life, and social kava drinking is a primary context where Tongans, especially males, interact within their community. For Tongans (and Pacific Islanders in general), "one's personhood is embedded in social relations and community" (Ritchie & Ritchie, 1989, p. 107) and this is particularly evident in the social interaction of the kava circle. Rubinstein (1987, p. 57) asserts that within the Pacific society of Vanuatu the drinking of kava includes "a private, in-body and in-mind experience which is also experienced by other men at the same time." In Tonga, the kava party offers a type of altered state, or kona experience that is meant to be eminently social in nature.

There is some discussion in the Pacific ethnographic literature of the importance of kava as a force for social cohesion. Lebot et al. (1992, p. 210) state that "psychoactive kava does enhance feelings of interpersonal universalism and does promote goodwill" and that "this attractive emotionally altered state is available for ongoing political and religious symbolic elaboration." A short historical note on the value of kava as social lubricant is provided by the naturalist Georg Forster who accompanied Captain Cook on a voyage through Eastern Polynesia: "The pepper-plant is in high esteem with all the natives of these islands as a sign of peace; perhaps because getting drunk together naturally implies good fellowship" (Forster, 1777, quoted in Lebot et al., 1992, p. 119). Katz (1993, p. 49) makes a more recent statement about modern Fijians: "People become more congenial with moderate drinking [of kava]; another common saying is that 'without yaqona [kava], we cannot have a good meeting,' meaning that yaqona encourages people to work together."

Clearly, such provocative, though brief, acknowledgments of the role of kava in engendering sociability need further clarification in order to understand the relevance of kava-drinking contexts for managing conflict. The recent work by Arno (1993) indicates that the kava event as an arena for appropriate styles of conflict management depends on more than the mild effects of the kava liquid. A careful examination of actual kava-drinking occasions in Tonga reveals the essential role of the cultural context in shaping the experience of the kava party. Lebot et al. (1992, p. 119) state that among Pacific Island societies, "kava drinking still signals good fellowship" and that "by sharing kava, Islanders create new relations with strangers and repair these relations when they falter." The kava-drinking event, whether in the private home or in a more public kava-club setting, brings with it certain norms that disallow physical violence and call for an atmosphere of general conviviality. In contrast to alcohol-drinking contexts, which lack traditional guidelines for nonaggressive behavior, the *faikava* is an event in which individuals can meet in social interaction without worry of violence or open conflict.

COMPETITION AND KAVA

The kava party is concomitantly a vehicle for strong forces of social control that prevent violent conflict from occurring and a culturally appropriate outlet for the expression of contentions, disagreements, and rivalry. On the one hand, the *faikava* allows unrelated persons of various positions within the social hierarchy to socialize together and experience a sense of camaraderie. On the other hand, "Kava symbolizes the ethos of hierarchy, status, latent competition, rivalry, and exclusion" (Rogers, 1975, p. 415) and *faikava* parties are occasions for status rivalry and competition (Marcus, 1978, p. 254). Status rivalry and competition have traditionally been major social forces in Tonga and other Pacific societies (cf. Goldman, 1983) and the kava drinking event, as a primary activity in Tongan society, offers a quintessential context for competition. For example, the club *faikava* generates excitement by encouraging individuals within a kava circle to compete with each other to donate the most money; each circle of males, in turn, competes with the other circles to donate the most money of any circle at the club. In this way, everyone has a chance to compete for the high status reputation of being a generous community member. The *faikava* is, then, a fairly controlled forum for individuals to safely compete actively against their cohorts and rivals for the good of the community.

In addition to competitive giving, the *faikava* held in either the club or the private home can also be a setting for courtship competition among the single males. In Tonga, there are relatively few socially acceptable settings for youth to interact with the opposite gender, and the presence of the female kava server at the *faikava*, whether in the club or private home, allows for a relished opportunity to engage in lengthy social exchange with the opposite sex. Such exchange inevitably involves competition among suitors. For example, Rogers (1975, p. 396), describing just one aspect of competition to gain the attention and favor of the female server, notes that there is keen competition for the sitting positions in the kava circle next to the female server and if "either the water-bearer or kava beater [seated next to the female server] slipped outside for a few minutes they would invariably return to find someone else in their place passing the cups from bowl to drinkers or helping to prepare more kava."

The group keenly observes the courtship competition among those sitting closest to the female server; the group, while serving as audience for the competition among those vying for the attention of the *tou'a*, also has the responsibility of sanctioning any inappropriate behavior. Those males sitting next to the female server are the most likely to misbehave and any hint of impropriety on the part of a male suitor may be enough for someone in the circle, perhaps a rival, to verbally chastise the culprit. In some cases, someone in the circle may even, for example, take a sandal and beat the offender about the head and shoulders. In more than one observed incident, there was real forcefulness to the blows upon an overly forward suitor seated next to the female server. Such punishment, often accompanied by a great deal of laughter by all (including the punished), usually has the approval of the group and illustrates the manner in which competition and rivalry within the kava circle is keenly observed and controlled by all participants. By comparison, other contexts for courtship, such as those found within the limited number of commercial establishments allowing dancing and/or the consumption of alcohol, are fraught with the danger of violence.

INSULTS AND KAVA

The *faikava* is a primary context for the expression of social frictions among male community members within the controlled revelry and rivalry of *faikava* discourse. Above all, the essential ingredient of the kava event, particularly one with a female server present, is verbal repartee: stories, jokes, and humorous insults are the most obvious form of competitive one-upmanship within the kava session. More than an opportunity to drink, the flow of social interaction in the *faikava* reveals the manner in which the group eagerly participates in the verbal and nonverbal competitive sparring within the circle. Humor, or *fakakata*, a primary part of Tongan social interaction in general, is imperative for the kava event. The expression of humor can concern a range of topics, but discourse within the *faikava* is frequently "a mix of sexual ribaldry, ridicule, and personal rivalry" wherein "sexual punning, allegorical and allusive comments are directed at particular individuals" (Rogers, 1975, pp. 393, 396). Such aggressive joking is most often between male rivals within a kava circle but can also occur between the female server and males. Though such humor is often derisive, the butt of the joke normally joins in the laughter.

LEAVING ANGER OUTSIDE OF THE KAVA CIRCLE: A CONTEXT FOR CONFLICT MANAGEMENT

Tongans believe it vital to maintain a mood of harmony within the kava circle and that anger, *'ita*, should remain outside. In contrast to the *faikava*, the situation involving the drinking of home brew or commercial beer often consists of individuals utilizing self-help (Black, 1989) and opting for a violent conflict strategy. Many cases of drunken violence eventually come to the attention of the police and end up in the local court; typically, the court punishes all parties involved in the drunken violence. However, at the kava bowl, unlike the situation in which alcohol is consumed, rarely will there be the appearance of open discord. Instead, the *faikava* allows contentions to be aired in the form of competitive humor that can be aimed at individuals without creating open conflict or violence (Riches, 1986, p. 10), whereas the same humor would provoke violence in an alcohol-drinking context.

The kava event, usually lasting into the early morning hours, serves as a type of informal means of social control via humorous insult of deviant or conflictual behavior of others. The following example was particularly humorous for all present within the circle. In this case, a male in his early 20s, referred to as Tevita, was repeatedly chided by his peers in the circle for not being able to handle the comparatively austere, restricted lifestyle of the theological seminary. Tevita had recently failed to finish his program in Tonga's main theological training school, and the accusation was that Tevita, behaving like a foolish young man who thinks only of his bodily desires, had irresponsibly spent his money on beer in order to become intoxicated, a forbidden activity for seminarians. Some individuals in the kava circle, who had been involved in past competitions and antagonisms with Tevita, were quick to point out the dismal failure of Tevita to resist being a beer-drinking fellow. One circle participant gleefully stated that Tevita had been "incredibly stupid," causing his own expulsion from the seminary.

Tevita's case is an example of the manner in which participants in the *faikava* express their hostility toward social deviants who may be openly questioning or violating traditional values; teasing can be seen as an indirect attempt to reject, modify, question, or bring into line the conduct of the recipient. Bernstein argues that "Tongan humor itself is often about self-control or its lack" (1983, p. 81). Tevita's drunken behavior caused embarrassment for family, friends, and the community and the kava circle served as a context to indirectly confront this conflict and to publicly sanction Tevita under the guise of joking discourse. In Tevita's case, it is important to note the presence of two older males who served to temper the joking with more serious admonishments for the future manifestation of socially appropriate behavior on the part of all the younger members of the kava circle.

Beyond general processes of social control, the kava circle also involves more clear-cut cases of conflict and personal grievance. Tongan conflict management can be characterized as ongoing processes of "disentangling" conflicts (White & Watson-Gegeo, 1990) that may express themselves in different ways in a variety of contexts, including the kava circle. An essential element to keep in mind is that talk is very important for Tongans and conflict management is accomplished in largely informal ways through extensive periods of talk. The observation by Arno (1993, p. 102) that in Fiji "among men ... informal yaqona [kava] drinking is an everyday event that provides ample scope for conflict talk" works equally well for Tongan kava drinking. Arno's work, the first concerted attempt to consider the conflict-management aspect to kava drinking in the Pacific, points out that conflict management is successful in the Fijian kava session because of the absence of strong clique formations, which would "tend to exacerbate conflict and restrict the flow of information and the variety of the opinion expressed." In Tongan kava sessions, the diverse age and social position of participants allows for the rather unrestricted flow of information and discussion of conflict. In addition, information flows beyond the boundaries of the *faikava* to reach individuals absent from the kava circle but implicated in conflict.

In the Tongan *faikava*, there is discussion of drunken behavior, fights, cases of petty theft, sexual misconduct, conflicts among churches, vandalism, and property damage done by a neighbor's wandering pigs. In one observed kava session, one participant, Sione, stated that he was tired. Another member of the circle, who was well-informed on village gossip, noted that this tiredness was due to Sione's efforts to chase the wandering pigs of Siale, a neighbor of Sione. Siale's pigs had, in fact, trespassed into Sione's yard and caused damage. Siale, who was seated across the circle, was humorously encouraged by a number of speakers to stop wasting his time in the kava circle and go home to mend his pig pen. There were then numerous comments on the laziness (a common theme in Tongan discussion) of Siale. Siale responded by describing how hard he had been working and by saying that Sione needed to stop doing the work of a dog and get himself a good watchdog to keep wandering pigs off his property. Another individual suggested that Sione should claim any trespassing pig for the next feast hosted by his family and the conversation moved to another topic. However, a few days later, Siale was observed mending a particularly decrepit section of his pig pen.

CONCLUSIONS

There is no readily apparent resolution of such conflicts within the kava circle but there are a number of reasons to categorize the *faikava* as a context for conflict management. First, the experience of kava consumption and entertainment into the early hours of the morning arguably offers a degree of personal catharsis in which pent-up emotions find a degree of release. Second, the freedom to air grievances in an indirect, friendly exchange allows for nonviolent means of handling conflict. Perhaps most important, the value on talk—the voicing of opinions and counter-opinions in the kava session—allows the fuller involvement of peer groups, elders, kin members, and community in the processes of conflict management.

The kava drinking event, in comparison to the alcohol drinking context or the courtroom, offers a more secure setting for individuals to indirectly express conflict without suffering either physical violence or public sanction. The kava session represents a middle ground between the open violence of the alcohol-drinking setting and the more controlled and punitive setting of the local court. The kava party is an informal arena for individuals—through joking, teasing, and scold-ing—to express conflict in a manner that allows for some dissipation or resolution. The important role of the kava party in social life suggests the continued vitality of the use of kava in the future for socializing and for conflict management. It is difficult to calculate precisely the effectiveness of the *faikava* for managing conflict, and perhaps it is best to see *faikava* as a key context of a wider process in which conflicts are expressed within the community. In Tonga, kava drinking offers one alternative to physical violence and suggests the significance of maintaining cultural institutions that call for a high degree of social interaction without violence.

ACKNOWLEDGMENT

Research in the Kingdom of Tonga was made possible by the Wenner–Gren Foundation for Anthropological Research and the National Science Foundation.

REFERENCES

Arno, A. (1993). *The world of talk on a Fijian island.* Norwood, NJ: Ablex.

Bernstein, L. (1983). *Ko e Lau pe (It's just talk): Ambiguity and informal social control in a Tongan village.* Unpublished doctoral dissertation, University of California, Berkeley.

Black, D. (1989). *Sociological justice.* New York: Oxford University Press.

Black, P. (1991). Surprised by common sense: Local understandings and the management of conflict on Tobi, Republic of Belau. In K. Avruch, P. Black, & J. Scimecca (Eds.), *Conflict resolution: Cross-cultural perspectives.* Westport, CT: Greenwood.

Goldman, I. (1970). *Ancient Polynesian society.* Chicago: University of Chicago Press.

Goldman, R. (1983). *Talk never dies: The language of huli disputes.* London: Tavistock.

Katz, R. (1993). *The straight path.* New York: Addison-Wesley.

Lebot, V., Merlin, M., & Lindstrom, L. (Eds.). (1992). *Kava: The South Pacific drug.* New Haven: Yale University Press.

Marcus, G. (1978). Status rivalry in a Polynesian steady-state society. *Ethos, 6,* 242–269.

Marshall, M. (1979). *Weekend warriors: Alcohol in a Micronesian culture.* Mountainview, CA: Mayfield.

Riches, D. (Ed.). (1986). *The anthropology of violence.* Oxford: Basil Blackwell.

Ritchie, J., & Ritchie, J. (1989). Socialization and character development. In R. Borofsky & A. Howard (Eds.), *Developments in Polynesian ethnology* (pp. 95–135). Honolulu: University of Hawaii Press.

Rogers, G. (1975). *Kai and kava in Niutoputapu: Social relations, ideologies, and contexts in a rural Tongan community.* Unpublished doctoral dissertation, University of Auckland.

Rubinstein, R. (1987). Card playing on Malo, Vanuatu. *Oceania, 58,* 47–59.

Shore, B. (1982). *Sala'ilua: A Samoan Mystery.* New York: Columbia University Press.

Watson-Gego, K., & White, G. (Eds.). (1990). *Disentangling: Conflict discourses in Pacific Societies.* Stanford, CA: Stanford University Press.

Part III

The Challenge
of Resolving Ethnic Conflict

Chapters in this section analyze ethnic or inter-group conflicts from various settings
and theoretical perspectives, and it is clear in all cases that an understanding of the
histories and cultures of the groups involved in conflict is critical. Nordstrom
conducted ethnographic research in war-torn Sri Lanka and Mozambique and
compares the violence and peacemaking endeavors in both places. One point that
emerges from her analysis is that people, through their daily actions following
divisive violence, can be viewed as the ultimate rebuilders of a peaceful society. A
challenge becomes one of designing appropriate institutional supports that facilitate
the role of individuals and local communities in developing and implementing
alternatives to ethnic or intergroup violence. Nordstrom writes, "People do not
merely voice the values of conflict mediation—they live them. ... It is the creativity
of the people themselves at the epicenters of often impossible violences that forge
solution instituted in practice."

Various preceding chapters, such as those by Hollan and Robarchek, stressed
and illustrated the critical impact of a culture's world view, values, and attitudes in
framing and affecting conflict behavior. The impact of world view, for example, is
reflected in the fact that the Semai fear a conflict more than they fear tigers and
place a high value on maintaining the peace. Another example is that the Toraja
reiterate the dangers of showing anger and engaging in aggression. In the chapter
by McCormick, we see a culture of conflict—part of a world view—in Northern
Ireland that strongly favors avoidance of interaction with the "other side." Paradoxically, the strongly held views and practices favoring curtailed interaction,
according to McCormick, may both reduce aggression and hinder reconciliation
efforts. McCormick notes that the vast majority of Northern Irish citizens have not
participated in violence: "Instead, they have diligently avoided it." But at the same

time—with some exceptions—they diligently have avoided associating with each other in positive, peace-building ways, many apparently considering cross-community contact to be nonsensical. Here we see a set of attitudes that hinder peacemaking contacts.

In his chapter on Islamic historiography, Hjärpe underscores the importance of how some historical events are selectively chosen and others ignored by leaders and other persons involved with the escalation or deescalation of conflicts. The broader point is that reference to historical elements, language, and culturally meaningful symbols, although often used to provoke antagonism through propaganda, also can be employed to defuse tensions and facilitate reconciliation between groups engaged in conflict. This point is illustrated and discussed in the chapter by Hjärpe as he relates the concept of historiography to conflict issues in Islamic culture. Conceivably this approach also has relevance for Northern Ireland.

Fry and Fry suggest in their chapter that Black's (1993) models have cross-cultural applicability. Landau demonstrates the utility of Black's typology of conflict management by using it to categorize and analyze conflict processes in Israel. Landau shows how virtually all forms of conflict management discussed by Black—toleration, avoidance, self-help, bipartisan negotiation, and third-party settlement—are utilized in some manner within Israeli society.

In the final chapter of this section, Glazer focuses on interethnic relations between African Americans and Jews in the New York neighborhood of Crown Heights, where a 4-day race riot occurred in 1991. She recounts how members of both groups compete with each other over certain resources and that elements of their cultural values and lifestyles clash at times. Glazer suggests that inter-ethnic relationships can be enhanced, and consequently that violence can be prevented, through enhancing meaningful interaction across sub-groups. This is one of the four ways discussed by Rubin, Pruitt, & Kim (1994, pp. 138–139) for combating polarization and conflict escalation in communities consisting of subgroups with few bonds between them. Rubin, et al. (p. 139) noted that when some individuals from one group work with some members of the other group—in essence paralleling what Glazer calls "special interest friendships"—a common group identity can develop allowing "them to engage in problem solving about matters of mutual concern." Glazer's ethnographic data correspond to such a model. The chapters in this section show that ethnic and intergroup conflicts are challenging to resolve, but also offer some insights about the dynamics of such conflicts.

REFERENCES

Black, D. (1993). *The social structure of right and wrong*. San Diego: Academic Press.
Rubin, J. Z., Pruitt, D. G., & Kim, S. H. (1994). *Social conflict: Escalation, stalemate and settlement* (2nd ed.). New York: McGraw-Hill.

9

The Eye of the Storm: From War to Peace— Examples from Sri Lanka and Mozambique

Carolyn Nordstrom

University of California, Berkeley

Nordstrom compares violence and peacemaking in Sri Lanka and Mozambique, noting how local level conflict resolution and peacemaking efforts occurred in both cases. In Mozambique, the government actively encouraged and supported local peacemaking initiatives, whereas in Sri Lanka, the local practices to ameliorate violence went unnoticed and unreinforced. Following the comparison of these two cases, Nordstrom discusses the broader global context of "dirty wars" in which, she notes, unarmed civilians are by far the most numerous victims. She discusses facets of the international system that both allow and augment the outbreak of wars. Finally, Nordstrom argues that in any war zone, the people are engaged not only in reproducing but also in resisting the war and rebuilding some semblance of a peaceful and healthy society.

—The Editors

Warfare is just an invention known to the majority of human societies by which they permit their young men either to accumulate prestige or avenge their honor or acquire loot or wives or slaves or grab lands or cattle or appease the blood lust of their gods or the restless souls of the recently dead. It is just an invention, older and more widespread than the jury system, but none the less an invention. (Mead, 1988, p. 134)

There is considerable concern with resolving conflicts in the world today. But how much can we say we know of conflict and the processes of peace? For in truth, is it conflict per se we want to resolve? Conflict is inherent, for example, in the democratic process, and even in the most basic disagreements of opinion. I suggest it is violence we really seek to resolve.

Both violence and peacebuilding, like all human behavior, are cultural phenomena. But they are often exceedingly difficult to study. Violence constitutes what Taussig (1992) calls a *public secret*: although it is something everyone knows about, it is kept hidden from the public eye of the everyday world. Other than in carefully controlled 15-second film bites offered by the media, battlefields, massacres, and torture chambers are seldom observed by impartial viewers and researchers. Without reliable ethnographic data, it is impossible to distinguish propaganda from fact, myth and misinformation from truth. Without access to the information that gives researchers clues to the reality of the situation, conflict resolution lives up to its name: resolving the same conflicts that resurface again and again over time and space because the core issues were never adequately addressed and ameliorated.

Peace building, though neither dangerous nor restricted to study, is often equally neglected. Global politics has handed down a legacy relegating conflict resolution to the realm of politico-military leaders and to the offices of specialists: in a word, to elites far removed from the epicenters and the impact of bloodletting. The fact that implementing peace is a long and complex process is largely lost in this orientation, as is the fact that peace is ultimately forged on the ground—by individuals and in communities—as soldiers, victims, and civilians react and interact in the attempt to (re)build their society. This process can be as unique as the conflict(s) that set it in motion—possibly resulting in a sustained peace, possibly fomenting further conflict. But without considered study into the complexities of the peacebuilding process, researchers are at a loss to identify the factors that lead to such divergent outcomes.

This study intentionally blurs the distinctions between macro- and microlevel analyses, and questions the validity of examining institutions in the abstract—depeopled from the agency and intentions of persons who comprise an institution at any given point in time. People do not live their lives, make decisions, or forge wars and peace accords apart from the national and international dynamics that affect them, and international relations are ultimately dependent on the biographies and histories of individuals.

We are coming to the end of an era when theorists could speak of states, wars, and institutions solely as structures, according to functions, in terms of policies—but devoid of people. There are no states without people, no ideologies forged apart from the hopes, dreams, and fears—the rationalities and irrationalities—that guide people. There are no wars, no peaces, without individuals: Someone stands behind every gun that fires a shot, behind every action to stem the flow of violence. There are no objective realities behind the people that live them—no natural truths beyond the cultures that define self and world. People's own biographies come to bear on the choices they make and the actions they perform, whether they be power elites brokering massive conflict or its cessation, or civilians facing the realities of these policies on the ground. To understand conflict and its solution is to delve into the complexities of human experience and cultural process.

I do not use the term *culture* here in the traditional or restricted sense of equating the lifestyles and world views of a particular people with a bounded geographical space such as the nation-state or a kin based system such as a tribe. Instead I draw upon current theory that sees all human action as culturally informed. Thus, nuanced concepts of culture can emerge that transcend specific geographies to include international processes that link numerous locales (cf., Abu-Lughod, 1991; Appadurai, 1990, 1991; Bhabha, 1994; Gupta & Ferguson, 1992). Multiple cultures can be seen to be operating at any given time and place. It is in this sense that violence, militarization, and peace can be seen as comprising cultural systems in their own right. They constitute spheres of thought and action performed by specific actors influenced by both local-level definitions and international dynamics.

THE CULTURES OF VIOLENCE

I love this country and I hate it. No one who has not lived like this can understand. The war has gotten into us all, it lives in us, affecting our every move and thought. If I walk outside, I wonder if today is the day I will die. If my brother is late coming to visit me, I wonder if he has been kidnapped or killed, and the terror lives in me. I have not heard from my mother—she lives in an area under enemy control, and I live daily not knowing if she is dead or alive. You do not have to see the war to live the war, and the war lives in all of us. (Fieldnotes, Mozambique, 1991)

Some of the most dangerous forms of violence are the least visible. The physical violence produced by sociopolitical conflict is staggering: But what happens when we consider the destruction to identity, community, society, and culture that accompanies physical violence—the common targets of dirty-war, specifically intended to destabilize both people (the generalized opponent) and political process (the threat of resistance)? Violence carries extensive social, political, economic, and cultural ramifications that permeate not only the military, but the whole of civil life within a war zone (cf. Nordstrom, 1992a, 1992b). Aggression dramatically reconfigures the lives of both perpetrators and victims. I define *dirty-war* as comprising those sets of strategies and tactics that use terror-warfare and human rights abuses against both combatants and noncombatants.

Civilians and civil society are a major target of dirty war, and the goal is to enforce political acquiescence among a society at large. Considering the fact that 80% to 90% of all casualties in war today are noncombatants (Sivard, 1993), the point of such violent tactics is to undermine the social and political will, and thus resistance, of the many by maiming and killing a selective part of the constituency. The irony in the use of such terror tactics is that they are counterproductive. As Foucault (1972, p. 142) noted: "There are no relations of power without resistances; the latter are all the more real and effective because they are formed right at the point where relations of power are exercised." People ultimately resist, turning their anger against the regimes that institute violent practices, and the destabilization created in the cycles of violence and counterviolence undermine perpetrators and victims alike. Curiously, dirty-war practices continue despite the fact that they do not quell, but provoke, resistance.

THE CULTURES OF PEACE

"Beneath the surface of [practical thinking] lie continuing acts of creativity—the invention of new ways of handling old and new problems" (Scribner, 1986, p. 28). There is cause for optimism in this analysis. The majority of people in war zones suffer the violence inflicted by a few. The majority, however, are not passive victims. I have found average citizens in war zones are far more informed, and involved, in the mitigation of conflict than national and international conflict research and resolution specialists suspect. An analysis of the practices and ideologies people institute at the ground level to counteract violence shows that key conflict-resolution processes are generated in the midst of war by those most affected—processes that can be widely implemented if recognized.

There is something of an irony in this observation. There is a tendency to view many conflicts today as internal. Agency—the impetus to act—is ascribed to local populations. Yet in matters of conflict resolution, agency is seldom seen as emanating from those same populations. Instead, it is granted to national and international bodies: superpower nations; sophisticated power elites; formal nongovernmental bodies; even academics. Our conflict–resolution approaches can be improved if these overarching bodies recognize, and work with, solutions to violence forged at the ground level by those seeking to mitigate the problems in which they find themselves embroiled.

Two examples provide illustration: Sri Lanka and Mozambique. Both document local level conflict–resolution practices, and the work among citizens to institute cultures of peace. In discussing Sri Lanka I focus on more general social dynamics affecting conflict and its resolution; for Mozambique I examine more specific actions individuals employ to ameliorate war's violence. In Sri Lanka, these practices went largely unrecognized by the government, and this lack of support hindered the peace process. In Mozambique, the government actively worked to support local-level initiatives, and the peace settlement in Mozambique has to date been more successful than in many other countries.

SRI LANKA: FAILED OPPORTUNITIES

The government of Sri Lanka has been fighting a war on two fronts during the past decade, both of which have roots that extend well back into history. Tensions between the minority Tamil population and the Sinhalese majority have periodically punctured long periods of peace for two millennia and have reached a pitch in the last decade with the Tamil separatist movement. On another front, the antagonisms between the government (a socialist democracy) and the JVP, a proscribed communist political and paramilitary movement originating among Southern Sinhalese has been heated since the failed 1971 JVP insurgency and government repression. Both conflicts together in the last decade have taken, as a conservative estimate, over 80,000 lives. The war between the Tamils and the Sri Lankan government is internationally visible, and the 30,000 killed are well circulated figures. The 50,000

Sinhalese killed in the JVP bid for power and the ensuing military repression are a less publicized story. As in most wars today, the vast majority of casualties in both instances have been unarmed civilians.

In 1986, I wrote that the sociopolitical violence had become institutionalized and routinized in the Weberian sense of becoming entrenched in institutional policy and public practice (Nordstrom, 1986). Observations during continuing fieldwork demonstrated I was wrong: Public attitudes towards violence are fluid and complex, and they undergo periods of both escalation and de-escalation.

I made the observation about the institutionalization of violence based on fieldwork spanning five years in Sri Lanka. I had witnessed the anti-Tamil riots in Ratnapura in 1981 and then the devastating anti-Tamil riots of 1983 that destroyed one sixth of the country's infrastructure and took more than 1,000 lives. I watched the development of the Tamil Eelam (separatist) movement to guerrilla warfare against the Sri Lankan State. In 1985, when I visited Jaffna, the stronghold of Tamil resistance, I found 33 different Tamil politico-militant groups. In addition, numerous armed military and civilian groups of Sinhalese had instigated aggressive actions against Tamil villagers.

I noted at this time that there was no clear unilinear evolution of violence. As armed aggressions and human rights violations mounted, so too did many people's sheer disgust and fatigue with the war. This was evident in late spring of 1985, when a Tamil paramilitary group was credited with the armed attack on the commercial and holy center of the city of Anuradhapura—an attack that left scores of Sinhalese dead and wounded. The Sinhalese saw the Anuradhapura attack as a particularly vicious assault, directed as it was against unarmed civilians in a religious center. The perpetrators felt it was a justified reprisal for a number of serious massacres conducted by military and government-sponsored paramilitary forces against Tamil civilians in the North.

Remarkable to many people at the time was the fact that no large scale civil violence erupted as a result of this assault.[1] This is particularly significant in light of the fact that the 1983 riots were provoked by a Tamil guerrilla retaliation against Sri Lankan military repression in the North that left 13 soldiers dead.

In fact, contrary to expectations, I found the reactions of many Sinhalese I talked with at this time had shifted to a less aggressive stance than that expressed after the riots two years before. Many people had begun to question seriously the role of the government in perpetuating the violence and committing atrocities against the Tamils. Instead of violent indignation among Sinhalese about the "Tamil threat" that had permeated discourse in 1983, there was widespread concern about the ineffectiveness and aggressiveness of government officials, and about the cruelty of the military and the inability of top military to control their troops. This concern aired people's disquietude with a deeper truth. In 1986, Amnesty International (1986a, 1986b) cited Sri Lanka as one of two countries with the worst record for

---

[1]However, the Tamils have documented a massacre of Tamil civilians on a ferry in the North afterward—an act they think was carried out by government-paid thugs as a reprisal for the Anuradhapura attack.

human rights violations. People began to realize the Sri Lankan government's military activities were not simply aimed at controlling the Tamil problem, but had to a large extent instigated it.

Sadly, the conversations I had with Tamils in the Jaffna and Trincomalee areas during this time showed that they were unaware of the antiwar sentiments among the Sinhalese. For the most part, they believed all Sinhalese were prejudiced against them and violent in their stance. Most of the residents in these areas had seen violence against civilians carried out by government forces or armed Sinhalese, and they concluded that this was done with the full sanction of the government and the Sinhalese population. Because there was little communication between Sinhalese and Tamils, and because few conflict–resolution groups paid attention to the dynamics of conflict resolution on the ground, Sinhalese and Tamils remained largely unaware of the sympathies each held for the other. Furthermore, because the government was unable, or unwilling, to implement peace accords, its forces met resistance with further military repression. The violence continued to escalate.

When I returned to Sri Lanka in 1986, a subtle but penetrating shift had taken place in many people's attitudes. It was this shift that lead me to conclude that the violence had become institutionalized throughout society. Although still worried about the government's excesses, there was now a feeling among the public that the violence had gotten out of hand, and that the government needed to take strong measures to rectify the situation. Terror tactics had worked: the population was fearful for their lives. At the time I noted that a number of the same Sinhalese who had, but a year before, decried both the government's and the Tamil's excessive use of lethal brutality now sided fully with the government's harsh suppression of Tamil militancy at the expense of the Tamil population as a whole. I concluded that, as the violence became more threatening to the daily lives of Sinhalese, they shed their more objective two-sided approach to conflict resolution in favor of a stark and dichotomous "us and them/good and bad" paradigm. During this time, I increasingly heard such conversations: "We have tried everything we could to solve the situation, but the Tamils have continued to violate our safety, they have asked for it, and the troops must go in and maintain order at any cost." When I asked people why they had adopted this sentiment when a year before they demonstrated a much more comprehensive approach that looked at the problems and injustices as they affected both sides, many responded: "I have become scared, the war now affects my daily life; maybe one of my family, maybe I myself, will become hurt or killed by the violence."

Ethnic antipathies were once again reminiscent of those found in the months after the 1983 rioting, with one major difference. Instead of focusing on the role of militant groups, people now tended to identify entire ethnic populations as responsible for the situation. People were frequently heard to say, "Those Tamils," or "Those Sinhalese are responsible . . . " rather than saying, "The situation," or "The Tigers [the main Tamil guerrilla faction] are responsible. . . . " The distinction between Tamil and Tiger, for example, or between militant Sinhalese and the general Sinhalese population, had become blurred.

What I missed in 1986 was the fluidity of conflict dynamics and the complexity of people's responses. When I returned again in 1988, I had to revise my original hypothesis. The intervening years had seen the introduction of the Indian peacekeepers to control the Tamil situation in the North, and the reemergence of the Sinhalese JVP antigovernment movement in the South (which provoked strong repression from the government). The dynamics of violence changed, but it did not lessen. Yet once again, people began to back away from demanding the government control the violence, and to see it as implicated in its continuance. Sheer disgust with the violence replaced fear yet again.

I have since concluded that although violent conflict can become institutionalized within a society, this is not a simple unilinear escalation. People hold complex notions of violence, and the balance among fear, repression, and resistance is a constantly changing dynamic. What terrorizes a community one day will provoke defiance the next, and these are not knee-jerk reactions but carefully considered political options.

Galtung (1992) argued that most conflicts are not new—they are new expressions of old conflicts that were never properly resolved in the first place. With the tensions still in place—simply momentarily quelled by security forces or by people's fatigue and aversion to violence—the society remains a powderkeg primed to reignite at a later date. This is the irony of the term "conflict resolution." We keep resolving conflicts that have never been adequately solved.

Had national or international conflict–resolution specialists recognized the local-level movements for peace, strongest in 1984 and 1985 and again in the late 1980s, they may have been able to make greater inroads in solving the political violence in Sri Lanka. A great many structures existed on which to build—from religious people who sought to implement peace accords to teachers who were trying to educate for peace. The majority of the population were behind such endeavors. But they remained unrecognized and silenced in the government's tendency toward harsh repression of political factions. Perhaps if conflict–resolution specialists recognize the depth to which violence affects communities and the tendency of conflicts to re-emerge when they have not been successfully solved, work can be done to ensure that Sri Lanka does not become inflamed in further political violence.

MOZAMBIQUE: REALIZED OPPORTUNITIES

The situation in Mozambique differs from Sri Lanka in a number of ways. The war and the rebel group Renamo were created externally by Rhodesian, and then South African, military intelligence. The rebel force Renamo never enjoyed widespread popular support, and toward the end of the war, actively provoked spontaneous civilian resistance in certain locales. Although the government was credited with certain dirty-war practices, most agreed the bulk of human-rights abuses were done by Renamo. The violence of the country's war ranks among the worst of contemporary times. Of a total population of 15 million, one million lost their lives to the war, and a quarter of the population were dislocated from their homes and livelihoods.

Mozambique, at the end of the 1980s, was the poorest country in the world. Not only was there a serious dearth of infrastructure, but what did exist was frequently paralyzed by warfare. There was virtually no road travel: Two million landmines and forces who preyed on people outside of fortified areas made travel extremely hazardous. The government of Mozambique had little to gain by prolonging the war, and so, unlike Sri Lanka, had no reason to impede popular practices aimed toward conflict resolution.

This does not reduce the significance of the conflict reduction practices average citizens promoted at the ground level. It is the creativity of the people themselves at the epicenters of often impossible violences that forge solutions instituted in practice. Far from abstract speculation answerable only to the epistemologies of political ideology or the academic theories of conflict resolution professionals, these ground-level theories-cum-practice carry a heavy penalty if they do not succeed. It is only at this level that success carries any real significance: the quality and possibility of life is at stake.

Before discussing some of the more formalized conflict resolution activities Mozambicans engaged in, I would like to stress that actions directed towards mitigating violence first and foremost take place as a constant process of everyday life, resonating through the minutiae of daily process. Conversations are constantly peppered with considerations of how to get through the day safely, who can and cannot be trusted, how assaults can be avoided, and how the dangerous can be placated. People help others track down missing relatives, help acquire medical attention for the wounded, assist people in fleeing attack zones, take in children whose parents have been killed, rebuild torched villages. A system of values emerges to reinforce peaceful behaviors: those who grow rich on war, who seek power in violence, who turn a deaf ear on the pleas of others, are ridiculed and stigmatized. Stories, songs, and parables develop alongside political and ethical discussions to convey these ethics and the practicalities of survival.

People do not merely voice the values of conflict mediation, they live them. I will start with examples that are not immediately obvious, and I choose them precisely for this reason: They are often overlooked in even the most considered analyses of conflict mitigation and local level resistance to the tyranny of terror-warfare.

Stumbling across a few rather rotten sea fish in the geographical center of a war-torn province in Mozambique first prompted me to look into the rational complexity behind seemingly frivolous behaviors. I was visiting an inland town that had recently been attacked and sacked a number of times as the competing militaries took, and lost, control of the area. Crops burned, animals killed, goods plundered, and trade and supply lines shut down by fighting, the markets had little to offer. I was, therefore, taken aback to find some fish that had seen better days for sale. This is particularly noteworthy for it entailed several men walking with baskets of ocean fish on their heads for 7 days from the coast through several language and ethnic communities and a number of severe war zones. This is a trip no formal trader would brave: The dangers were too high and the profit negligible. So why make such a trip? The men's answers to me, "Because that's how life goes on," did not make a lot of sense at first. But as I listened to them talk, I realized that through their journey they performed invaluable functions. They carried messages for families and friends separated by the fighting; they conveyed details on troop deployments and dangers; and they transmitted critical economic, crop, trade, and political news, not to mention gossip and stories, between communities severed from one another by the war. They linked different ethnic and language groups in a statement that the war was not about local rivalries, and could not be, if they were to survive. They forged trade and social networks through the disordered landscapes of violence, and, by walking for seven days with baskets of fish on their heads through lethal frontlines, they simply defied the war in a way that everyone they passed could enjoy and draw strength from. They were, literally, constructing social order out of chaos.

More systematic endeavors existed side by side with these informal ones. Health care workers and teachers undertook enormous risks to continue working in military hot spots. Both recognized that cultures of violence were reproduced throughout civilian society, and that rectifying this problem was a critical aspect of both health care and education. This took place in an almost total lack of infrastructural support, and the difficulty and danger of this cannot be overestimated. It is interesting how many people elected to stay and work in troubled areas rather than fleeing to safer ones. In traveling through battle zones, people from both professions developed strategies to combat the devastating repercussions of cultures of violence, shared them with others, refined them, and instituted them in their professional work.

The spectrum of those involved in working toward reestablishing a viable society in the midst of military chaos covered the whole of society. Traditional authorities and spontaneous civilian groupings variously decided on their own to do everything from establishing peace zones in their areas to protecting their communities from the excesses of troops and renegade bands of ex-military preying on unarmed populations.

One of the most interesting examples is that of the indigenous African healers. The healers demonstrated perhaps the most sophisticated understanding of the complex problems of violence, and offered some of the most considered solutions. The following quote shows a common approach to addressing the formative nature of violence, and redressing its insidious impact. I heard the same sentiments expressed across the length and breadth of Mozambique:

> We ask that everyone who arrives here be taken to a Curandeiro (African healer) for treatment. The importance of the Curandeiros lies not only in his or her ability to treat the diseases and physical ravages of war, but in their ability to take the violence out of a person and to reintegrate them back into a healthy lifestyle. You see, people who have been exposed to the war, well, some of this violence can affect them, stick with them, like a rash on the soul. They bring the war back home with them. They become more confused, more violent, more dangerous, and so too does the whole community. We need to protect against this. The Curandeiro cuts the person off from any holds the war has on him or her, scrapes off the effects of violence from their spirit,

and makes them alive and part of the community again. (Fieldnotes, Mozambique, 1991)

In refugee camps, in informal dislocation centers, in burned out villages trying to rebuild, I found Curandeiros performing treatments to take the war out of the community, the violence out of the people, and the instability and terror out of the culture.

These peace-building dynamics exist in every war zone.[2] But what is noteworthy about Mozambique is the way in which formal political institutions recognized and began to support local-level peace-building dynamics. The government dropped Marxist-Leninist politics to institute democratic elections. Even Renamo was granted free party status. Recognizing that repressing Renamo soldiers after the war would in all likelihood only produce more Renamo soldiers, Frelimo agreed to integrate a set percentage into existing governmental forces at the end of the war. Equally, a set number of Renamo leaders were to be granted political positions in the government at peace.

The bottom line is that Mozambique has managed a successful cease-fire, and has not yet encountered repeating cycles of violence. It is my opinion the care given to recognizing the impact violence has on social process as well as on individual bodies, and the support given to local level peacebuilding movements, helped broker a more successful peace than that found in many countries.

THE GLOBAL CONTEXT: CULTURES OF MILITARIZATION

Comparing the dynamics of wars across international contexts demonstrates that a sprawling international system allows and supports the occurrence of any localized outbreak of political hostilities. There is a growing recognition that international dynamics are as important to understanding political processes and cultural identities as are local ones. We can no longer see our subject matter in terms of isolated, self-contained cultural communities. Even the most particular is set within a larger context of international influences, indelibly changing the character of both the local and the translocal (Appadurai, 1990). Violent conflicts we label "internal" or "regional," far from being particular expressions of unique conditions and specific tensions, are strongly influenced by cultures of militarization operating throughout the world today.

Consider, for example: foreign strategists and advisors, arms and supplies, soldiers, mercenaries, power brokers, and development and interest groups move among countries; guerrillas and soldiers travel to other countries for training and strategic planning; refugees and displaced people flow across borders time and again; and black marketeers negotiate networks of profit on everything from land, ivory, and drugs to computer technology and nuclear weapons components. Wars are

---

[2]In all likelihood, they were more developed in Mozambique because of a culture that sees disorder not simply as a physical and individual concern, but also as a societal and cultural one, and because the majority of average citizens were not overly supportive of either Renamo or Frelimo, and preferred to be left in peace altogether.

dependent upon these international networks—public and private; political, military, and civilian; legal and illegal. This international, and often intentional, interweaving of alliances, antipathies, and resources on both sides of a conflict enables fundamental ideological assumptions, strategic orientations, and specific tactical practices to be transferred from group to group across international boundaries and political affiliations.

Transferred with these are the cultural-belief systems in which strategic knowledge and action are embedded: Beliefs about what constitutes acceptable battlegrounds, who comprises acceptable targets, and what kinds of violence can be employed. It also addresses how dirty-war practices can coexist with treaties banning such actions. Like specific strategies, these core cultural assumptions defining the fundamental relationships of power and violence are not forged anew with each outbreak of violence, they are continuously transmitted, shared, reformulated, and reproduced across borders as goods and personnel move around the world.

These transnational dynamics are not unilateral forces. Local and translocal concepts of violence and war intersect and influence one another (Nordstrom, 1994). International associations reconstruct orientations toward violence at the local level. These are transmitted down through the ranks to ground troops, who accept certain cultural definitions of war while reinterpreting ideology, strategy, goals, and the role of violence in the most immediate and individual of ways. At the level of practice, military and paramilitary process becomes infused with local-level culture, personal biography, and individual motivation. These actions are then translated back to the international level as soldiers, profiteers, refugees, and foreign experts (to name but a few) interact with people across different countries.

The ideas and ideals shaping contemporary wars permeate all militaries to some extent. They have become institutionalized in military epistemology, and embedded in training and practice. Cultures, including military ones, do not change overnight. No matter where war occurs, it is likely to share many fundamental similarities to those currently taking place in terms of acceptable strategies, targets, and amounts and kinds of violence. The war in former Yugoslavia, like virtually all the wars in the last several decades, has relied heavily on dirty-war tactics. Civilians and civil infrastructure have been heavily targeted, and human rights violations, including the now infamous rape, detention, and death camps, have shocked the world. Yet such tactics do not differ substantially from those employed in El Salvador, Guatemala, Cambodia, Burma, Sri Lanka, Mozambique, Sudan and a host of other countries.

Unless we begin to understand the cultures of militarization and violence that exist in a preponderance of the world's militaries—and the ideologies, assumptions, norms, values, and beliefs about the conduct(ing) of war that have been internationally forged—we are likely to find all upcoming wars, where ever they occur, will share many of these characteristics. Given the research on the formative nature of violence—that it is capable of long-term social destabilization—the levels of instability and cultural violence unleashed within societies may have serious consequences for the world at large.

CONCLUSION

As a stream of soldiers, private militias, foreign advisers, mercenaries, arms merchants, war suppliers, quasilegal enterprisers, black marketeers, and a host of others attracted to the power and profit of war carry the war effort throughout a region; and as a host of jackals, informers, thugs, and collaborators carry the war into the heart of societal relations—a fluid and largely invisible "un-army" work to resist violence and rebuild some semblance of a healthy society.

In any region embroiled in war, people are variously engaged in both reproducing and resisting the war effort. The very outbreak of hostilities prompts at least part of the population to begin working to dismantle the harmful effects of violence. Equally, regions that may be labeled *peace zones* by virtue of the fact that they are free of actual warfare are often implicated in the processes of war. War as we know it would not exist without the international cast of characters already identified who grease the machinery that makes war possible. A significant proportion of these people and resources originate in countries that are not themselves at war.

In addressing these issues, it seems appropriate to end where I began, with the question of the nature and culture of violence. I have found that people living in the midst of violent conflict challenge us in the West to reassess our notions of violence. Western discourse on violence is littered with phrases such as *controlling violence, surmounting violence, avoiding violence*, and so on, leading to the conception that violence is rather "thing-like:" something that exists as a forever fixed entity and must be dealt with as such.

Yet it has been my experience that the average person who has been forced to live face to face with violence does not find violence to be inherent to human nature or society, or a fixed entity unchanging across time and space. Instead, people have stressed to me time and again that violence is a fluid human construct. If people construct violence, and if people reproduce cultures of violence, then they have not only the ability, but the obligation, to un-construct them.

This dynamic view of violence is much more likely to yield positive lasting solutions to violence. In fact, a number of people living on the frontlines of wars have stressed to me that the orientations Western conflict–resolution specialists hold can actually be detrimental to the peace process. By accepting that violence is an inherent fact of human society, one that must be controlled rather than un-constructed, such specialists forge policies that leave in place destructive tensions rather than solving them—a process, people note, that is likely to ensure that new conflicts erupt. Solving, rather than re-solving, the problems of the destructive violence unleashed by war involves recognizing the cultures of violence and militarization that drive wars, and supporting the cultures of peacebuilding that are instituted by people living in the midst of war. It also involves subjecting our own assumptions and theories about violence to the closest scrutiny.

REFERENCES

Abu-Lughod, L. (1991). Writing against culture. In R. Fox (Ed.), *Recapturing anthropology* (pp. 137–162). Santa Fe, NM: School of American Research Press.

Amnesty International. (1986a). *Sri Lanka: Disappearances. ASA 37/08/86.* New York: Author.

Amnesty International. (1986b). *Sri Lanka: File on Torture. ASA 37/20/86.* New York: Author.

Appadurai, A. (1990). Disjuncture and difference in the global cultural economy. *Public Culture, Volume 2(2)*, 1–24.

Appadurai, A. (1991). Global ethnoscapes: Notes and queries for a transnational anthropology. In R. Fox (Ed.), *Recapturing anthropology* (pp. 191–210). Santa Fe, NM: School of American Research Press.

Bhabha, H. (1994). *The location of culture.* New York: Routledge.

Foucault, M. (1972). *Power/knowledge.* New York: Pantheon.

Galtung, J. (1992, July). *Conflict resolution as conflict transformation: The first law of thermodynamics revisited.* Paper presented at the International Peace Research Association meetings, Kyoto.

Gupta, A., & Ferguson, J. (1992). Beyond "culture": Space, identity, and the politics of difference. *Cultural Anthropology, 7(1)*, 6–23.

Mead, M. (1988). False heroes. In D. Gioseffi (Ed.), *Women on war* (p. 134). New York: Simon & Schuster.

Nordstrom, C. (1986, December). *The 'rationalization' of violence—From riot to conflict.* Paper presented at the American Anthropological Association meetings.

Nordstrom, C. (1992a). The backyard front. In C. Nordstrom & J. Martin (Eds.), *The paths to domination, resistance and terror* (pp. 260–274). Berkeley: University of California Press.

Nordstrom, C. (1992b). The dirty war: Civilian experience of conflict in Mozambique and Sri Lanka. In K. Rupesinghe (Ed.), *Internal wars and governance* (pp. 27–43). London: Macmillan Press.

Nordstrom, C. (1994). Contested identities/essentially contested powers. In E. Garcia (Ed.), *War and peacemaking* (pp. 55–69). Quezon City, Phillipines: Claretian Publications.

Scribner, S. (1986). Thinking in action: Some characteristics of practical thought. In R. Sternberg & R. Wagner (Eds.), *Practical intelligence: Nature and origins of competence in the everyday world* (pp. 13–30). Cambridge, England: Cambridge University Press.

Sivard, R. L. (1993). *World military and social expenditures, 1993.* Leesburg, VA: World Priorities Press.

Taussig, M. (1992). *Public secrets.* Paper presented at the University of California.

10

Avoidance Strategies
in Northern Ireland

M. Melissa McCormick
University of Arizona

In this chapter, McCormick reports on the "Troubles" of Northern Ireland, violence that began in 1969. She emphasizes that the paramount strategy for managing this ethnic conflict, especially in the most violent areas, has been avoidance of the "other side." Ethnographic data on Protestants of South Armagh reveal, however, that this taken-for-granted alternative to violence also contradicts reconciliatory logic. The point is that avoidance and violence are not necessarily mutually exclusive, and that avoidance, like violence, can be counter to conflict resolution.

—*The Editors*

Since 1969, Northern Ireland has been lacerated by more than 3,200 killings, 33,000 serious injuries, and approximately 10,000 paramilitary explosions related to the so-called Troubles. Yet, most of the 1.6 million citizens of the unstable United Kingdom province have not participated directly in sectarian or paramilitary violence. Instead, they have diligently avoided it by avoiding the "other side." This mundane form of managing what militarists call *low-intensity conflict* appears to be related to the perception that community reconciliation efforts are "dangerously naive," "counterproductive," or "a trick." More than 25 years of curtailed interaction between Protestants and Catholics, along with other forces, seems to make conciliatory catchphrases such as "mutual understanding" and "cross-community contact" appear nonsensical to many people living in Northern Ireland's hot-spots, including members of South Armagh's Protestant enclave. This chapter illustrates ways in which the language and logic of avoidance informs some of their responses to formal reconciliation efforts.

TIT-FOR-TAT VIOLENCE

A local euphemism, the Troubles refers to the highly structured and often predict-
able range of violence that emanated from historically contested national and
ethnic identities as well as discriminatory practices of the Protestant-dominated
Stormont government (dismantled by London in 1972). Despite conflicting political expectations, most Catholics and Protestants interpret much Troubles-related
violence as retaliatory, in local parlance "tit-for-tat," violence that is to be avoided
(e.g., Arthur, 1990, p. 56; Bruce, 1992).

In South Armagh, a sparsely populated, hilly farming area, where one is never
more than a few minutes away from the Irish border, the rate of killings per capita
due to the Troubles is three times greater than in Belfast (Poole, 1990, p. 71). A
statistical assessment of all documented deaths reveals that Republican paramilitants are responsible for about 82% of the deaths in this overwhelmingly Catholic
and nationalist area. Victims include the security forces, local civilians, and scores
of people from all over the province (mostly Catholics) whose corpses were dumped
in the area following Provisional Irish Republican Army (PIRA) interrogations.
Despite a seemingly oppressive military presence (e.g., Curtis, 1994), the PIRA has
been adept at routine terrorism, public relations, and their own brand of policing.
Mortar attacks, deadly shootings, parading weapons, vehicle checkpoints, and
"disciplining" Catholic youth for so-called antisocial behavior, for example, were
common up until the PIRA ceasefire that began on September 1, 1994—punishment shootings and beatings by loyalist and republican paramilitants have actually
increased throughout the province since the most recent ceasefire (which came to
a dramatic end on February 9, 1996 when the PIRA bombed London's Canary
Wharf, killing two newspaper vendors and injuring 100).

It has been alleged that republican paramilitants, mostly the PIRA, have engaged
in a sectarian campaign of violence against South Armagh's declining Protestant
community of about 2,700 people, 12 percent of the area's total population.
Standard wisecracks made in Belfast about my research among South Armagh
Protestants reflect this view: "Oh, all two families?" or "Oh, are there any left?" The
PIRA is suspected of having "organized attacks or threats against any remaining
Protestant families in some predominately nationalist areas with a view to forcing
them to move out and make way for Catholic families" (Boyle & Hadden, 1994, p.
73). Father Denis Faul, a well-known human rights activist, recently denounced
the PIRA for trying to intimidate a family into leaving their farm and called on all
of the farmers from South Armagh to "unite and make a stand against the IRA"
(*Belfast Telegraph*, 1993, p. 6). In 1992, one Protestant woman, a relative of several
local men who were shot by the PIRA, expressed to me a commonly held sense of
besiegement: "They [PIRA] probably wanted to destroy, maybe not a whole
Protestant community, but if there was enough fear within Protestant families,
they're goin' to get up and move out of the locality. . . . Exactly what they [PIRA]
would do with Protestants if it were to become an all-Ireland, I sort of dread to
think."

The image of a decimated Protestant enclave in South Armagh, exploited by some loyalist propagandists and disregarded by their republican counterparts, primarily emerges from three widely condemned massacres. In 1975, the South Armagh Republican Action Force (thought to be a flag of convenience for local PIRA units during an official PIRA ceasefire) broke into a meeting at the Tullyvallen Orange Hall and opened fire, injuring 12 and killing 5 men. A bomb planted at the hall failed to explode. At least one local Catholic went on television to condemn the attack. A few months later, the same group claimed responsibility for what one IRA expert (Coogan, 1993, p. 337) called "outright sectarian murder," the "Kingsmills Massacre." On their way home from work, 11 Protestants were sprayed with machine-gun fire; only one survived. Years later, in 1983, Irish National Liberation Army (INLA) gunmen opened fire on the small, hymn-singing congregation at the Darkley Pentecostal Church. Three elders died and seven others were wounded.

"PASS NO REMARKS"

Black (1993, pp. 5–6) defined a *form* of social control as "a mechanism by which a person or group express a grievance." The quotidian form of managing the Troubles in Northern Ireland for well over two decades has been avoidance (Buckley, 1989, p. 148; Darby, 1986). "Violence makes movement outside of the communal worlds actually (and imaginatively) dangerous" (Ruane & Todd, 1992, p. 90; cf. Whyte, 1993, p. 103). A landmark of the Troubles is the peace line that separates predominately Catholic and Protestant areas in an often turbulent part of Belfast. Night and day, sturdy barriers proclaim that direct contact between Protestants and Catholics is inherently dangerous.

This dominant anxiety is reflected in the fact that throughout the province, including South Armagh, residential segregation is more prevalent now than it was before the most recent Troubles (Pollak, 1993, pp. 91–92). Several older people I met in South Armagh complained, for example, that the traditional rural ethic of neighborliness had been eroded by the Troubles (as well as by the TV). Shortly after I moved to the area I was chastised by two elderly Catholic women, on separate occasions, for "digging [or kicking] with both feet." In other words, it was unacceptable and possibly dangerous for me to be socializing with my Catholic neighbors while I was focusing on Protestants.

An often-heard phrase, "Pass no remarks," is an extended metaphor for the avoidance style expressed by many members of South Armagh's minority Protestant population. This powerful trope also reflects the reality that certain types of talk in so-called Bandit Country (not just what the PIRA has labeled loose talk or the passing of information that could harm the cause) have resulted in injury or death. The language and logic of avoidance permeates many of the choices made by Protestants concerning the Troubles.

For most ordinary Protestants as well as Catholics, it is considered tactless and imprudent to talk about the Troubles in "mixed" company. A group of local

Protestants and Catholics who regularly attend a free lunch for pensioners in one village, for instance, would never "pass remarks" at the luncheon about a particular Protestant woman's son being tortured to death by the PIRA or one Catholic woman's PIRA son having been shot dead by the British Army. Likewise, once when I was on a bus heading into South Armagh, no one, except for a little girl who was quickly shushed by her mother, said anything about the driver having to turn the bus around because of cars being hijacked and burned up ahead by supporters of the Irish People's Liberation Organization (IPLO), recently shattered by the PIRA.

Many a young man, Protestant and Catholic alike, knows full well how quickly a sectarian remark or gesture can escalate into immediate or eventual violence. Several Protestant women have forbidden their sons from joining the security forces, knowing that they could rarely visit home and, most important, could not raise families in the area without risking intimidation or assassination. Protestants who do socialize with Catholics, especially those Catholics who are rightly or wrongly suspected of being "involved," risk being scorned by more hard-line Protestants. An elderly Protestant woman who continually yelled at young "skitters" who painted republican paramilitary slogans on the walls of her home was partly responsible for the ritualized harassment because she "passed remarks," according to some other Protestants.

CROSS-COMMUNITY CONTACT

Historical conflicts of interest left unresolved by inequitable postcolonial institutions, unabated violence, and sectarian fear have all been powerful forces of polarization and confrontation in Northern Ireland. They have always been challenged, however, by social, cultural, political, and economic forces of conciliation and toleration. A variety of peace and reconciliation groups are a part of the latter dynamic. "While they have different emphases, nearly all see lack of cross-community contact, misunderstandings created by community division, and difficulties in making and sustaining friendships across the divide as central to the conflict" (Pritchard, 1993, p. 30).

One of the oldest challenges to centrifugal forces in Northern Ireland is the Corrymeela Community, founded in 1965 by university students and an ecumenical Protestant clergyman. Early on, it was a sanctuary for hundreds of families who had been intimidated or bombed out of their homes. Since then it has organized cross-community activities and workshops for youth, families, community leaders, politicians, and especially those most victimized by the conflict. "We know from first hand experience that many of the young people who have supported us [Corrymeela] have turned their backs on the paramilitants and have opted for the alternatives we offer" (McCreary, 1986, p. 6). Many church people from various denominations, especially ecumenists, have engaged in cross-community and peace activities. Very often "the Churches contain and support the only people seriously committed to inter-community relationships. . . . In some areas the Roman Catholic Church has been the refuge for all those opposed to the IRA. In many working-class areas it is the only local institutional opponent" (Morrow, Birrell, Greer, & O'Keefe, 1994, pp. 262–263).

Scores of reconciliation projects, organized by trade unions, housewives, students, academics, and the business community, color the Northern Irish landscape. There are dozens of student groups like the Student Campaign for Peace. The Irish Congress of Trade Unions' Counteract program is aimed at reducing intimidation and sectarianism in the workplace. The Confederation of Irish Industry and the Confederation of British Industry are attempting to strengthen the island economy by increasing joint ventures between Northern Irish and Irish businesses. The Peace Train Organization challenges the PIRA's routine disruption of rail services between Belfast and Dublin. Likewise, Families Against Intimidation and Terror (FAIT) protests paramilitary cruelty, especially so-called "punishment shootings" and forced exile.

Peace groups have accelerated their efforts in response to particular atrocities. The Nobel Peace Prize-winning organization Peace People (like the recently created Dublin-based Warrington Project, which emerged after two children were killed by a PIRA bomb in England in 1993) erupted in the late 1970s after three children were crushed to death by a fatally wounded PIRA gunman's runaway car. Tens of thousands of people flooded into the streets to demand a stop to the killing (Deutsch, 1977). By the early 1980s, however, Peace People lost its momentum due, in part, to strident republican accusations that the organization was a British front. This indictment is a codified republican response to reconciliation groups that threaten its sense of legitimacy and the strong partisanship on which it thrives. During the same decade, for example, members of Sinn Féin, the legal political wing of the PIRA, disrupted meetings of Women Together, a peace movement made up of Protestant and Catholic working-class women who engaged in activities like stopping the hooliganism and vandalism of armed youth gangs or negotiating with the security forces if innocent youth were detained. Generally, Sinn Féin calls community relations initiatives "middle class," "neo-Unionist" schemes, despite evidence to the contrary (McThomas & Friel, 1993, p. 20).

The British and Irish governments have been committed to policies that create incentives for greater integration. The reconciliation of the so-called two traditions is one of the main aims of the 1985 Anglo-Irish Agreement. As clearly argued by others, the terms *two traditions* or *two communities* are problematic because they reinforce the idea of dichotomous, monolithic camps and mask multiple identities within any particular community. Nevertheless, they have become an integral part of the conciliatory lexicon. Following a report by the Standing Advisory Commission on Human Rights, the Northern Ireland Community Relations Council was reestablished in 1990 in the spirit of the two-traditions approach. The Council provides grants for community relations and cultural traditions work, among other projects.

The government also funds the small but expanding integrated-education movement. Most parents who have placed their children in such schools believe in the *contact hypothesis*, "the idea that relationships between potentially or actually antagonistic groups can be ameliorated through regular meetings and joint activities" (Morgan, Dunn, Cairns, & Fraser, 1992, p. 32). All schools are now required to enact reconciliation programs, such as Education for Mutual Understanding, aimed at breaking down barriers between pupils across the sectarian divide. Religious tolerance is being promoted through a common-core school religion syllabus.

Boyle and Hadden (1994, p. 39) pointed out that involvement in and the impact of cross-community activities in places like South Armagh have been relatively small. Before the 1990s, organized community-relations work and peace activities were almost nonexistent. A small number of South Armagh Protestants—mostly churchmen and lay women—are pursuing a broader sense of community, despite PIRA force, Protestant fears, and the constant deluge of sectarian and hard-line political rhetoric. Working with local Catholics who have initiated most of the recent reconciliation activities in the area, they are well aware that many of their coreligionists see them as naive because, among other factors, they are violating the widely accepted alternative to violence, that is, avoidance of primarily Catholic or nationalist (especially Republican) spaces and groups.

A brief consideration of three cross-community events that took place in 1991 and 1992 emphasizes the difficulty of overcoming normative avoidance in South Armagh, although the fact that some Protestants are participating in such activities should not be overlooked. Furthermore, participation in formal reconciliation programs should not be thought of as the only measure of local interests. Many more Protestants have participated in informal ways of handling particular incidents or potentially dangerous situations than have been willing to attend, for example, a cross-community Christmas concert.

While I was in South Armagh, a handful of parents protested the implementing of the Education for Mutual Understanding (EMU) initiative at a local Protestant primary school. None of the parents objected to Protestant and Catholic children interacting in a classroom environment, but for a few parents, joint teams for sporting events "had gone too far." Local school-board officials as well as unionist and nationalist politicians tried to reassure them that they were overreacting, in part by agreeing to modify the nature of school-sponsored, cross-community contact. The parents were not persuaded. About a dozen children transferred to another school.

In another South Armagh village, with one of the smallest proportions of Protestants, an interdenominational service of Prayers for Peace was held at a Church of Ireland site whose baronial grounds are important historically and archaeologically for both Catholics and Protestants. One of the few remaining Episcopalian churches in South Armagh, it has a dwindling congregation of nine families. At the time of the event, a professionally drawn sign located across the road from the church's main gates depicted a PIRA man in full combat uniform. His machine gun was aimed at the church.

The media excitedly reported that an overflowing crowd of Protestants and Catholics from the infamous "Bandit Country" had come together to forge reconciliation during the special church service. Unfortunately, this was not the case. Most South Armagh Protestants probably did not even know about the event until they saw it on the evening TV news. I did attend, and it was an uplifting ecumenical service at which we heard words such as, "Never pay back evil for evil. As far as it lies with you, live at peace with everyone." No more than a dozen Protestants, however, joined the overwhelmingly Catholic majority.

Although all the other Protestant churches in the area, mostly various Presbyterian denominations, had received invitations, ministers either did not announce the event to their congregations or discouraged them from attending. According to fundamentalist doctrine, it is wrong to hold a joint Roman Catholic–Protestant religious service. "Fundamentalist vigilance against ecumenism," as Ruane and Todd (1992, p. 86) noted, reproduces polarization by making cross-community contact spiritually risky. From a more secular perspective, some Protestants from South Armagh said that they had not been to that particular village in years because it is essentially a "no-go" area for Protestants, that is, a threatening social space to be avoided. Others dismissed the service as irrelevant: "No Provo [PIRA] is going to pay attention to the church."

The last example of a sizable cross-community event was a traditional hiring fair organized in a South Armagh village that has a somewhat larger number of Protestants than other villages in the predominately Catholic region. It attracted some Protestant support and participation. Still, a good number of Protestants stayed away, interpreting the event not as a benign expression of cultural traditions (historically, farm workers hired themselves out during the fair, and various goods were bought and sold) but rather as an assertion of Irish Catholic power to be avoided. When the fair was recreated the following year, in 1993, a PIRA sniper took advantage of the crowd and shot dead a teenage soldier, after which, to the abhorrence of many Protestants, some local Catholics continued to celebrate the fair, if not the killing. Once again, from the point of view of those who perceive cross-community contact as potentially dangerous, the distinction between the sharing of cultural traditions and violence was made nonsensical.

LESSONS FROM SOUTH ARMAGH

The language and logic of avoidance of the "other side" has discouraged many South Armagh Protestants, who reject unilateral aggression as a form of conflict management, from participating in reconciliation projects. As two Northern Irish mediators who seek existential change in community relations explain, the people of Northern Ireland "often prefer to remain apart or to meet politely, avoiding anything that touches on the dominant social contest. Avoidance certainly enables much of life to continue, at least in the short term, but the contest remains unchanged" (Morrow & Wilson, 1993, p. 13).

Using comparative survey data designed to detect changes in the attitudes of people participating in community relations programs, Knox (1994, p. 614) found that "there are signs of a more tolerant society emerging, albeit slowly, through integrated education, EMU, and the cross-community contact scheme." Although, it is unclear to what degree this trend exists in South Armagh, my sketch of its declining Protestant community does coincide with a couple of Knox's less optimistic findings. He notes that violence, especially sectarian killings, negatively influences reconciliation projects and that such initiatives have had "little, if any, impact on Protestant alienation" (Knox, 1994, p. 613).

The relationship between rural Protestants' avoidance practices and their unenthusiastic responses to reconciliation activities in Northern Ireland's most violent area also indicates that Black's (1993, p. 82) universal claim that "violence varies inversely with avoidance" does not bear out in such divided societies. Instead, violence engenders not only more violence but also intense forms of avoidance which, in turn, result in increased polarization conducive to "strong" partisanship, "hard" moralism, and making enemies (Black 1993, pp. 131, 151).

ACKNOWLEDGMENT

This research was funded by the National Science Foundation, the Wenner Gren Foundation for Anthropological Research, Sigma Xi, and the University of Arizona.

REFERENCES

Arthur, P. (1990). Republican violence in Northern Ireland: The rationale. In J. Darby, N. Dodge, & A. C. Hepburn (Eds.), *Political violence: Ireland in a comparative Perspective* (pp. 48–63). Belfast: Appletree Press.

Black, D. (1993). *The social structure of right and wrong*. New York: Academic Press.

Boyle, K., & Hadden, T. (1994). *Northern Ireland: The choice*. London: Penguin Books.

Bruce, S. (1992). Northern Ireland: Reappraising loyalist violence. *Conflict Studies, 249*, 1–21.

Buckley, A. D. (1989). "You only live in your body": Peace, exchange and the siege mentality in Ulster. In S. Howell & R. Willis (Eds.), *Societies at peace: Anthropological perspectives* (pp. 146–162). New York: Routledge.

Coogan, T. P. (1993). *The IRA: A history*. Niwot, CO: Roberts Rinehart Publishers.

Curtis, L. (1994). All along the watchtowers. *The New Internationalist, 255*, 10–12.

Darby, J. (1986). *Intimidation and the control of conflict in Northern Ireland*. Dublin: Gill & Macmillan.

Deutsch, R. (1977). *Maired Corrigan, Betty Williams*. Woodbury, NY: Barron's.

Knox, C. (1994). Conflict resolution at the microlevel: community relations in Northern Ireland. *Conflict Resolution, 38*(4), 595–619.

McCreary, A. (1986, December). Ulster group celebrates 21-year commitment to reconciliation. *The Christian Science Monitor*, p. 6.

McThomas, H., & Friel, L. (August 1993). Same old story. *Fortnight, 320*, 20–21.

Morrow, D., & Wilson, D. (1993, Winter). Three into two won't go? From mediation to new relationships in Northern Ireland. *Forum* 13–18.

Morgan, V., Dunn, S., Cairns, E., & Fraser, G. (1992). *Breaking the mould: The roles of parents and teachers in the integrated schools in Northern Ireland*. Coleraine, Northern Ireland: Centre for the Study of Conflict, University of Ulster.

Morrow, D., Birrell, D., Greer, J., & O'Keeffe, T. (1994). *The churches and inter-community relationships*. Coleraine, Northern Ireland: Centre for the Study of Conflict, University of Ulster.

Pollak, A. (Ed.). (1993). *A citizen's inquiry: The Opsahl report on Northern Ireland*. Dublin: The Lilliput Press.

Poole, M. (1990). The geographical location of political violence in Northern Ireland. In J. Darby, N. Dodge, & A. C. Hepburn (Eds.), *Political violence: Ireland in a comparative perspective* (pp. 64–82). Belfast: Appletree.

Priest slams IRA "bullying." (1993, August 24). *Belfast Telegraph*, p. 6.

Pritchard, D. (January 1993). Hard to reconcile. *Fortnight*, 313, 30.

Ruane, J. & Todd, J. (1992). Diversity, division and the middle ground in Northern Ireland. *Irish Political Studies, 7*, 73–98.

Whyte, J. (1993). Dynamics of social and political change in Northern Ireland. In D. Keogh & M. Haltzel (Eds.), *Northern Ireland and the politics of reconciliation* (pp. 103–116). Washington, DC: Woodrow Wilson Center Press.

11

Historiography and Islamic Vocabulary in War and Peace: A Memento for Conflict Resolution in the Muslim World

Jan Hjärpe
University of Lund

This chapter suggests the application of a new subdiscipline, historiography, in conflict studies. By analyzing the vocabulary of parties in conflict, with a focus on historical events alluded at in their speech, it is possible to get a deeper understanding of the ongoing conflict process. Any change in the political situation is immediately reflected in a change of historical allegories. As a consequence, historiographical analyses have prognostic value. A conscious implementation of historiography in mediation can serve the promotion of peace by suggesting reconciliative historical precedents. Examples are provided by an analysis of Islamic vocabulary in war and peace.

—*The Editors*

Most of the past has left no traces whatsoever; hence the historian is working on a jigsaw puzzle where most of the pieces are lacking. On the other hand, only a very small number of all the remainders of the past can ever be analyzed, and a still smaller number become a part of the general public's historical consciousness. Historiography, the use of history, is a process of choice. We choose our past. We must ask: What are the criteria for our choices? In what way, and why, do we choose to regard some (documented) events in the past as important, as significant?

To an audience of history teachers from Swedish schools, I once posed the question: What happened in the year 1389? No one among the Swedes could remember anything connected with that year, but two Serbs in the audience reacted immediately: The Battle of the Thrush's field (*Kosovo polje*), the historical event that in Serbian historiography serves as a legitimization for the claim to Serbian character of the Kosovo region. As an event that happened more than 600 years ago, that is, an event that no contemporary person can personally remember, it belongs to the historiography of one party of a contemporary conflict. The parties in any conflict choose their significant historical events differently. It is not that one party is lying and the other is speaking the historical truth. The parties in a conflict present events in the past that really have happened, but they do not present the *same* events. The present situation of the particular determines the choice of history.

This means that a change in the political situation, ambition or goal, immediately is reflected in a change of historiography. A consequence is that the study of the historiography presented by those involved in a conflict, the analysis of the use of history of a specific group, has a prognostic value. It is also valuable in a process of mediation to be able to suggest other historical precedents, such precedents that can serve the idea of reconciliation. Such was the case when President Anwar Sadat alluded to the Prophet Muhammad's treaty at *al-Hudaybiya* (in the year 628) with the tribe Quraysh as a legitimization for the Camp David treaty in 1978. The same allusion was used by Yasir Arafat in a speech in a South African mosque, in May 1994, regarding the ongoing peace process with Israel, a speech that provoked much attention and got very different interpretations, especially his use of the ambiguous word *jihâd*. We can take this as an example of change in vocabulary, used as a signal; the most common use of the word *jihâd* in the religiopolitical language is as a designation for a legitimate war (*bellum iustum*), or war as a religious duty. But the term is also used, even if less frequently and mostly in other contexts, to connote "endeavor" (its primary lexicographic meaning), or "spiritual struggle." In the Palestinian political vocabulary the more common words for struggle or fight, have been *qitâl*, *kifâh* or *nidâl*, words that are unambiguous. By choosing the word *jihâd*, Yasir Arafat has said nothing that his militant opponents can stigmatize as defeatism. The word still includes the meaning of militant struggle, even military battle, but not exclusively so, because it can be used in the sense of peaceful spiritual struggle. The choice of the term was clever.

Another example of change in historiography involves the Iran–Iraq war (1980–1988) and the long diplomatic efforts to bring about a cease fire. In the Iranian propaganda during the war (as well as before and during the revolution in 1978–1979) the most important historical event was the tragedy of Karbala (in 680), where the third *Shii Imam*, the Prophet's grandson Husayn, was martyred in his rebellion against the Umayyad calif Yazîd. Imam Husayn was the impeccable example of martyrdom and bravery, the infallible who performed unflaggingly against tyranny: "War to victory or death," no cease-fire as long as "Yazîd" (or, in the Iran–Iraq war, Saddam) was still in power in Baghdad. The battle of Karbala was the most significant event in history, giving the battle its meaning. But, in the Iranian newspapers and propaganda pamphlets, the reader could observe that during the spring of 1988, the stories about Imam Husayn became less frequent, and there were more articles, speeches, and booklets featuring different aspects of the life of the second *Shii Imam*, Hasan. I made then the prognosis that the regime in Teheran was now ready to accept a cease-fire. The articles on Imam Hasan were a way to prepare the public for a change in policy. In contrast to the fighting martyr Husayn, Imam Hasan was the one, still an infallible Imam, who had accepted a cease-fire, a settlement with the Umayyad calif Mu'âwiya, in a situation where a rebellion was not possible.

United Nations Security Council Resolution 598 had recommended a cease-fire in the Iran–Iraq war, followed by an international arbitration on the question of war guilt. Baghdad accepted the resolution without condition, but the answer from Teheran had been more complicated. Its content could be accepted, but not its sequence: The arbitration must go before the cease-fire. Why? Because of the precedent, the battle of Siffîn (in the year 657), where the first *Imam*, the Prophet's cousin Alî, had accepted a cease fire in the battle with Mu'âwiya, followed by an arbitration later on, which eventually went against him. So: Arbitration first, cease fire afterwards.

During 1988, it became obvious that Teheran had to yield. The public was prepared by the articles on Hasan. When Resolution 598 was accepted in July, the leader, Khomeini, made the comment that this was a necessity, although "it was worse than drinking poison." Why this formulation? Who had drunk poison? According to the Shiite historiography, Hasan, the second Imam, was murdered by poison—but still, he had accepted a settlement with the calif Mu'âwiya. The historical allusion to the death of Imam Hasan served, in a subtle way, as a legitimization of the change in policy from war to a cease fire.

The Kuwait crisis provided ample examples of conflicting historiographies. In the European (and U.S.) debate, as well as in the propaganda, the Kuwait crisis was analyzed in a series of historical comparisons: with the preludes to World War I, with the war of Abyssinia, with the beginning of World War II, with the Suez crisis, with the Vietnam War, with the Soviet adventure in Afghanistan—and with the chaos of Europe in the 16th and 17th centuries. These comparisons are all intelligible for a European public. Every one of them serves as a kind of prognosis: World War I resulted in a total reshuffling of the political map of Europe, World War II led to the defeat and death of Hitler (or, in this case, Saddam), Vietnam and Afghanistan both ended badly for a Superpower. The Suez crisis showed that a military victory can be followed by a political defeat (Saddam as Nasser, the political victor), all of these historical comparisons, can be regarded as warnings: Do not repeat former mistakes (such as at Munich).

But all these events are from European (and U.S.) historiography. The perspective is European, even when the examples support opposite sides in the debate. The comparisons were comprehensible (and effective) for a European public but lacked the same meaning elsewhere.

After the Iraqi invasion in Kuwait in August 1990, King Fahd of Saudi Arabia asked for help, and U.S. and European troops began to arrive. We saw then that people in the Middle East, and in the entire Muslim world, were seriously alarmed by the non-Muslim military presence in the region of the two Holy Cities, Mekka and Medina. An historical comparison was then made between Saddam Husayn and Salâh ad-Dîn drawing mental associations with the Crusades (*as-salîbîya*). Salâh ad-Dîn/Saladin was the chivalric and valiant hero who defeated the crusaders and put an end to the Latin Kingdom of Jerusalem. President Bush was called "the Crusader." The Iraqi propaganda made full use of the theme. It was stressed that Saddam was born in the same region as Salâh ad-Dîn—Takrit. The airplane that took the Iraqi foreign minister Târiq 'Azîz to Cairo for the meeting of the Arab League bore the name of Salâh ad-Dîn. Also, this comparison had a prognostic point: Salâh ad-Dîn did vanquish the crusaders. Then it was of less importance that Saddâm, as a person, could not possibly be characterized as a chivalric hero like the valiant Sultan, and that he was an Arab and not a Curd, as was Salâh ad-Dîn.

The abdication of the Soviet Union from the position of a superpower was of importance for the development of the crisis. Saddâm made his mistake: A conflict with Washington did not provoke support from Moscow. In this desperate situation Saddâm played very skillfully with the only cards left, those of the propaganda, using Islamic vocabulary and historiography to the utmost. In that new situation he appropriated much of the themes used by his previous main enemy, those of the Iranian revolution. He could enjoy the dictator's privilege of having access to the language of religion without being bound by its content.

Already the date of the invasion could be used as a propagandistic signal. It was the night after August 1st, which that year coincided with the night after the 10th of *Muharram* in the Islamic calendar, the night after the '*âshûrâ*', the commemoration of the tragedy of Karbala in 680 and the martyrdom of Imam Husayn.

In the Iranian revolution, as discussed, this commemoration was crucial as a pattern of interpretation: When the headquarters of the Islamic Revolutionary Party were destroyed in a bomb attack the on July 28, 1981, the (false but effective) rumor was immediately spread that the number of victims was 72—the same number of martyrs as in the tragedy of Karbala. Bomb attacks and suicidal actions have often happened during the first ten days of *Muharram* (also, for instance, those in Paris during September 6th to 16th, 1986). In 1994, a bomb exploded in the famous shrine of the eighth *Imam* in Mashhad in Iran: on June 20—exactly in connection with the '*âshûrâ*' celebration the 10th of *Muharram*!—the rumor again was heard that the number of victims was "about 70," although it later became clear that the number was considerably less (24). In 1990, Saddâm Husayn chose the '*âshûrâ*' for the invasion of Kuwait. It might have been meant as a signal to the Shii population in the nearby Qatif province of Saudi Arabia (a province rich in oil, and with social and political disturbances in the past, especially in 1979). The city of Karbala was "taken hostage" in the war.

Another more emotionally charged question involves sovereignty over the two Holy Cities, Mecca and Medina. For the Islamic revolutionary groups, after the Iranian revolution, this question had become very important: Among them, the rituals of the Pilgrimage had taken on a symbolic revolutionary interpretation. The main ideologist behind this was the very influential sociologist Ali Shariati. The Pilgrimage was interpreted as a symbolic revolution against the tyrants, the devils, especially the ritual of stoning the Satan. The great Satan now was the United States, and the small Satans were the non-Islamic rulers in the Muslim World. The rituals became opportunities to demonstrate against them, which led to serious disturbances, with the clashes in 1987 as the peak, with more than 400 dead. For the revolutionaries (as well as at that time for the regime in Teheran) the two Holy Cities could not be legitimately the property of a family (i.e., Saudi Arabia).

In May 1989, the governments of the states in the Islamic Conference Organization sent representatives to a Pilgrimage Conference in Saudi Arabia. Its final statement implied that the governments in the Muslim world (then with the exception of Iran) supported the Saudi administration of the Pilgrimage and the Cities, and accepted King Fahd as the *Khâdim al-haramayn*, Guardian of the Holy [Cities].

By invading Kuwait in 1990, Saddâm was in conflict with almost every government in the world including the Muslim world. He then had one option; to try to work upon the popular opinions, the tensions between ruler and ruled, rich and poor, and, more importantly, to stress the symbolic value of Mecca as belonging to all Muslims. By the 8th of August, U.S. troops arrived in Saudi Arabia. Did this mean that there now was a non-Muslim sovereignty over the Holy Cities? In a Teheran newspaper, a cartoon appeared with the inscription "Guardian of the Holy Cities," the picture not showing King Fahd, but three female U.S. soldiers.

In most of the debate in Europe and in the United States, the focus of the Kuwait crisis was on the sovereignty of Kuwait. For much of the Muslim World, the Kuwait crisis was centered around the question of Mecca, and the Muslim or non-Muslim sovereignty over the Holy Cities. A non-Muslim sovereignty there was unacceptable. Should a situation arise where non-Muslims have power over Mecca, then a war against the intruders becomes an individual duty (*fard al-'ayn*) for every believer.

The position was very delicate for Saudi Arabia and the other regimes in the region. It was, therefore, very important for the Arab League to resolve to send Muslim troops to protect Saudi Arabia. The symbolic value of their presence was the main purpose: Muslims around Mecca and Medina. Their military importance was very small. They constituted perhaps 10% of the number of soldiers, so the military victory was in no way due to their weapons, but their propaganda value was immense.

King Fahd very quickly called an Islamic Conference in Mecca, to be held September 10 to 12 in order to get the support of religious authorities for the Islamic legitimacy of the struggle against Saddâm; the offender and un-Islamic usurper and despot and war criminal, the hypocrite (*munâfiq*) and renegade (*murtadd*). A legal statement (*fatwâ*) by the *Imam* of Ka'ba supported the legitimacy of getting help from the United States and Europeans—they were not heathens, but *ahl al-kitâb*, "people of the Book," Jews and Christians. Still, the important problem was not that of Kuwait, but of Mecca. The conflict was expressed in Islamic vocabulary and historiography.

For his part, Saddam claimed Hashimite descendence as another legitimization of his power; he too belonged to the family of the Prophet's cousin 'Alî. The counterpropaganda denied this very vehemently. Rizvi (1991, p. 21) enumerated

Saddâm's anti-Islamic misdeeds: He was no Muslim, not even an Arab, he was "*the illegitimate son of an unknown German, Hitleric, youth fighting in the second world war in the remainder of the ottoman caliphate* [italics added]."

During three months of the Islamic lunar year 1413, from the beginning of the month of *Rajab* to the beginning of *Shawwâl*, roughly corresponding to the end of December 1992 to the end of March 1993, I recorded the shortwave news broadcasts from Saudi Arabia in order to analyze the news evaluations and the use of religious vocabulary. A few of the main observations related to conflict or its resolution are as follows. The choice of news items and ways of presenting them were regularly made to support the Saudi claim not only to Islamic legitimacy but also to a leading position. One very obvious example has to do with the calendar. At the end of every month, one of the main themes in the news is the exhortation to observe the new moon. This is more controversial than it seems at first. The moon must be observed, so the date of the new month can be declared. The problem is that in order to have a practically applicable calendar, it must be calculated in advance. How does one combine a calculated calendar with the actual observation? And who has the authority to proclaim a calculated calendar? The Saudi regime claims that right, and those opposed to the Saudis in the Muslim world regularly reject or question the Saudi proclamation of the new month and dates of the religious festivals.

Saudi Arabian initiatives on the international Islamic scene had, of course, a high priority in the news evaluation: conferences, the international engagements of the Grand Mufti 'Abd al-'Azîz ibn Bâz, and the measures taken by the Saudi dominated World Muslim League (*râbitat al-'âlam al-islâmî*). King Fahd was without exception, mentioned with the title *khâdim al-haramayn* ("Guardian of the Holy [Cities]"). At the turn of the month to *Sha'bân*, on January 23, 1993, most of the time was taken by the report on the inauguration in Mecca of the International Koran Recitation Contest for Youth. The broadcast included the entire speech given by the vice emir of Mecca, Sa'ûd ibn 'Abd al-Muhsin, as substitute for *Khâdim al-Haramayn*, to the youth from all over the Muslim World, assembled for the contest. One of the points in the speech was the implicit repudiation of all kinds of militant revolutionary interpretation of Islam. *Da'wa*, the "invitation," shall always be made with kindness, with courtesy and a good example, not by "being harsh" (cf. Koran, Sura 3: 159).

The inauguration on January 26th by the Saudi ambassador, emir Bandar ibn Sultân, of the Saudi-sponsored Islamic Institute in Washington, DC, was of course an important matter. Although not explicitly stated in the broadcast, the institute is important because it can propagate the Saudi view on Islam, and it can work against the militant revolutionary interpretation of the religion.

The immense political problems and conflicts in the Muslim world were reflected by the mentioning of the Saudi engagements in help projects, and in the international diplomatic efforts of mediation. A considerable part of the news during the mentioned three months was taken by the mediation in the Afghanistan civil war, where a settlement, although not very durable, was reached at this time, and confirmed by a visit to the shrines of Mecca and Medina by the leaders of the different factions. The visits to the shrines constitute a reminder of the Holy History, establishing the connection with the Prophet and his time. The intention is to make the peace settlement psychologically more binding.

There were reports on all the regions of conflict and disaster in the Muslim world; Caucasus, Central Asia, Somalia, India (Ayodhya), Jammu-Kashmir, Albania, the problems of Muslim minorities in Sri Lanka, Burma, the Philippines, Jerusalem, and, of course, the tragedy in Bosnia. But there was one phenomenon that was never mentioned, perhaps the most important one of all: Despite all those oppositions and revolts against the power, and the existing regimes, in the Muslim world, and despite all those rebellious groups that use the Islamic terminology and interpret their revolt in religious categories, not a word was said about Algeria and nothing about the ongoing crisis in this respect in Egypt and elsewhere. Indirectly, the problem was reflected in other news, for instance, in reports about security questions as an important issue in the meetings of the Gulf Cooperation Council, and about international cooperation on internal security measures. Obviously the main con- cern was the instability due to internal opposition in the States of the Muslim world. External enemies often get the blame, but the point is that these external enemies have ideological affinities with the internal opposition. The opponents' use of Islamic terminology makes it dangerous even to mention them, because this same terminology is used in order to show the legitimacy of the Saudi regime. Here is a struggle for the right to use the religious language and historiography, as they serve both as legitimization of power and as expression of opposition.

A risk group, the basis of a possible radical Islamist opposition, is constituted mainly by those with scientific or technical education, and the Saudi regime has tried a rather clever solution: the creation of a consultative assembly (majlis ash-shûrâ), a kind of parliament, not elected, however, but to which the king has appointed the 60 members in a special decree issued on August 20, 1993. If we look at the categories of people chosen by the king, we can see that he appointed neither traditional tribal shaikhs or emirs, nor (with a few exceptions) members of the class of 'ulamâ,' those two traditionally influential categories, often designed as "those who unfasten and bind." (ahl al-hall wa-l-'aqd). Almost all the members appointed to the parliament were instead persons with Western-type academic educations. More than half the number were PhDs (several from European or U.S. universities). We should note that two were Shiites, which is a direct provocation for the traditional wahhâbî 'ulamâ.' This new institution is evidently intended to involve the technocrats in the function of the state and in the process of political decisions, and in that way—if possible—diminish the risk of that group forming a basis for organized opposition (as was the case in Algeria and Egypt). Important still is the religious legitimization: The designation of the Assembly of Consultation, the majlis, is an allusion to Koranic terminology (shûrâ, cf. Koran, Sura 42: 38). The new institution, which is a change in policy, and a change in relation to the traditional power structure, is legitimized by this Koranic word. Simultaneously it is a part of the appropriation, by those in power, of the vocabulary of the opposition groups. The religious terms and history constitute a language, the message and meaning of which has to be discerned in the actual situation. The changes, sometimes very subtle ones, in the use of that language can be a very interesting indicator of new political developments.

In conflict resolution there is, thus, a need for analysis not only of economic, social, and political factors, but of the use of religious vocabulary and historiography in the present day Muslim world. It can also be used consciously in conflict resolution. For instance, during the ongoing and very delicate Israeli–Palestinian peace process, there has been a stress in the general debate, in Europe and in the Muslim World, on certain aspects of the history of Muslim Spain. The point is that an historical, flourishing, multireligious cultural milieu exists in Spain in contrast to what happened after the Catholic (i.e., European) *reconquista*. Instances of peace and coexistence are thus more interesting in the historiography than the traditional enumeration of conflicts and atrocities in the past. In other words, it is possible to choose a conflict-resolving historiography.

REFERENCE

Rizvi, Y. (1991). *The renegade: A narration of the mother of all retreats*. (Available from Dr. Yaseen Rizvi, P.O. Box 1312, Islamabad, Pakistan)

12

Conflict Resolution in a Highly Stressful Society: The Case of Israel

Simha F. Landau
The Hebrew University of Jerusalem

In this chapter, conflict management in Israel is analyzed in accordance with the conceptual framework of Black (1993). Israel has to cope with conflict on several levels: individual, group, and national, and a variety of methods are applied. The external Israeli–Arab conflict, the Jewish–Arab conflict within the country, the ethnic–economic conflict between Eastern and Western Jews, the normative, value-system conflict between religious and secular Jews, and the political–ideological conflict between left and right are discussed. The effect of social stressors and social heterogeneity are analyzed, and three distinct patterns of changes in conflict resolution within Israeli society are identified.

—The Editors

In this chapter, I attempt to analyze conflict resolution in the Israeli context. Clearly, conflict resolution can be applied to disputes at various levels: between individuals, social groups, and nations. Israeli society has to cope with conflict on all these levels. Indeed, the very creation of Israel as a sovereign state in 1948 came only after a long and bitter struggle between the Zionist movement and its many opponents, both internal, within the Jewish community, and external, with the ruling British Mandate and the Arab population in Palestine, as well as with neighboring Arab countries.

Israel is basically a society of immigrants with the majority of its members either born elsewhere or born to immigrant parents. Mainly because of massive immigration from around the world, the Jewish population of the country grew more than sevenfold, from 650,000 in 1948, to about 4,700,000 in 1993 (Smooha, 1994). During this period, the country experienced several major wars and endless terrorist incidents, as well as rapid economic development which, apart from raising the standard of living in general, also included periods of economic recession, high rates of inflation, and unemployment. Thus various demographic, political, economic, and social processes have contributed to the formation of a dynamic yet highly stressful society. Although this chapter focuses mainly on the macronational level, attention is drawn to the effects of macrosocial stress factors on conflict resolution on the microindividual level.

CONCEPTUAL FRAMEWORK

I attempt to apply some of the conflict management concepts used by Black (1993) to the Israeli context. Black's conceptual formulations in this area are particularly useful in view of the fact that his theory of social control (in which conflict resolution is an integral part) encompasses all levels of human organization and grouping, from the microindividual level to the level of social groups, to the macronational level of analysis.

Black (1993) described five major forms of conflict management:

1. *Self-help*: "The handling of a grievance by unilateral aggression" (p. 74). This form ranges from simple gestures of disapproval, to assaults, killings, wars, and so on.
2. *Avoidance*: "The handling of a grievance by the curtailment of interaction" (p. 79). Examples here include secession from a nation, running away, divorce, and suicide.
3. *Negotiation*: "The handling of a grievance by joint decision" (p. 83). In this form, one party, but usually both, must move toward the other with or without the intervention of a third party.
4. *Settlement*: "The handling of a grievance by a nonpartisan third party" (p. 85), which includes mediation (the third party does not take sides), arbitration (the third party decides how to resolve the conflict, but cannot compel compliance), adjudication (the judge both makes a decision and, if necessary, enforces it), and repressive pacification (the third party crushes the conflict by force).
5. *Toleration*: "Inaction, where a grievance might otherwise be handled" (p. 88).

THE EXTERNAL ISRAELI–ARAB CONFLICT

The Israeli–Arab conflict in which Israel has been involved for so many decades has been and still is the cardinal and the most demanding stress factor affecting Israeli society. In applying Black's classifications, it is clear that self-help (i.e., war and belligerence) on both sides, has characterized the relationship between Israel and its neighbors for most of the country's history.

This conflict casts its shadow on almost every aspect of daily life in Israel. Since its establishment in 1948, Israel has been involved in five major wars and in endless hostilities with its Arab neighbors and the Palestinian population under its control (since 1967). Acts of terrorism create a constant sense of insecurity, and the need to take precautions and to be on guard constitute a continuous threat to daily routine. As would be expected, the permanence of the threat of war and acts of terrorism, and the lifetime commitment of Israeli men to national service in the military have an inevitable effect on Israeli society. National surveys have indeed shown that the fear of war and related issues (e.g., fear of terrorism, prolonged army reserve service) became the most salient concerns of Israelis from 1968 onwards (Katz, 1982a, 1982b; Stone, 1982).

A number of Israeli studies have investigated the effects of wars and other security-related events on a wide range of topics, from its direct effects on soldiers on the front line (Yarom, 1983) to its more generalized effects on public morale (Guttman & Levy, 1983), on children (Raviv & Klingman, 1983), on the level of psychopathology (Landau, 1990), on changes in gender roles (Bar Yosef, 1975), on emigration from Israel (Cohen, 1988), and on the functioning of various segments of society (Kimmerling, 1985).

The number of casualties caused by wars and various terrorist acts. (i.e., collective self-help) in Israel's history far exceeds the number of casualties caused by "regular" crimes of violence (i.e., individual self-help). For example, Landau (1994) reports that during the first five years of the Palestinian *Intifada* (uprising) (1988–1992), politically motivated violence (e.g., terrorist attacks, military operations) accounted for the great majority (82.3 percent) of all the people killed by violence in Israel and the occupied territories.

The first major breakthrough on the way to a peaceful solution of the Israeli-Arab conflict took place in 1978–1979 when Israel and its most powerful enemy, Egypt, chose to switch from almost total reliance on self-help (war and belligerence) to conciliation by means of mediation and negotiation (with the help of mediating countries such as the United States, Morocco, and Romania). In this settlement, both sides succeeded in accommodating one another: Israel pulled out from the Sinai Peninsula, which it had conquered in 1967 and, in return, received recognition and peace with Egypt.

A further positive step in this direction was the Madrid Conference in 1991, in which Israel and its Arab neighbors (including the Palestinians) started negotiating a comprehensive peace in the Middle East under the auspices of the United Nations and the major world powers. In 1993, negotiations between Israel and the Palestinian Liberation Organization (PLO) through the mediation of Norway culminated in the signing of the Declaration of Principles between the two parties as a first step on the way to a permanent settlement of the conflict.

The Israeli–Palestinian conflict, an intense conflict between two national movements with strong ideological claims for the same piece of land, lies at the heart of the Israeli–Arab problem. The aim of the current peace negotiations is to attempt to resolve this conflict by means of physical separation of the two peoples in neighboring territories (i.e., avoidance), with each side compromising on its original territorial claims and aspirations.

As is typical of deep ideological national conflicts of this kind, it has taken many years and thousands of casualties on both sides for the two parties to recognize the futility of attempting to resolve this conflict by physical violence (self-help) and a total denial of the rights of the opponent (enemy). Although the prolonged duration of this conflict and the many casualties caused by it provide an incentive for a peaceful solution, they also pose a psychological barrier for reconciliation, because each side is required to unlearn and/or change the long-held stereotypes of the enemy. The realization that in the long run this is the only feasible solution gives hope (threatening setbacks notwithstanding) that we are slowly approaching the end of the long period of belligerence and violence in Israeli–Arab relationships.

THE JEWISH–ARAB CONFLICT IN ISRAEL

The most significant division and source of internal conflict in Israeli society is between its Jewish majority and its Arab minority. Arabs comprise 18.6% of the Israeli population. About 76% of the Arabs are Sunni Moslems, about 15% are Christians of various denominations, and about 9% are Druse (Central Bureau of Statistics, 1994). The geopolitical situation of Israel in the Middle East poses a dilemma for the Arab population in the country. The sense of loyalty to their brethren in the neighboring countries and the occupied territories puts them in conflict with their required civil loyalty to the Jewish state, the declared enemy of most Arab countries. This internal conflict is exacerbated by the fact that many Israeli Arabs have relatives who fled in the wake of war to the neighboring Arab countries (or to the West Bank and the Gaza Strip, then occupied by Jordan and Egypt, respectively).

The problematic situation of Israel's Arab citizens has a number of practical consequences that prevent them from being fully integrated in Israeli society, thus increasing the areas of conflict between them and the Jewish majority. The most prominent distinction between Jews and Arabs in Israel is that the Arabs are exempt from military service. Conscription (three years for men and two years for women) is perceived as both a duty and a privilege. Moreover, it is a prerequisite for many occupational positions, especially in the public sector, and, in effect, it has become a way of legitimizing the exclusion of Arabs from many occupations on the labor market, and not only for job openings directly related to national security. The Israeli political structure is aimed at the realization of Jewish national interests and, as a result, it is much less responsive to claims made by Arabs. In practice, Jews enjoy a greater share of resources allocated by the state as well as more favorable educational and occupational opportunities (Shavit, 1990).

There is also some evidence that the criminal justice system operates more strictly in the Arab sector (Cohen & Palmor, 1985; Haj-Yahia, Rahav & Teichman,

1978), but the findings are not uniform in this respect (Cohen, 1989). There is, however, specific evidence of discrimination against Israeli Arabs in other areas, including both legal and administrative practice related to agriculture, social, education and health services. The fact that Israeli Arabs are exempt from military service also results in their exclusion from many benefits restricted to veterans and their families (cf., Kretzmer, 1988; Al-Haj & Rosenfeld, 1988).

Given the gravity of the division between Jews and Arabs in Israel and the intense feelings of discrimination among Arabs, the relatively peaceful coexistence of Jews and Arabs within Israel is somewhat surprising. There are several structural explanations for this. First, the two communities live in almost total residential segregation (i.e., avoidance). The great majority of Israeli Arabs live in exclusively Arab towns and villages, with their own municipal councils, educational system, social and health services, and so on. This arrangement provides occupation opportunities to qualified and educated Arabs that would be less available to them in the Jewish sector. Another result of this residential segregation is the minimization of interethnic friction between Jews and Arabs on a daily basis.

However, the most important mechanism in the peaceful regulation of the Jewish–Arab conflict in Israel is the full participation of the Arab population in the democratic process in Israeli society, that is, their participation in general national elections to the parliament (the *Knesset*) as well as in municipal elections and in membership in the trade union congress (the *Histadrut*). Thus, by recourse to electoral power, through political negotiation, and legitimate forms of self-help (e.g., public demonstrations, the use of the media), they manage to fight for their rights, improve their situation, and strive toward greater equality with the Jewish majority. Another related mechanism is the use of the justice system by Israeli Arabs (i.e., adjudication) which, on several occasions, has forced the government (and other public institutions) to rectify discriminatory practices (e.g., full entitlement to family benefits).

In spite of the foregoing regulatory mechanisms, the conflict between Jews and Arabs in Israel does erupt on occasion, as in the case of Land Day demonstrations in 1986 (against land confiscation by the government), which became violent and claimed a number of casualties. Since the onset of the *Intifada* in 1988, there have been several Israeli Arabs involved in terrorist acts such as stone throwing. However, such examples have been the exception rather than the rule.

Thus the nature of the conflict between Israel and its external Arab enemies differs from the conflict between Jews and Arabs within Israel. The former is on the international level, whereas the latter is an intranational conflict between a distinct minority group and the majority. Though the *Intifada* has led to increased national feelings among Israeli Arabs, on the whole, they cope with the situation and struggle for their rights within the bounds of the democratic process, utilizing the political, legal, and social mechanisms provided by the institutions of a democratic society. It would be safe to assume that the peaceful resolution of the external Israeli–Arab conflict will have a positive effect on areas of conflict between Jews and Arabs within Israel.

ETHNIC–ECONOMIC CONFLICT:
EASTERN JEWS VERSUS WESTERN JEWS

The Jewish population in Israel can be divided into two major ethnic groups: Eastern Jews (originating mainly from Middle Eastern and North African countries) and Western Jews (originating mainly from Europe and America). Following massive waves of immigration to Israel, the proportion of Eastern Jews increased from 23% in 1948 to 52% in 1970 (Smooha & Peres, 1980). Originating from developing countries, Eastern Jews found themselves in an inferior and disadvantaged position in comparison to that of their Western counterparts. They had less formal education and lacked technical skills and experiences of living in an industrial, democratic society. As a result, they found themselves occupying lower status positions in terms of occupation, income, and education (Smooha & Kraus, 1985).[1] Despite official policy aimed at reducing the gap between Eastern and Western Jews, ethnic inequality in the above spheres has not been significantly reduced, and in some aspects has even increased (Bernstein & Antonovsky, 1981; Nahon, 1984, 1987).

The feeling of relative deprivation among Eastern Jews, reinforced by their underrepresentation in political and social power positions, has given rise to a number of protest movements (a form of self-help), some of them quite militant and violent by nature. Of significance were the riots of Wadi Salib (a North African slum area in Haifa) in 1959 and the violent protests of the Black Panther movement in a rundown neighborhood in Jerusalem (Musrara) in 1971 (Cromer, 1976).

However, on the whole, interethnic conflict among Jews in Israeli society is nonviolent. There are a number of reasons for this. First, both groups share a common Jewish heritage and identity. Second, the constant threat from Israel's external enemies acts toward maintaining internal solidarity and has a cohesive unifying effect on Jews of all origins, thus defusing the intensity of internal conflicts. It is of significance that the two aforementioned eruptions of ethnic violence occurred during lulls in the Israeli–Arab conflict: in 1959, a time of relative peace following the Sinai/Suez campaign of 1956–1957, and in 1971, a period of economic prosperity and tranquility on the borders following the end of the War of Attrition with Egypt in 1970.

An additional factor that mitigates the ethnic conflict is the increasing participation and representation of Eastern Jews in elite positions in the political, military, economic, judicial, and social spheres. Thus, in spite of ongoing underrepresention of Eastern Jews in positions of power, it is unlikely that ethnic conflict in Israeli society will take a serious violent turn. However, a peaceful solution of the Israeli–Palestinian conflict may have the effect of increasing the salience and intensity of internal rifts, including the aforementioned ethnic conflict.

---

[1]During the years 1989–1993, about 500,000 Jews immigrated from the former Soviet Union to Israel (Smooha, 1994). As a result, the proportion of Eastern Jews in the Jewish population decreased. However, this slight demographic change did not change the essence of the economic–ethnic conflict, as described following.

NORMATIVE, VALUE SYSTEM CONFLICT:
RELIGIOUS VERSUS SECULAR JEWS

Israeli Jews can roughly be classified along the following continuum of religious ritual observance: secular, traditional, orthodox, and ultraorthodox. The main normative conflict is between the two extremes of this spectrum: the secular majority and the small ultraorthodox minority. The secular–religious conflict is very high on the public agenda and in the internal political arena; it is rated higher than the ethnic conflict between Eastern and Western Jews (Ben-Rafael, Shteyer, & Lewin, 1989). The ultraorthodox political parties, although small in size, have disproportionate influence and power in the government because the major political parties are usually forced to rely on their support in order to form a coalition government. As a result, there is a general feeling among the secular majority that their lifestyle is being threatened by concessions to the religious parties (e.g., the ban on public transportation on the Sabbath). These feelings lead to expressions of aggressive sentiments by the secular majority towards the ultraorthodox minority (Struch & Schwartz, 1989).

As with the ethnic conflict, this normative conflict is mainly dealt with nonviolently by forms of self-help, negotiation, and settlement (e.g., political agreements, use of the media, the courts, public protests, demonstrations). The only exception to this rule relates to a very small splinter group of ultrareligious zealots (*Neturei Karta*) who, on a number of issues, over extended periods of time, have indulged in individual and organized violence, such as throwing rocks, blocking roads, and burning down bus shelters displaying advertisements portraying "overexposed" females. On the ideological level, the conflict with this small group is deep and unsolvable in view of the fact that they accept neither the authority of any secular Jewish government, nor the legitimacy of the State of Israel. However, because of their small numbers and their isolation in public opinion, their sporadic outbursts of violence do not pose any real danger to the social fabric of Israeli society.

POLITICAL–IDEOLOGICAL CONFLICT: LEFT VERSUS RIGHT

The conflict between right and left in Israel is multifaceted and touches on a number of areas, including the economy and welfare policies. However, the most salient aspect of this conflict has to do with the approach to the Israeli–Palestinian conflict and the territories occupied in 1967. In brief, the various right-wing factions are against the return of the territories to non-Israeli rule, whereas the left-wing factions advocate pulling out of most of the territories (pending appropriate security arrangements) in order to preserve both the Jewish and democratic character of Israel. It is worth noting that there is considerable overlap between the secular–religious and the left–right divisions, with most of the religious parties and their electorate located in the right-wing of the political map.

This conflict has been managed so far mainly by nonviolent forms of democratic political struggle. However, the outbreak of the Palestinian *Intifada* intensified this political conflict. The 1993 agreement between Israel and the PLO, and the ensuing escalation in terrorist attacks on both sides, has brought the cleavage between left and right to the brink of civil war and the possibility of armed Jewish resistance to the legitimate government has became a feasible danger for the first time in Israel's history. The most violent opposition to current peace talks and official policy comes from a nucleus of right-wing religious-messianic zealots settled in the occupied territories who believe in an ideology of "Greater Israel." In July of 1995, a group of right-wing rabbis issued a religious judgment delegitimizing the evacuation of Jewish settlements from the occupied territories, ordering their followers in the army to refuse to take part in such actions.

This internal conflict is currently the most intense and potentially the most violent and dangerous because it addresses the very existence and future of Israeli society. The way this conflict is resolved will be determined largely by how the Israeli–Palestinian conflict is resolved. A successful peaceful settlement of the Israeli–Palestinian problem will probably serve to defuse the intensity of the conflict between the left and the right within Israel.

In conclusion, I reiterate that given the number and intensity of the structural cleavages in Israeli society, the relatively low level of violence between the various social groups mentioned above is indeed surprising. The grievances and conflicts of most of these groups find their outlet mainly through legitimate forms of self-help, negotiation, and settlement. In the age of the media, self-help in the form of public protest and demonstration are increasingly used by various minority and interest groups (e.g., new immigrants, the unemployed, and women) to place their grievances on the public agenda and force the political elites to respond to them (Lehman-Wilzig, 1986).

THE EFFECTS OF SOCIAL STRESSORS ON AGGRESSION

Conflict and stress are related in more than one way. Stress can cause conflict (i.e., scarcity of resources as a source of conflict between individuals or social groups). On the other hand, conflict, by its very nature, is a major source of stress. Do the macrostress factors resulting from some of the structural conflicts already discussed have any measurable effects on the microindividual level? The extreme forms of self-help (i.e., physical aggression) and avoidance (i.e., suicide), often referred to as outward-directed aggression and inward-directed aggression, respectively, are considered.

The detrimental effects of macrosecurity-related stress on the level of individual aggression in Israel has been shown in a number of studies. Regarding crimes of violence, whether the units of analysis are the short major wars (Fishman, 1983; Hassin & Amir, 1974; Segev, 1975; Shoham, 1985) or extended periods of conflict and stress (Landau & Pfeffermann, 1988), research results support the legitima-tion–habituation hypothesis (Landau & Pfeffermann, 1988), which assumes that in the long run, violence resulting from conflicts with out-groups (enemies) is general-ized and directed towards in-group members of society. Landau and Pfeffermann (1988) found that the number of security-related casualties had a significant positive effect on the number of regular criminal homicides using monthly data for 1967 through 1982. More recently, Landau (1994), reported a strong similarity between the trends of politically motivated (terrorist) homicides and regular criminal homicides during the first five years of the *Intifada*. Among the findings of this study was a sizable increase in homicides resulting from domestic disputes since the onset of the *Intifada* in 1988. These findings can be interpreted in relation to the increased exposure of Israelis to violence in the occupied territories, thus lending additional support to the legitimation–habituation hypothesis (Landau & Pfeffermann, 1988).

A new approach was introduced in this line of research by investigating the relationship between the subjective perception of external stress factors and levels of aggression in society on the aggregate level (Landau, 1988). The theoretical basis of this approach assumes that the prevalence of aggression in society will be positively related to the intensity of stress factors and negatively related to the intensity of social support or solidarity. In general, this theoretical model is supported empirically. Violent crime (homicide and robbery) was positively related to most subjective stress indicators (e.g., security-related stress and economic stress) and negatively related to social-solidarity indicators (e.g., positive attitudes regarding the relations between various segments of the population). The model was also successfully applied to inward-directed aggression: suicide and attempted suicide. Landau and Rahav (1989) showed that suicidal behavior in Israel was positively related to subjective social stress indicators (mainly among males) and negatively related (among both males and females) to subjective social-solidarity indicators. The main conclusion from these studies is that the macrostress factors in Israeli society (mainly security-related and economic stress) have a measurably significant effect on the levels of both outward-directed and inward-directed aggression on the microindividual level.

SOCIAL HETEROGENEITY AND CONFLICT RESOLUTION

This section discusses the differential distribution of the extreme forms of self-help and avoidance (i.e., physical aggression and suicide) in varies ethnic groups in Israel. It focuses mainly on the effects of cultural and social norms on the use of aggression as a means of conflict resolution.

Comparison between the Jewish and Arab populations reveals that the prevalence of violence among Arabs is considerably higher than among Jews. According to traditional Arab culture, certain interpersonal situations or circumstances dictate self-help in the form of violent behavior. This is the case in killing to preserve family honor (usually related to alleged sexual misconduct of a female in the family), blood feud, or participating in individual or collective acts of violence between clans (*Hamulahs*; Kressel, 1981). An analysis of homicides in Israel between 1950 and 1964 found that the homicide rate in the Arab population was almost 4 times higher than among Eastern Jews, and almost 7 times higher than among Western Jews (Landau, 1975b). In recent years, this gap between the homicide rates of Jews and Arabs has narrowed, but still exists. For example, the number of Arabs convicted of homicide and attempted homicide in 1992 (2.73 per 100,000 population) was 3.62 times higher than the corresponding number among Jews (.75 per 100,000 population; Central Bureau of Statistics, 1995).

Comparison between Eastern and Western Jews reveals that the great majority of violent offenders (and most of the Jewish prison population) are of Eastern, especially North African origin (Landau, 1975a; Shoham, Rahav, & Markovsky, 1987). It should be noted that in Israel, as in many other societies, homicide is basically an intraethnic rather than interethnic phenomenon (Landau, Drapkin & Arad, 1974).

Marx (1980) provided an analysis of violence in a small development town inhabited by Moroccan Jews. On occasion, violence and the threat of violence are used instrumentally by individuals against public officers, either to achieve specific material goals (e.g., subsidized accommodation or increased welfare support) or out of despair in an attempt to draw the attention to a distressing personal situation.

Another example of instrumental aggression among Eastern Jews is the collective violence of Jewish immigrants from the former Soviet Republic of Georgia (Eilam, 1975, 1978). This group has a long history of collective violence against the oppressive communist regime in their country of origin. After immigrating to Israel, absorption difficulties (mainly economic) increased their internal community cohesiveness and intensified their use of collective violence with Israeli authorities or members of other ethnic groups. In the community context of this group, assisting a fellow member by the use (or threat) of violence, is considered a substitute for material help; without the threat of severe punishment (because of the more tolerant nature of Israeli authorities), investment in violence represents an economical way for forging and strengthening both interpersonal ties and community identity.

The foregoing examples facilitate the understanding of the social function of violent behavior in various ethnic groups in Israeli society. The higher prevalence of violence among Arabs and Eastern Jews in Israel can be seen as closely related to the inferior social position that these ethnic groups occupy in the Israeli social system.

The ethnic distribution of suicide in Israel confirms Black's (1993, p. 82) observation that violence varies inversely with avoidance. The rate of suicide is the highest among Western Jews and lowest among non-Jews (particularly Moslems) with Eastern Jews falling in between these two extremes (Landau, 1975b; Levav & Aisenberg, 1989). Total avoidance (such as suicide) is most likely under conditions of social fluidity, social fragmentation, and individuation (Black, 1993, pp. 81–83). In the Israeli context these conditions are more characteristic of Western Jews than of Arabs and Eastern Jews. For example, when measures related to family ties are considered, Western Jews exhibit the lowest fertility rates and the highest divorce rates, Arabs are highest in fertility rates and lowest in divorce rates, and Eastern Jews are located in between these two extremes (Davids, 1983). In recent years, because of the increased adoption of Western lifestyle, these gaps between the ethnic groups have narrowed to some extent (Katz & Peres, 1986). Consequently, a corresponding increase in suicide among Arabs and Eastern Jews can be expected.

The contrast between homicide and suicide in Israel is very similar to that found in other industrialized societies: Population groups in the higher social strata are underrepresented in violent crime rates and overrepresented in suicide rates, whereas those of lower socioeconomic status are overrepresented in categories of outward-directed aggression and underrepresented in inward-directed aggression (Henry and Short, 1954; Holinger, 1987).

CONCLUSIONS

This examination of Israel's short history suggests that the time dimension is an important factor in the analysis of human conflict. Three distinct patterns of changes in conflict resolution over time can be identified.

1. Initial mode: unilateral self-help—Subsequent mode: negotiation and settlement. For many decades the external Israeli–Arab conflict was characterized by unilateral self-help (war and belligerence). The futility of this mode led the aggrieved parties to opt for negotiation and settlement in the attempt to achieve a durable and peaceful resolution of the conflict.

2. Initial mode: toleration—Subsequent mode: negotiation and settlement. The conflicts between Jews and Arabs within Israel and between Eastern and Western Jews were dealt with for many years by various degrees of toleration (i.e., ignoring their respective legitimate grievances). Only with time, through the increased participation of these groups in political life and the utilization of their civic and constitutional rights, were these underprivileged parties able to negotiate and reach settlements aimed at procuring greater equality.

3. Initial mode: negotiation and settlement—Subsequent mode: unilateral self-help. The conflicts between religious and secular Jews and between left and right have been an integral part of political life since the establishment of the state in 1948 and have been dealt with mainly by means of negotiation and settlement. However, with regard to the left-right conflict (which, as already mentioned, overlaps the religious–secular conflict), there is a serious danger of "regression" and recourse to self-help in the form of extreme violence against the legally elected government.

In closing, it would seem safe to predict that overall the conflicts and divisions in Israeli society are not likely to disappear in the foreseeable future and will probably just change in form and intensity.

Postscript

On November 4th, 1995 shortly after this chapter was completed, Israeli prime minister Yitzhak Rabin was assassinated at a mass rally supporting the peace process and opposing violence. The assassin, a law student, Jewish, religious, and a member of an extreme right-wing organization, considered the Israeli peace agreement with the Palestinians to be an act of treason. This tragic event, which has traumatized Israeli society, surely represents the most extreme expression of the self-help mode in the left–right conflict. However, its repercussions will be felt in all the other areas of conflict analyzed in this chapter.

ACKNOWLEDGMENTS

This chapter was written during my stay as a visiting professor at the John Jay College of Criminal Justice, New York, in Spring 1994. I would like to thank Menachem Amir, Stanley Cohen, and Maya Landau for their valuable comments.

REFERENCES

Al-Haj, M., & Rosenfeld, H. (1988). *Arab local government in Israel*. Tel Aviv: International Center for Peace in the Middle East.
Bar Yosef, R. (1975). *Nashim ugvarim b'milchama: Shinuei tafkid b'matzavei lachatz* [Women and men during war: Role changes in stressful situations]. Jerusalem: Hebrew University of Jerusalem.
Ben-Rafael, E., Shteyer, H., & Lewin, E. (1989). Israel as a multi-cleavage setting. *Plural Societies, 19*, 21–40.
Black, D. (1993). *The social structure of right and wrong*. New York: Academic.
Bernstein, J., & Antonovsky, A. (1981). The integration of ethnic groups in Israel. *Jewish Journal of Sociology, 23*, 5–23.
Central Bureau of Statistics. (1994). *Statistical abstracts of Israel, 1994*. Jerusalem: Government Press.
Central Bureau of Statistics. (1995). *Criminal statistics, 1992*. Special Series No. 988, Jerusalem: Government Press.
Cohen, B., & Palmor, S. (1985). The impact of ethnicity on probation officer's recommendation and dispositions in Israel. *Justice Quarterly, 2*, 197–212.
Cohen, S. (1989). *Crime, justice and social control in the Israeli Arab population*. Tel Aviv: International Center for Peace in the Middle East.
Cohen, Y. (1988). War and social integration: the effects of the Israeli-Arab conflict on Jewish emigration from Israel. *American Sociological Review, 53*, 908–918.
Cromer, G. (1976). The Israeli Black Panthers: Fighting for credibility and cause. *Victimology, 1*, 166–171.
Davids, L. (1983). What's happening in the Israeli family? Recent demographic trends. *Israel Social Science Research, 1*, 34–40.
Eilam, Y. (1975). Dfussei hitargenut shel olim migruzia: Shimush b'koach k'emtzai l'gibush kehilati [Patterns of organization of Georgian immigrants: The use of force as a means of community cohesion]. *Megamot, 21*, 377–393.
Eilam, Y. (1978). Shimush b'koach etzel olei Marocco v'etzel olei gruzia [The use of force among Morrocan and Georgian immigrants]. *Megamot, 24*, pp. 169–185.
Fishman, G. (1983). On war and crime. In S. Breznitz (Ed.), *Stress in Israel* (pp. 165–180). New York: Van Nostrand, Reinhold.
Guttman, L., & Levy, S. (1983). Dynamics of three varieties of morale: The case of Israel. In S. Breznitz (Ed.), *Stress in Israel* (pp. 102–113). New York: Van Nostrand, Reinhold.
Haj-Yahia, M., Rahav, G., & Teichman, M. (1978). *The distinction between Jews and Arabs in the process of judgment and punishment of juveniles*. Tel Aviv: Institute of Criminology and Criminal Law, Tel Aviv University.

Hassin, Y., & Amir, M. (1974). Business (crime) as usual in wartime conditions among offenders in Israel. *Journal of Criminal Law and Criminology, 66,* 491–495.

Henry, A. F., & Short, J. F. (1954). *Suicide and homicide: Some economic, sociological and psychological aspects of aggression.* Glencoe, IL: The Free Press.

Holinger, P. C. (1987). *Violent deaths in the United States.* New York: Guilford.

Katz, R. (1982a). Concerns of the Israeli: Change and stability from 1962 to 1975. *Human Relations, 35,* 83–100.

Katz, R. (1982b). Dynamic patterning of concerns: A long term comparison of the structure of hopes and fears of Israelis. *Social Indicators Research, 10,* 359–388.

Katz, R., & Peres, Y. (1986). The sociology of the family in Israel: An outline of its development from the 1950s to the 1980s. *European Sociological Review, 2,* 148–159.

Kimmerling, B. (1985). *The Interrupted System: Israeli civilians in war and routine times.* New Brunswick, NJ: Transaction Publishers.

Kressel, G. M. (1981). Sororicide/filiacide: Homicide for family honour. *Current Anthropology, 22,* 141–158.

Kretzmer, D. (1988). *The legal status of Arabs in Israel.* Tel Aviv: International Center for Peace in the Middle East.

Landau, S. F. (1975a). Future time perspective of delinquents and non-delinquents: The effect of institutionalization. *Criminal Justice and Behavior, 2,* 22–36.

Landau, S. F. (1975b). Pathologies among homicide offenders: Some cultural profiles. *British Journal of Criminology, 15,* 157–166.

Landau, S. F. (1988). Violent crime and its relation to subjective social stress indicators: The case of Israel. *Aggressive Behavior, 14,* 337–362.

Landau, S. F. (1990). Subjective social stress indicators and the level of reported psychopathology: The case of Israel. *American Journal of Community Psychology, 18,* 99–39.

Landau, S. F. (1994). Violent crime in a society at war: Israel and the "Intifada." In J. M. Ramirez (Ed.), *Violence and some alternatives* (pp. 63–84). Madrid: Centreur.

Landau, S. F., Drapkin, I., & Arad, S. (1974). Homicide victims and offenders: An Israeli study. *Journal of Criminal Law and Criminology, 65,* 390–396.

Landau, S. F., & Pfeffermann, D. (1988). A time series analysis of violent crime and its relation to prolonged states of warfare: The Israeli case. *Criminology, 26,* 489–504.

Landau, S. F., & Rahav, G. (1989). Suicide and attempted suicide: Their relation to subjective social stress indicators. *Genetic, Social and General Psychology Monographs, 115,* 273–294.

Lehman-Wilzig, S. N. (1986). Public protest and systemic stability in Israel: 1960–1979. In S. A. Cohen & E. Don-Yehia (Eds.), *Comparative Jewish politics: Public life in Israel and the Diaspora* (pp. 171–210). Ramat-Gan: Bar-Ilan University Press.

Levav, I., & Aisenberg, E. (1989). Suicide in Israel: Crossnational comparisons. *Acta Psychiatrica Scandinavica, 79,* 468–473.

Marx, E. (1980). Ein lachatz bli matara [There is no pressure without a purpose]. In S. Orr (Ed.), *On violence and non-violence* (pp. 11–178). Tel Aviv: Social Workers Union.

Nahon, Y. (1984). *Megamot bata'asuka—Hameimad ha'adati* [Trends in the occupation status—The ethnic dimensions 1958–1981]. Jerusalem: The Jerusalem Institute for Israel Studies.

Nahon, Y. (1987). *Dfussei hitrachavut hahaskala umivne hizdamnuiot hata'asuka—Hameimad ha'adafi* [Patterns of educational expansion and the structure of educational opportunities-The ethnic dimension]. Jerusalem: The Jerusalem Institute for Israel Studies.

Raviv, A., & Klingman, A. (1983). Children under stress. In S. Breznitz (Ed.), *Stress in Israel* (pp. 38–162). New York: Van Nostrand, Reinhold.

Segev, H. (1975). *Patterns of juvenile delinquency during the Yom Kippur war in the Tel-Aviv area.* Unpublished master's thesis. Institute of Criminology, Tel-Aviv University.

Shavit, Y. (1990). Segregation, tracking and the educational attainment of minorities: Arabs and Oriental Jews in Israel. *American Sociological Review, 55,* 115–126.

Shoham, E. (1985). *Shinuim b'hitnahagut dfussei avarianut ktinim batkufa shelifnei milchemet Yom Kippur ula'achareha* [Changes in the behavior patterns of minors' delinquency before and after the Yom Kippur war]. Unpublished master's thesis. Bar-Ilan University, Ramat-Gan.

Smooha, S. (1994). Hashpa'at ha'alyah hahamonit michever hamedinot al hachevra ha'Israelit [The effect of the mass immigration from the Commonwealth of Independent States on Israeli society]. *Sociology Newsletter*, 6–7.

Smooha, S., & Kraus, V. (1985). Ethnicity as a factor in status attainment in Israel. In R. V. Robinson (Ed.), *Research in social stratification and mobility* (pp. 151–176). Greenwich, CT: JAI.

Smooha, S., & Peres, Y. (1980). The dynamics of ethnic inequalities: The case of Israel. In E. Krausz (Ed.), *Studies of Israeli Society* (Vol. 1, pp. 165–181). New Brunswick, NJ: Transaction Publishers.

Stone, R. A. (1982). *Social Change in Israel: Attitudes and events, 1967–79*. New York: Praeger.

Struch, N., & Schwartz, S. H. (1989). Intergroup aggression: Its predictors and distinctness from in-group bias. *Journal of Personality and Social Psychology, 56*, 364–373.

Yarom, N. (1983). Facing death in war-an existential crisis. In S. Breznitz (Ed.), *Stress in Israel* (pp. 3–38). New York: Van Nostrand, Reinhold.

13

Beyond the Competition of Tears: Black–Jewish Conflict Containment in a New York Neighborhood

Ilsa M. Glazer

City University of New York, Kingsborough Community College

Glazer presents ethnographic data on Jews and African-Americans living in the Crown Heights neighborhood in New York, where, in 1991, a 4-day race riot rocked the community. She suggests that some issues represent unresolvable conflicts between these two groups, but that conflict can be contained or limited in some regard. Glazer describes how following the 1991 riots, the first coalition with members from both subgroups was established to recommend long-term solutions and to prevent future problems. Several projects and programs implemented to facilitate communication, interaction, and the working together of both adults and youth in the two groups are described as ways to reduce tensions and improve intergroup relations.

—The Editors

This chapter concerns the evolving relations of Blacks and Jews in the Crown Heights neighborhood of Brooklyn in New York City. Crown Heights was the site of a 4-day race riot in 1991. After the riot, neighborhood leaders made efforts to engage in dialogue. In this chapter, I propose that conflict containment can be considered a form of conflict resolution and analyze the process by which the people of Crown Heights developed mechanisms of conflict containment. Communal conflict containment is successful if neighbors themselves develop mechanisms that facilitate finding solutions to resolvable conflicts, learn to control rather than solve tension-provoking unresolvable issues and bring antagonists together around a common effort. I suggest that it is critical during conflict containment to develop and keep open channels of communication through sustained purposeful interpersonal interaction between members of different subcultures, and that one effective way to accomplish this goal is through the fostering of special-interest friendships. I present a community profile, followed by a discussion of intergroup relations and conflict containment.

COMMUNITY PROFILE

Crown Heights is a densely settled culturally and linguistically diverse Black and Jewish neighborhood with a population of 207,000, which is 80.5% Black, 9.8% Hispanic, 8.2% Jewish and 1.5% "other." The Crown Heights Coalition (1992) reported that Jews speak English, Yiddish, Farsi, French, and Hebrew, whereas Blacks speak English, French, Dutch, Spanish, and Creole. Crown Heights' per capita income averages $10,799, lower than the rest of Brooklyn. Unemployment stands at 13.2% for men and 10.1% for women. One third of the population is under the age of 24. The number of AIDS deaths is skyrocketing, and the infant mortality rate is the highest in the city (higher for Whites than Blacks). Overcrowding affects the quality of life: Crown Heights has 137,550 housing units, 20% of which are overcrowded, high schools are at 108% capacity; and day-care centers are at 107% capacity.

The neighborhood stretches about 19 blocks east-to-west and 28 blocks north-to-south at its widest points. It is bisected by Eastern Parkway, internationally known in the Jewish and Caribbean worlds (cf., Glazer, 1992; Kasinitz, 1992; Mintz, 1992).

The neighborhood is economically mixed. There is a middle class along with a large number of poor. It is generally characterized as economically depressed with a high rate of violent crime and drug abuse. At the same time, by day there is a lively street life in which all groups actively participate. Young Black and Jewish boys play together, racing their bicycles on the sidewalk. Their mothers, living next door to each other, constantly help each other. Day-to-day relations among Black and Jewish women and young children tend to be peaceful, warm, and cordial. Quarrels between neighbors are based on specific complaints, not prejudice.

The neighborhood has important institutions: museums, churches, hospitals, and a branch of the City University of New York, Medgar Evers College, with an overwhelmingly Black student body. It is the world headquarters of a Jewish sect.

Jews

The majority of Jewish residents are from a subculture known as Lubavitcher Hassidim. The Lubavitchers are members of an endogamous fundamentalist sect, open to all who follow its teachings. The sect originated in 18th century Europe. Those who escaped the European Holocaust before World War II, and remnants who survived the genocide, rebuilt their community in Crown Heights in the 1940s and developed a highly successful international movement. When the Lubavitch settled in Crown Heights, it was a middle-class Jewish community. When the middle-class Jews left in the mid-1960s, the Lubavitch stayed on. The sect was headed by the Grand Rebbe Menachem Mendel Schneerson until his death in 1994. Many revere the Rebbe as the Messiah (*Moshiach*). The address 770 Eastern Parkway was his residence, and the international headquarters of the movement. "770" became famous in the Jewish world, as hundreds of religious pilgrims visited weekly.

The Lubavitch community attempts self-sufficiency by maintaining its own institutional structures, including schools (*yeshivas*), charities, social welfare agencies, houses of worship, ambulance service, real estate, publishing, and specialty shops. They are effective politically, voting as a block, and active in pursuing government funding for their school, social service, and community development. They wear distinctive clothing and hair styles and have a precisely constructed way of life based on a belief in revealed religion, with specific rules governing every aspect of daily personal and social life, varying significantly from those of mainstream America. They are an enclave in the neighborhood and indeed wherever in the world they settle. Their interactions with non-Lubavitch are as limited as possible. As adults, they do not socialize with non-Lubavitch, nor do men and women socialize together. Children receive gender segregated education in Lubavitcher *yeshivas*. In per capita income, some Hassidim are the poorest of the poor in the neighborhood. Hence they are eligible for various government sponsored antipoverty programs.

Blacks

African Americans and Caribbean Americans form different Black subcultures, each having its own religious affiliation, music and literature, historical memories, food preferences, social ties, values, and attitudes towards one another. Jamaicans, Haitians, and Guyanese are the majority of the Caribbean population, but there are also people from several other islands and from several African countries.

African-Americans have lived in Brooklyn since 1660, and some Crown Heights residents are their descendants. A community of freed craftsmen called Weeksville began in 1830. As Brooklyn developed, some migrated from surrounding areas of New York; others came from the south as part of the Great Migration. The harsh experiences of poor Blacks in Brooklyn is widely documented (Donaldson, 1993).

Caribbean Americans have lived in Crown Heights since the 1920s. The Immigration and Naturalization Act of 1965 opened large scale Caribbean immigration to the United States. Fifty-eight percent of the Caribbean Crown Heights population, half legal and half illegal, moved to the neighborhood between 1980–1990. Caribbeans bought the homes and small shops of Jews and Italians. The most outstanding feature of Caribbean Crown Heights life began in 1969, when Eastern Parkway became the site of the annual Carnival, now attracting 1,000,000 to 2,000,000 visitors per year. Each island represented in Brooklyn has at least one parade float behind which costumed crowds dance. The Carnival parade takes place on Labor Day.

Many middle-class Caribbean peoples maintain ties to their islands and resist assimilation to African-American culture. Through school and the workplace, young Caribbean and African-Americans are mixing socially. Youth are developing a new bicultural urban musical style, combining elements of rap, reggae, and calypso.

BLACK–JEWISH DIALOGUE

The challenge of Black–Jewish dialogue is getting beyond a *competition of tears*, a competition of who suffered more—the Blacks because of the experience of slavery or the Jews because of the experience of the Holocaust. In an effort to move beyond the competition of tears there is a substantial body of literature about Black–Jewish relations in the United States (cf., e.g., Davis, 1984; Kaufman, 1988; Salzman, Back & Sorin, 1992). This literature tends to ignore subculture and class. The main generalizations from this literature appropriate in Crown Heights are the existence of White racism and Christian and Muslim anti-Semitism. Prejudice adds to tensions caused by issues specific to Crown Heights. In part, these come from competition for resources. Blacks feel they consistently lose in competition with Jews. For example, citizen influence over distribution of community resources rests in access to Community Boards. In the 1970s, the Lubavitchers won a struggle to divide the neighborhood into two Community Boards. Through the early 1980s, Lubavitchers dominated one and Blacks the other; later Blacks dominated both. This issue has left a legacy of resentment (Girgenti, 1993a). Ongoing competition is over housing, the use of public space, public funding, and police protection.

The supply of housing is not expanding to meet the needs of exploding Caribbean and Hassidic populations. The Caribbean community's growth has been by immigration. The Hassidic community's growth has been more by natural increase. One basic competition is over the use of public space for ethnic group activities. Hassidic religious practice brings hundreds of people onto the streets. Once a week on the Sabbath and throughout the year at religious holidays, the police close the streets around "770." Hassidim claim closing the streets protects everyone. Blacks claim it is inconvenient and an example of favoritism by the police and the city administration. Every year on Labor Day, Carnival passes by "770." The costumes of paraders violate Hassidic rules of propriety, as do the street drinking and dancing style. Nevertheless, in recent years, representatives of the Hassidic community ride on one of the floats as a symbolic gesture of good will.

The New York Police Department is a major source of tension. Most police are suburban White Christians and lack identification with the neighborhood. Neither group sees the police as protecting them adequately. Blacks feel that innocent Black males are just as likely to be targeted by police as by criminals. Hassidim say they, too, are conspicuous targets for bias crimes and that police do not protect them.

Blacks say police give Hassidim preferential treatment. When the Grand Rebbe was alive, police gave him round-the-clock protection since he was threatened by a rival Jewish sect. They also escorted the Rebbe and his followers once a week to a cemetery in Queens. This was greatly resented by Blacks.

THE CROWN HEIGHTS RIOTS

Tensions in Crown Heights resulted in many instances of marches and demonstrations by both Blacks and Hassidim over the years. A tragedy on a hot summer day in August 1991 precipitated the worst street riot in New York City in twenty years. En route to the cemetery, a car in Rebbe Schneerson's entourage went out of control, killing a Guyanese immigrant child. The accident and ensuing rumors triggered an incident six blocks away. A group of 15 Black teenagers, yelling "kill the Jew," attacked and killed a Jewish man. The riot followed. The ensuing days of violence and destruction were traumatic to the neighborhood and the police. The police were thought to be so incompetent that the Governor of New York ordered an inquiry (Girgenti, 1993a, 1993b). Howard Golden, the Brooklyn Borough President, orchestrated the formation of a neighborhood coalition, to be described in the following paragraphs.

CONFLICT CONTAINMENT

Committees aiming at conflict containment formed within days following the riot. One, the New York Tolerance Committee, consisted of Black and Jewish museum directors and their supporters. They undertook an ambitious and successful joint museum project educating the public to the history of Black–Jewish relations in Crown Heights (Crown Heights History Project, 1994; Young, 1994).

A second project was organized by the Brooklyn Borough President's Office of Racial and Ethnic Affairs, which created the Crown Heights Coalition. This marked the first time that Crown Heights Blacks and Jews formed a coalition. Their mandate was to explore the underlying causes of the riot and recommend long-term solutions. Thirty-six Hassidic, Caribbean, and African-American community leaders, including ten women were appointed in approximate proportion to their representation in the neighborhood. There were politicians, educators, clergy, socialservice executives, carnival organizers, community activists, and a businessman. They were given a year to issue a formal report on the underlying tensions in the neighborhood and recommendations to ameliorate them (Crown Heights Coalition, 1992).

In comparing Black and White "styles of conflict," Kochman (1981, p. 40) wrote that in dialogue, Blacks believe emotion must be included whereas Whites believe emotion must be excluded. In this and many other respects, unassimilated Jews are *not* White. Jews and Blacks are alike in the importance they attach to emotional expression, which is one reason why dialoguers refer to a *competition of tears*. Coalition partners were faced with emotions they felt personally and with emotional issues that deeply affected their communities. All people in Crown Heights feel vulnerable. Faced with irreconcilable differences of belief and opinion, coalition members agreed to disagree in certain areas, and to focus instead on issues in which cooperation was possible.

Because the Coalition's report included many recommendations that required outside funding, some people dismissed the report. I maintain, however, that by working together, Coalition colleagues created an important breakthrough in conflict containment: the production of the report generated special-purpose friendships. This type of friendship is defined as socializing in pursuit of common community rather than personal interests. When people from antagonistic groups engage in regular goal-directed contact, they can become comfortable and honest with each other as they get to work together and to know each other. Dynamic intergroup special purpose friendships among leaders also create new possibilities beyond their specially mandated purpose—special purpose friends cooperating with each other as a strategy to achieve the short and long term goals of each, as well as those they share—they can maximize the use of existing resources to benefit all groups, attract more funding for joint projects, settle disputes on practical matters, and enhance bridge building. This is what occurred in Crown Heights.

An early test of cooperation-as-strategy—special purpose friends cooperating with each other as a strategy to achieve the short and long term goals of each, as well as those they share—came just after the report was issued. In 1993, Labor Day and the first day of *Rosh Hashanah*, the Jewish New Year, came on the same date. The competition for public space on Eastern Parkway caused anxiety in both Hassidic and Caribbean circles. *Rosh Hashanah*, a solemn time of prayer and meditation, attracts hundreds of visitors to "770"; thousands are on the streets going to and from synagogue from sundown of the day before and then throughout the next two days. There was likely to be conflict—in culture and mood—between the Jews' new year religious observance and the Caribbeans' joyously playful carnival celebration. Several months of highly charged negotiation produced an agreement. The parade was rerouted to bypass the area around "770." The police cooperated, and the day, which so many feared would result in violence, passed peacefully.

The common interests and values that Coalition members found helped produce new networks. Rabbi Jacob Goldstein, head of one of the Community Boards, used his personal networks at the state level to recommend a grant for a program at Medgar Evers College, honoring a request from administrator Dr. Betty Shabazz, widow of Malcolm X. Goldstein had previously worked on a Coalition committee with Edison O. Jackson, the President of Medgar Evers. Shabazz and Goldstein now consider themselves friends, meeting to cooperate because both believe that higher education for Black students betters the entire community.

Among the most important efforts at conflict containment through bridge building is aimed at teenage boys, the main perpetrators and victims of ongoing communal violence. Project C.U.R.E. (Communication, Understanding, Respect, Education) began with months of teen dialogue. Like the dialogue between adults, the teens agreed to disagree and get on with joint Black–Hassidic activities. They formed a rap group, basketball teams, tutoring services, neighborhood beautification projects, *Kwanzaa* and *Hanukkah* celebrations, a model *Seder*, and visits to public schools and *yeshivas* to discuss strategies to "increase the peace."[1] In 1995, four years after the riots, they attended a special computer class at Medgar Evers College together and created a traveling street fair around Brooklyn, demonstrating their own fitness training and nutrition program.

The bonds created by the described projects are based on fostering respect and mutual understanding among members of the subcultures. Conflict-containment activities, such as those of the Coalition and Project C.U.R.E., function mainly to develop channels of communication, linking members of antagonistic communities. Conflict containment is successful because it is based on the combination of personal ties and a mutual commitment to keep communication open. Unlike the assimilationist we're-all-alike approach to friendships, the personal ties are special-purpose friendships. They are links that entail ongoing goal-directed contact, out of which mutual respect and demystification of diverse subcultures gradually emerge. Special-purpose friends can count upon each other to work towards keeping communities tolerant. Given the warm expressiveness of both subcultures, such sentiments as those of an African-American man towards his Jewish friend—"I love the guy"—are telling.

ACKNOWLEDGMENTS

Data for this chapter were gathered as part of a project on Black–Jewish relations conducted in 1991–1993. Research began in conjunction with New York's Jewish Museum exhibition, *Bridges and Boundaries: African Americans and American Jews* (Glazer, 1992; Salzman et al., 1992) and continued subsequently. An earlier draft was presented at the Meetings of the American Anthropological Association in 1992. This chapter benefitted from critiques by Benjamin Schuster and Douglas Fry, and I gratefully acknowledge a research grant from City University of New York's Dispute Resolution Consortium.

REFERENCES

Crown Heights Coalition. (1992). *Crown Heights: A strategy for the future. A report of the Crown Heights coalition.* Brooklyn, NY: Office of Brooklyn Borough President Howard Golden.

Crown Heights History Project (1994). Teacher's Guide. Brooklyn, NY: Brooklyn Children's Museum, Brooklyn Historical Society, and Society for the Preservation of Weeksville and Bedford-Stuyvesant.

Davis, L. G. (1984). *Black–Jewish relations in the United States, 1752–1984: A selected bibliography.* Westport, CT: Greenwood.

Donaldson, G. (1993). *The Ville: Cops and kids in urban America.* New York: Ticknor & Fields.

---

[1]*Kwanzaa* is an African-American holiday celebrated in the Christmas season; Hannukah is a Jewish holiday celebrated around the same time. The *Seder* is the joyful ritual and special dinner marking the beginning of the Jewish Passover holiday. Passover celebrates the exodus from slavery in Egypt, and it inspired generations of Christian African-Americans.

Girgenti, R. H. (1993a). *A report to the governor on the disturbances in Crown Heights: An assessment of the city's preparedness and response to civil disorder* (Vol. 1). Albany: New York State Division of Criminal Justice Services.

Girgenti, R. H. (1993b). *A report to the governor on the disturbances in Crown Heights: A review of the circumstances surrounding the death of Yankel Rosenbaum and the resulting prosecution* (Vol. 2). Albany: New York State Division of Criminal Justice Services.

Glazer, I. (1992). *Intersections and parallels of Blacks and Jews: Shaping the dialogue in New York City.* Brooklyn, NY: Unpublished manuscript, Kingsborough Community College, City of New York.

Kasinitz, P. (1992). *Caribbean New York: Black immigrants and the politics of race.* Ithaca, NY: Cornell University Press.

Kaufman, J. (1988). *Broken alliance: The turbulent times between Blacks and Jews in America.* New York: Scribner's.

Kochman, T. (1981). *Black and white styles in conflict.* Chicago: Chicago University Press.

Mintz, J. R. (1992). *Hasidic people: A place in the new world.* Cambridge, MA: Harvard University Press.

Salzman, J. with Back, A., & Sorin, G. (Eds.). (1992). *Bridges and boundaries: African Americans and American Jews.* New York, George Braziller in association with The Jewish Museum.

Young, J. (1994, March 27). Crown Heights under glass. *Daily News,* p. 1.

Part IV

Conflict Resolution
as an Alternative to War

In this section, we turn to an examination of examples of successful conflict resolution at the international level. The first examples are drawn from Latin America, a region sharing common historico-cultural elements. Two chapters describe cooperative, problem-solving orientations to diplomacy and crises. Problem solving has been defined as "any effort to develop a mutually acceptable solution to a conflict" (Rubin, Pruitt, & Kim, 1994, p. 168), and the chapters consider approaches and tactics that build peace based in part on emphasizing the collective, shared interests of the nations involved and/or their joint membership in the regional community. We also see bilateral as well as multilateral conflict–resolution processes in action, including positive—but also negative—effects of third parties.

The first chapter in this section is written by former President of Costa Rica, Nobel Prize laureate Oscar Arias, architect of the Arias Peace Plan and organizer of Esquipulas I and II. He provides first-hand experience with the recent peace processes in Central America, in which he played such a central role. An important point that he stresses is the idea that peace, democracy, and development must go hand in hand: One element cannot exist without all the others. This, in fact, is a variation of the *Pax Democratica* principle referred to by Klicperová, Feierabend, and Hofstetter in their chapter: Without democracy, there will be no peace.

The second chapter in the section, written by Meyer, follows as a natural continuation of the chapter by President Arias. Meyer demonstrates that Latin American states have a long history of active and concerted diplomatic cooperation when confronted with foreign military threats and interventions from outside powers. This history shows a distinct diplomatic style, from which other regions may learn useful and important lessons. Hers is a careful analysis of the specific characteristics of the Latin American diplomatic style, stretching over Bolivar's ideal, the Congress of Panama, the Esquipulas I and II, the Contadora Group, and Latin American cooperation in general.

The third chapter in this section, by Klicperová, Feierabend, and Hofstetter, describes specifics in conflict resolution, Czech style. During the 20th century, there were seven occasions involving a serious conflict or dramatic change in Czechoslovak society: the gaining of independence in 1918, the Munich agreement in 1938, the 1948 Communist party coup, the 1968 Prague Spring, followed by the August invasion of the Warsaw pact armies the same year, the "Velvet Revolution" of 1989, and the "Velvet Divorce" of Czechs and Slovaks in 1993. Never did the situations trigger a substantial level of aggression and violence. The authors analyze possible reasons for this fact, and use the Black (1993) typology of conflict management as a helping instrument in this analysis. Last, but not least, they provide a vivid, first-hand description of what actually took place during the Velvet Revolution.

REFERENCES

Black, D. (1993). *The social structure of right and wrong*. San Diego: Academic Press.
Rubin, J. Z., Pruitt, D. G., & Kim, S. H. (1994). *Social, conflict: Escalation stalement and settlement* (2nd ed.). New York: McGraw Hill.

14

Esquipulas II: The Management of a Regional Crisis

Oscar Arias

Arias Foundation for Peace and Human Progress

Oscar Arias is the former President of Costa Rica and recipient of the 1987 Nobel Peace Prize. He continues to promote peace, human rights, democracy, and development through the Arias Foundation for Peace and Human Progress. In this chapter, President Arias describes personal experiences and the role of Costa Rica in the management of regional crises in Central America. Costa Rica abolished its army in 1948. In 1986, a meeting known as Esquipulas I was held, in which the Central American presidents agreed to advocate democratization within the region. The Arias Peace Plan proposed the peaceful resolution of the Central American conflict, beginning with the inception of electoral, democratic, and pluralist processes in all countries. When in August 1987 the five presidents signed the Esquipulas II Accords, which incorporated the idea that peace, democracy, and development are inseparable, the region moved much closer to ending the arms race. President Arias compares the Esquipulas process with the Contadora group initiative, and lists a number of reasons why Esquipulas was more effective in promoting peace. He suggests that the style of Esquipulas might well be applied to other regional crises.

—The Editors

COSTA RICA, DEMILITARIZATION, AND DEMOCRACY

Costa Rica's prolonged democratic experiment supports the theory that democracy is the form of government most conducive to peace and progress in the Central American region and in developing countries in general. However, rather than expounding upon the achievements of my country in particular, I feel it is more important to highlight the achievements of democracy in general. These successes are particularly encouraging at a time when (regional) conflicts seem intractable and interminable in Europe.

The stability of Costa Rican democracy stems primarily from the fact that it possesses no military institution. In most countries of the developing world, the armed forces are a burden on the political and economic systems. The overwhelming economic and human costs of supporting an army prevent many governments from attaining even minimum levels of essential health care, education, and social security.

Costa Rica abolished its army in 1948, under the leadership of President José Figueres. President Figueres succeeded in converting a small, relatively poor country into the first totally disarmed state in America and, possibly, the world. The Constitution of 1949 expressly prohibited the subsequent creation of an army. Both the Constitution and the underlying spirit of peace live on to this day in a country that has proven the seemingly utopian hypothesis that a small, poor, demilitarized country can survive amidst mighty and wealthy neighbors. Costa Rica serves as an example of peace and democracy in a region of war and dictatorship, a leader of the future in a present that has too often been without joy or hope.

Our tradition of neutrality has never meant that the people of Costa Rica are uninterested in the serious political and social problems that pervade the rest of Central America. When I assumed the presidency of Costa Rica in May 1986, these problems had led to a series of violent confrontations that endangered our country's peace and stability. The magnitude of the war efforts and the direct and indirect intervention of the great powers in those conflicts made it practically impossible to distinguish between civil and international war.

While maintaining a commitment to provide refuge to victims of political persecution throughout the world, Costa Rica has adhered to a firm policy of neutrality, broken only when the country united with the democracies of the world against fascism during the World War II. But the democratic and independent attitude expressed by my country was not always well regarded by dictators in other Latin American countries, who repeatedly tried to involve Costa Rica in their bloody regional power plays.

THE COSTA RICAN INITIATIVE

Despite my government's firm decision not to permit Costa Rican territory to be used to attack any neighboring nation, even peaceful Costa Rica seemed destined to become involved in the Central American crisis of the 1980s. Thus, for many reasons, including self-interest, our country had to initiate dialogue and negotiation immediately.

In late 1986, the direction of our foreign policy changed in several important ways. We reaffirmed the principle that all Central Americans were entitled to the same liberties and social and economic guarantees that our democracy promised. We maintained that each nation had the right to select—through free and fair elections—the type of government that could best meet its desires and interests and those of its people, and that neither armies nor totalitarian regimes were entitled to make this decision. We also recognized that no country, great or small, should impose forms of organization or government upon others.

After the fall of the Somoza dictatorship in 1979 and the introduction of the Sandinista regime in Nicaragua, the situation in Central America rapidly approached a state of generalized war. Still entrenched in the Cold War, the superpowers interfered ideologically and militarily in the region, transforming the Central American conflict into a significant cause of global tension. Their interference exacerbated the internal unrest in El Salvador and Nicaragua as well as the border tension between Nicaragua and Honduras. It also worsened the state of civil war that probably already had claimed more than 100,000 lives in Guatemala.

We in the Costa Rican government began our efforts at mediation by resolutely objecting to the U.S. military intervention in Nicaragua. Based upon our dedication to democratic values and demilitarization, we decided to distance ourselves from the sectarian attitudes that had previously impeded dialogue between governments and leaders with diverse ideologies. Although we considered the undeniable Cuban and Soviet influence upon important protagonist groups, we rejected the belief that dialogue with Marxist governments and movements was impossible. As Costa Rica continued to express its desire for an American continent free of any form of totalitarianism, we also continued to establish contact with all potential participants, including insurrectional organizations.

In 1986, even before assuming the presidency, I traveled throughout our subcontinent to invite the Latin American heads of state to visit Costa Rica for the inauguration. On the day I took office, the presidents of nine Latin American countries met in San José. At this meeting, I called for a continental alliance for the defense of democracy and liberty. This policy would constitute the principle guiding factor of Costa Rican foreign policy in the upcoming years: "Costa Rica believes that the Americas need an alliance for liberty and democracy. We should not ally ourselves economically or politically with governments that exert pressure on their peoples. I convoke an alliance for liberty and democracy in the Americas and the Caribbean. Liberty and democracy for development. Liberty and democracy for justice. Liberty and democracy for peace" (Arias, 1987, p. 13).

The alliance I spoke of would be based on respect for differences between peoples. It would recognize that justice and democratic pluralism are the pillars of international coexistence. I informed the U.S. government of our decision to oppose any political or military activities within Costa Rican territory by any type of armed groups. Then, in late May 1986, the Central American presidents convened a meeting known as Esquipulas I. We agreed to formalize the presidential meetings and advocate democratization in the region. We endorsed a concept of democracy that clearly incorporated pluralism. This was both surprising and encouraging considering that one of the participants presided over a Marxist regime and at least two others represented a recent transition to dictatorships from the right.

At Esquipulas, we outlined the fundamental ways in which the Costa Rican government would openly and frankly differ with the Reagan Administration. At the same time, internal and external pressures urged Costa Rica to consider its new stance. There were indications that the United States would cut, or even eliminate, its economic aid to our country. The Costa Rican press began to question whether a possible Arias–Reagan meeting could ever take place. Then, in August 1986, the U.S. Congress appropriated substantial military aid to the Nicaraguan insurgents.

In the face of these obstacles, I intensified my actions to promote peace by expressing the position of the Costa Rican people to the United Nations General Assembly. In December, I met with President Reagan and insisted that we seek a nonmilitary solution to the Central American problems together. I also talked with Vice-President Bush about the peace plan, which I presented to various political figures of democratic countries and to the leaders of international organizations.

THE ARIAS PEACE PLAN

I met with the presidents of Guatemala, Honduras, and El Salvador in San José on February 15, 1987. There we agreed on the document *A Time for Peace*, which proposed the peaceful resolution of the Central American conflict, beginning with the inception of electoral, democratic, and pluralist processes in all countries. Once we had signed that document, presidents Cerezo of Guatemala, Duarte of El Salvador, Azcona of Honduras, and I decided to invite President Daniel Ortega of Nicaragua to join us at the meeting scheduled to be held in Esquipulas, Guatemala within the next 90 days.

At the San José meeting, the Central American presidents decided to distance themselves from the Reagan Administration's insistence upon using military pressure to overthrow the Nicaraguan regime. Instead, we considered the Costa Rican peace plan to be a "viable, opportune, and constructive instrument to find peace in Central America through political negotiation" (Arias, Duarte, Arévalo, & Hoyo, 1987, p. 14).

Although the President of Nicaragua accepted our invitation, the U.S. government pressed us to modify or abandon the peace plan. We responded by intensifying our diplomatic activities. In February of 1987, we traveled to Mexico to solicit the Contadora Group's endorsement of our plan. We maintained constant communication with U.S. senators and congressmen. We also conversed with many Latin American leaders, receiving positive responses from everyone. In March 1987, the U.S. Senate approved the Arias Peace Plan in a historic vote of 97 in favor and 1 opposed. In May, I traveled to Europe. I spoke with the leaders of Portugal, Spain, Britain, Belgium, Germany, France, Italy, the Vatican, and the European Community.

The Reagan administration's pressures did influence President Duarte, who asked us to postpone the Esquipulas II meeting planned for June 25 and 26, 1987. He conditioned his participation on the convocation of prior meetings of foreign ministers to discuss various modifications proposed by El Salvador, Honduras, and the United States. Guatemala and Nicaragua objected to the Salvadoran request.

When I privately visited the United States in June, President Reagan expressed his interest in speaking with me. However, after our conversation, he refused to alter his position favoring a military solution in Nicaragua. I told him that we would take all steps necessary to hold the second Esquipulas meeting on August 7.

On August 3, I began an unannounced tour of the Central American nations in order to speak with the presidents. I embarked upon this tour when I learned that the foreign ministers of El Salvador, Guatemala, and Honduras were preparing an alternative peace plan and that a third Wright–Reagan bipartisan plan was underway in the United States. Although we were willing to discuss any of these plans, I realized that the Reagan administration was prepared to hinder any advance toward agreement that excluded a military solution in Nicaragua.

THE ESQUIPULAS II PEACE ACCORDS

During the Esquipulas meeting, held on August 7, 1987, the five Central American presidents signed an accord agreeing to work toward peace and democracy in the region. The agreement, entitled *Procedure to Establish Firm and Lasting Peace in Central America*, included the following stipulations: (a) national reconciliation; (b) exhortation of the ceasing of hostilities; (c) democratization; (d) free elections; (e) ceasing of assistance to outside forces within a country or to insurrectional movements of another; (f) refusal to use one's own territory to attack other states; (g) negotiations in matters of security, verification, control, and limitation of armaments; (h) attention to the problem of refugees and displaced persons; (i) cooperation, democracy, and liberty for peace and development; (j) international verification and follow-up; (k) a schedule for executing the agreements.

The Esquipulas II Peace Accords, moved much closer to ending the arms race than had previous initiatives. The Peace Plan incorporated the idea that peace, democracy, and development are inseparable. It consecrates the premise upon which our administration based its foreign relations—true development cannot be achieved without peace, and peace cannot exist without democracy.

The Peace Plan received almost universal support and recognition, especially in Latin America, Europe, and Canada. In September of 1987, I was invited to speak before a joint session of the U.S. Congress. My purpose in giving this speech was to convince the congressional leadership of the United States to give peace a chance, and I was very pleased at the positive reception expressed by U.S. legislators. The level of this recognition and moral support for the Peace Plan was perhaps best expressed when I was awarded the 1987 Nobel Peace Prize. This honor clearly indicated that the Peace Accords had acquired an important universal dimension, and that its success or failure would no longer result from a diplomatic confrontation between various small states and a great power. The possibility that a complex regional conflict could be peacefully resolved without the influence of the great powers was recognized and became a realistic option for many countries and regions around the world.

Costa Rica then intensified its efforts to ensure that the Esquipulas II agreements were respected. Ours was not an easy task, because external pressure never subsided. It was also difficult to replace a world view that had been determined by decades of violence. We were concerned about the strict scrutiny to which our plan would be submitted. Delays and adjustments, normal and acceptable in other international negotiations, would be interpreted as failures. Each country contained groups that opposed the Peace Plan. There was an undeniable interest in eliminating the Marxist government of Nicaragua, even at the cost of replacing it with a totalitarian regime from the right. We aimed to establish governments that respected pluralism and agreed to submit themselves to the electoral will of their peoples in all of the region's nations.

Our initiative resulted in a second presidential meeting, in Costa Rica, on January 15 and 16, 1988. Before the meeting, Nicaragua was accused of failing to respect the agreements of Esquipulas II, whereas El Salvador, Honduras, and Guatemala claimed to have met them. Many people were discouraged and feared that much of the hope inspired by the Peace Plan had been lost. However, the fact that this was the first occasion on which President Ortega had visited our country produced an extremely positive effect. His visit was a violation of the implicit prohibitions on relations with the Nicaraguan Marxist regime.

After a frank dialogue among the presidents, new expectations emerged as the five leaders agreed to ratify the Esquipulas II agreements and to emphasize its fulfillment. The Central American presidents realized the urgency of our undertaking, but we also knew that an inflexible or overly detailed schedule would generate expectations which, if unfulfilled, would discourage the citizens and undermine the credibility of the process. This observation is extremely important in the sense that, on at least one previous occasion, setting a deadline for the fulfillment of an act endangered world peace. I refer to the Persian Gulf crisis. The risk of eliminating opportunities for peace by setting inflexible deadlines is too great. The deadline, transformed into an end in itself, confounds the search for new options for understanding.

THE IMPLEMENTATION OF THE PEACE PLAN

This consideration did not deter Costa Rica from insisting upon the need to reach a cease fire in Nicaragua as soon as possible. In Sapoá, the Sandinista government and the Contras agreed upon the following: cease-fire; free elections; commitment to representative democracy; nonpartisan national armed forces; and dismantlement of the military and entrance of the Contras into the formal political life of Nicaragua.

The dialogues between governments and insurgent forces in El Salvador and Guatemala did not initially yield such positive results, but the fact that they began at all signifies an important advance that, in the Salvadoran case, eventually led to a cease-fire at the start of 1992.

The five Central American presidents also directed efforts toward eliminating extraregional intervention in Central American conflicts. During the inauguration of President Borja of Ecuador, in August 1988, I spoke with other Latin American leaders once again about the situation. I was especially interested in meeting President Fidel Castro, whom I encouraged to stop Cuban military aid to Central American guerrilla movements.

In February, 1989, during the inauguration ceremony of President Carlos Andrés Pérez of Venezuela, I had the opportunity to resort to informal diplomacy to defend the peace plan before several continental leaders, including U.S. Vice-President Dan Quayle and Cuban President Fidel Castro.

Meanwhile, a Central American summit, to take place in Tesoro Beach, El Salvador, on February 14 and 15, 1989, was being planned. Once again, dialogue produced positive effects and led to the following agreements: (a) the advancement of Nicaraguan elections; (b) the demobilization and repatriation of the Nicaraguan Contras; (c) the urgent approval of the Central American Parliament; (d) the incorporation of insurrectional forces into the political processes of every country; (e) a call for the international community to support the socioeconomic recovery processes of the Central American nations; (f) the creation of a Central American commission for the environment and development; (g) support for an international conference on Central American refugees; (h) the agreement for regional coopera-tion to eradicate illegal drug traffic; and (i) a call for the involvement of the United Nations and the Organization of American States (OAS) in the first peacekeeping operation in Central America.

Afterward, in March 1989, an initiative of the Bush Administration offered a measure of hope to the Peace Plan advocated by Costa Rica. In an environment of agreement between our two governments, I spoke with President Bush, in Wash-ington DC, in April, 1989. During these conversations, President Bush revealed to me that the U.S. government had adopted a new attitude that encouraged support of the Peace Plan.

At this point, it is appropriate to reflect upon the importance of this official change in U.S. policy with respect to Central America. For many years, the United States had impeded the efforts to reach negotiated agreements, primarily because of its prejudice against a Marxist regime, by neglecting to guarantee noninterven-tion, political pluralism, and the protection of human rights. These were the declared objectives of the military assistance to the Contras, despite the fact that at least certain sectors of the Contras would be unable to meet those requirements if they rose to power. Subsequent events demonstrated that the United States would faithfully follow this unfortunate policy, as it continually attempted to obstruct proposals that favored democracy over the continuation of military confrontation. The support that the Bush administration offered to the peace plan was interpreted as a positive indicator that the United States would permanently modify its Latin American policy so that it would no longer intervene unilaterally as it had done throughout the 20th century. The 1989 invasion of Panama, however, dashed many hopes and led us to question whether the United States had truly learned the Central American lesson.

Under the Peace Plan, Central Americans took the initiative to solve their problems. We gained the respect of the United States and Latin America for our decisions. We adopted dialogue as a method of conflict resolution. For the first time, leaders spoke face-to-face and openly discussed sensitive issues. The governments and guerrillas in El Salvador and Guatemala spoke with one another. The Nicaraguan Contras and the Sandinista government spoke. The cease fire in Nicaragua heralded the Sandinista compromise to hold free elections and to maintain a representative democracy. The U.S. government curbed its military aid and granted only humanitarian aid to the Nicaraguan Contras. Amnesty was declared in Nicaragua, and many Central Americans who had been incarcerated for political reasons were released.

In addition, economic aid for development increased. The European Community (EC) agreed to grant special aid to Central America. The United Nations acted similarly. Canada offered generous aid to Costa Rica. Our country adopted the Brady Plan to solve the problem of foreign debt. The establishment of the International Commission for the Recuperation and Development of Central America, sponsored by U.S. Senator Terry Sandford, further endorsed Costa Rica's peace initiatives. The Commission reported that poverty and injustice must be eliminated, and that development must be promoted in order to construct peace in Central America. The EC has supported our region, both economically and morally. The EC has developed and strengthened bilateral and multilateral cooperation programs with Central Americans. Costa Rica has benefited from the EC's loans for development programs. In early 1989, members of the European and Latin American parliaments met in Costa Rica, recognizing the struggle for peace and the values of the Costa Rican people. The President of the European Parliament, Lord Plumb, centered his speech around the importance of the democratic nations' interest in the Peace Plan. He urged respect for the agreements and the initiation of political collaboration to maintain the Central American dialogue.

As the Central American leaders had agreed in Tela, Honduras, the execution of the Peace Plan was guaranteed at the beginning of August, 1989. All the previous agreements were ratified, and the United Nations Secretary-General was given the liberty to send a mission to the region to create a body to supervise the Peace Plan. Subsequently, United Nations Central American Operations initiated a heightened United Nations involvement in Central America, heralding the timely involvement of Secretary-General Perez de Cuellar in the negotiations that led to the Salvadoran cease fire.

The later evolution of the Nicaraguan situation merits a separate comment. The United States questioned the Sandinista regime's will to fulfill its obligation in the Peace Plan. However, we, the participants in the process, trusted that Nicaragua would comply with the agreements. Our trust was based upon the presidents' commitment to achieve peace and dedicate all our national resources to the economic and social development of our countries. This commitment resulted from a combination of mutual concessions based upon a group of common principles established to encourage the formation of electoral commissions with pluralistic participation.

The rescheduling of the Nicaraguan elections for an earlier date represented an important concession on the Sandinistas' part. We trusted that the Nicaraguan regime would not offend international public opinion by deviating from the purity of the electoral process. The Sandinistas could not afford to commit the same mistakes that General Noriega had made in Panama.

Substantial progress toward democratic pluralism already had been achieved in Nicaragua to allow political opposition groups to participate freely and permanently in the political process. I was certain that the Sandinistas would not win the election, because the Nicaraguan people knew that a Sandinista regime would mean the continuation of war. Nevertheless, the Sandinistas themselves were convinced of victory. The electoral defeat of the Sandinistas undoubtedly helped to rapidly discredit the opponents of the Peace Plan, who maintained that it postponed the elimination of the Nicaraguan Marxist regime.

SEEKING LESSONS FROM THE ESQUIPULAS PROCESS

I am satisfied with the path that we have chosen. All the Central American countries currently have democratically elected governments. The violent internal conflicts have been reduced to levels that, although still of concern, are much less severe than those that prevailed when I assumed the presidency of Costa Rica in 1986. Important steps have been taken to demilitarize the region, and periodical presidential meetings now serve as an established forum to vent and discuss problems of mutual concern. I have presented the history of the Esquipulas process and will leave further analysis to the reader. However, it is interesting to compare two processes, related to the same group of problems, that developed consecutively but had entirely different results.

CONTADORA AND ESQUIPULAS:
AN ANALYTICAL COMPARISON

The Esquipulas process was initiated shortly after the unsuccessful conclusion of the Contadora initiative. This last mediation process was conducted by four countries that were not direct parties to the conflict: Mexico, Panama, Venezuela, and Colombia.

The Contadora group was officially created in January 1983. During its first months, the group established a very complex agenda that included numerous points that were not necessarily related to one another. In its first meeting, the group advanced a sufficiently general platform, stating that Latin American nations should intensify dialogue among themselves as a step to facilitate the solution of the political, social, and economic problems of the Western Hemisphere. They also discussed aid for development and the importance of the Movement for Non-Aligned Countries to the Third World. They emphasized the recessive tendencies of the world economy and its negative effects upon Latin America. They expressed their desire to contribute effectively to "fulfill the purpose of coordinating and setting forth a joint negotiation posture for the developing nations at the VI

UNCTAD to be held in Belgrade." They addressed other diverse points in the agenda, emphasizing the indefinite nature of their goals. In fact, this lack of clarity was reflected in Contadora's tardiness to publish its diagnosis of the points in dispute in Central America. Upon publication, the report read:

Among the matters which, in the view of the Contadora Ministers (of Foreign Affairs), require the most attention, the following should be mentioned: the arms race, arms control and reduction, the transfer of armaments, the presence of military advisors and other forms of outside military assistance, actions aimed at disrupting the internal order of other countries, threats and verbal aggression, warlike incidents and border tensions, the violation of human rights and individual and social guarantees, and the grave economic and social problems which are at the heart of the region's present crisis. (Contadora, 1986, p. 249)

Based on this diagnosis, the Contadora Group conducted a series of actions through June of 1986. Ultimately, the group was unable to persuade the five countries of the region to sign an agreement. In contrast, the Esquipulas process, which included direct dialogue between the parties, required less than one year to reach important agreements about concrete points relating to the fundamental causes of the problems that it sought to resolve.

Contadora attempted to deal with all the goals of the conflicting groups in only one document; its negotiations were basically an exercise in confrontation and nonconcession. However, Esquipulas reflected a coordinated effort by the five presidents, the parties involved in the conflict, to resolve their common problems.

In the Contadora case, the mediating group allowed bargaining to focus on the most immediate and obvious causes of the conflict. Through this approach, the parties blamed one another for recent incidents and fixed or modified their positions in light of those conflicts. In the Esquipulas process, on the other hand, the parties studied and tried to solve the fundamental causes of the problem. This approach allowed them to surpass their most superficial differences, to build confidence, and to create a climate of trust and solidarity among the negotiators. They soon shared the desire to advance the process rapidly, as it was in everyone's interest that such achievements resulted from consent and not from confrontation. This is only possible when the negotiators have decision-making power.

Esquipulas, as a cooperative negotiation, fulfills all the phases that in theory conform to an ideal negotiation: deliberation, communication, debate, and transaction. However, it is not possible to reach cooperative negotiations when one party has a different expectation of appropriate conduct. When, for cultural, military, economic, or political reasons, some groups maintain expectations of an appropriate way of life that others do not share, they must seek a consensus through international law. Although international law is ambiguous, the parties may take advantage of this ambiguity in order to reach consensual interpretations. They can do so, depending upon their abilities to find effective ways to clarify the law and develop a common interpretation of appropriate behavior.

In view of its demonstrated intention to act independently and democratically, Costa Rica's ability to lead the Esquipulas process effectively was also an advantage.

It is unlikely that mediation conducted by four countries with different objectives, such as the Contadora group, would provide strong and definite leadership.

In the realm of international law, we can conclude that Contadora was unable to clarify certain basic principles for the parties, namely: the prohibition of the use or threat of force, the principle of nonintervention, and the right of peoples to self-determination. Each party interpreted these principles to suit its own interests. In Esquipulas, on the contrary, we, the presidents, agreed from the start on a similar interpretation of these principles. This consensus was fundamental because the various parties were able to derive common criteria to resolve their conflicts; this ability guided our transactions as we modified our negotiation styles and political objectives.

CONCLUSIONS

Can the style of Esquipulas be applied to other regional crises? Although certain aspects of Esquipulas are not necessarily replicable or guaranteeable, such as the presence of a demilitarized nation in the midst of the crisis, I believe that another crucially important factor affecting the outcome of the negotiations—a region's determination to solve its crises without external interference—can be duplicated in other regional crises.

The Esquipulas accords saw the internal resolution of a crisis that commanded international attention and interest. In an era when superpower tensions still reigned supreme, we were able to deny superpower influence. I believe that the most important factor that allowed us to achieve peace in Central America is a quality that does not depend upon economics, international politics, or geography. Ultimately, strong leadership determined our success. Particularly in conflict situations, people need leaders with vision and courage—leaders who will tell them not what they want to hear but what they must know. We need leaders whose concerns surpass personal good and political maneuvering; we need leaders concerned with a greater good—leaders who can understand the plight of a people at war, and dedicate themselves fully and absolutely to the peaceful well-being of a nation or region. Without such leadership, and without the good faith that can be nurtured among leaders, the resolution of conflicts will become immeasurably more difficult. Heroes of war live on in the memories of their people as great and glorious men. Their courage cannot be disputed. But it is too often forgotten that the decision to declare peace rather than war, to choose life over death, has a greatness and a glory—and a courage—all its own.

REFERENCES

Arias, O. (1987). *Paz en centroamérica: Libertad y democracia para cinco pueblos* [Peace in Central America: Freedom and democracy for five communities]. San José, Costa Rica: Imprenta Nacional.

Arias Sànchez, O., Duarte, J. N., Arévalo, V. C., & Hoyo, J. A. (1987). *Plan de paz para centroàmerica* [Peace plan for Central America]. San José, Costa Rica: Imprenta Nacional.

Contadora. (1986). *Las relaciones interamericanas: Crisis y perspectivas* [Interamerican relations: Crisis and perspectives]. Mexico City: Centro de Investigación y Docencia Economicas, A. C.

15

Cooperation in Conflict:
The Latin American Diplomatic
Style of Cooperation in the
Face of Foreign Threats

Mary K. Meyer
Eckerd College

In this chapter, the Latin American cooperative diplomatic style is discussed. Despite the fact that violent domestic struggles are frequent, there are remarkably few cases of interstate war in Latin America. Meyer suggests that the Latin American diplomatic style has characteristics that may offer an explanation for this circumstance: There exists a pattern of regional cooperation aimed at mediation rather than war, especially in preventing and curtailing extraregional military interventions. This style takes the form of international congresses and multilateral diplomacy, and is based on such principles as security through unity, mutual defense against outside intervention, mutual recognition and respect, and rule-governed behavior. The author provides examples of this diplomatic style from the 19th-century congress movement and the Central American peace process of the 1980s.

—The Editors

Let us avoid war by reducing everything to mediations.
—Don Manuel Lorenzo de Vidaurre
Peruvian delegate to Congress of Panama, 1826
(United States Senate, 1890; p. 105)

Despite the media images we are accustomed to seeing, war is not common between Latin American states. If the region's history is marked by violent domestic civil struggles, and if its recent experience includes serious human rights violations under military dictatorships, it is nevertheless remarkable that the diplomatic history of Latin America includes so little interstate war. In fact, Latin American diplomatic history over the past 170 years shows a pattern of regional cooperation and harmonization (*concertación*[1]) that has sought to limit interstate war. This pattern constitutes a distinct Latin American diplomatic style of regional conflict management and conflict resolution.

This diplomatic style has not eliminated all interstate war; territorial disputes have erupted in bitter wars between Latin American states from time to time. However, there has been a clear tendency for neighboring countries to cooperate in seeking mediation between belligerents. Even more clear is the pattern of Latin American diplomatic cooperation aimed at preventing or curtailing wars involving extraregional powers. During the 19th and early 20th centuries, the threat of war or military intervention by an extraregional power against a Latin American country commonly evoked a collective and concerted diplomatic response from sister republics, most remarkably in the form of an international congress like the Congress of Panama (1826) and the Congresses of Lima (1847 and 1864). Such congresses sought to present a united, defensive front aimed at deterring, limiting, or resolving military conflicts. The 19th-century congress movement became the focus of the regional diplomacy—and mutual survival strategy—of the Latin American republics.

In more recent times, Latin American states have continued to practice a concerted, multilateral diplomacy to mediate interstate conflicts involving both regional and foreign powers. A notable recent example of the Latin American diplomatic style of cooperative conflict resolution is the Central American peace process of the 1980s, originally created and sustained by the diplomatic work of the Contadora Group—Mexico, Venezuela, Colombia, and Panama. The Contadora Group worked together to build a diplomatic framework for a regional peace agreement among the Central American countries.

This chapter analyzes this Latin American diplomatic style of multilateral cooperation in response to regional security threats. I look first at the 19th-century congress movement. Drawing from the diplomatic correspondence, documents, and treaties of the congress movement[2], I identify the common themes that diplomats used to explain and justify what they were doing. I then discuss how these ideas and practices continued to be manifested in the Central American peace process of the 1980s. Although there is no direct causal link between the 19th-century congress movement and the Central American peace process of the 1980s, there are clearly similar practices and rationales that constitute a distinct Latin

---

[1]The Spanish word *concertación*, from the verb *concertar*, is best translated as harmonization and includes the idea of some kind of a concerted policy, arrangement, settlement, or accord.

[2]The 19th-century diplomatic correspondence, documents, and treaties forming the data set for this part of the study can be found in the following sources and volumes: Gobierno de Venezuela (1976); Lecuna and Bierck (1951); Medinaceli (1862); Mexico. Secretaria de Estado y del Despacho de Relaciones Exteriores (1897); Peru. Archivo Diplomatico del Peru, II (1938); Peru. Ministerio de Relaciones Exteriores (1942); Peru, Secretaria de Relaciones Exteriores (1867); Unites States Senate (1890); and Zubieta (1912).

American diplomatic style of cooperation. This diplomatic style has produced innovative strategies and rationales for finding peaceful methods of managing or resolving regional conflicts.

THE 19TH-CENTURY CONGRESS MOVEMENT

The congress movement grew out of Simón Bolívar's vision of creating a unified Latin American voice in international affairs, recognized and respected by European powers. The movement was a series of international congresses and calls for congresses by Latin American states to ensure their independence and sovereignty. Between 1822 and 1896, Latin American diplomats issued nearly two dozen calls for international Latin American congresses. Most of these calls came after one or more states perceived a serious threat of intervention from some outside power. In 1822 and again in 1824, Simón Bolívar issued the first calls for a congress of Latin American states as they fought for their independence from Spain. These calls led to the Congress of Panama of 1826.

Seven congresses were actually opened between 1826 and 1896. Of these, two accomplished little, but at five congresses—the Congress of Panama, 1826; the Congress of Lima, 1847–1948; the Second Congress of Lima, 1864–1965; the Congress of Jurists at Lima, 1877; and the Congress of South American Jurists at Montevideo, 1888—as well as the special diplomatic activity of 1856 in Washington, DC and Santiago, Latin American diplomats succeeded in producing significant multilateral treaties and experiences. The diplomatic agreements, protocols, and related correspondence of the 19th-century congress movement develop clear themes, values, and rationales that have guided Latin America's regional diplomacy ever since. Seven distinct but often overlapping themes of the congress movement can be summarized under the following headings: security through unity, sovereignty, recognition, relationship/outreach, lawmaking, conflict resolution, and leadership.

Security Through Unity

One of the most important themes centered on the need for unity among the young Spanish American republics. For the Latin Americans, union through a congress of plenipotentiaries meant diplomatic union only: The congress was to be a confederation, league, or alliance of independent sovereign states that would come to each other's aid. This unity centered on collective security principles, pledging mutual defense against outside intervention or aggression. This point is clear in all the documents under consideration, including Bolívar's writings as well as the various treaties of union signed at the Congress of Panama and the two Lima congresses. The type of congress that Bolívar had in mind when he first proposed a Spanish American congress was the type held by European states in the early 19th-century, such as the Congress of Vienna in 1815 and of Aix-la-Chapelle in 1818 (Meyer, 1992).

The theme of unity was often bolstered by arguments stressing the common origin, history, and institutions in the region, and references to "one family" of Spanish American nations punctuate period documents. These kinship arguments were marshaled either to justify the exclusion of non-Spanish American states from the call for union (e.g., the United States, Brazil, Haiti) or, more commonly, to explain why Spanish American diplomatic union was possible. The serious proponents of union never argued for some kind of regional superstate.

Security through unity also meant pooling regional resources for a common defense force. Despite subsequent lack of ratifications, Latin American diplomats wrote several treaties meant to create multinational armies and navies (e.g., the 1826 Convention on Troop Contingents; the 1848 Treaty of Confederation; the 1865 Treaty of Union and Defensive Alliance, and so forth). They sometimes provided for burden sharing, with distant states, unable to furnish troops in case of war helping instead to pay the costs of the alliance's defense effort (Gobierno de Venezuela, 1976; Peru. Archivo Diplomático del Perú II, 1938. These multinational military forces, like the unity theme itself, were always cast in terms of mutual defense against threats from outside powers. Through unity, Latin American diplomats sought to find mutual strength and security.

Sovereignty

The unity theme related closely to sovereignty. The 19th-century congress movement always defended and asserted the sovereignty of the individual Latin American republics in the face of extraregional threats. The diplomatic calls for a congress were usually sparked when at least one state perceived its sovereignty or its neighbor's to be threatened by military actions or interventions involving extraregional powers (i.e., Spain, France, Great Britain, or the United States) or forces apparently supported by these powers (i.e., the General Flores expedition in the mid-1840s, the William Walker episode in the mid-1850s).

Sovereignty includes the legal principles of equality, autonomy, self-determination, territorial integrity, and nonintervention/noninterference. The principles of territorial integrity and nonintervention were most often and most clearly asserted in the congress documents, but those of self-determination and autonomy were also prominent. For example, the first article of the Treaty of Confederation signed at the Lima Congress, in 1848, stated emphatically:

> The high contracting parties unite, bind, and confederate themselves in order to sustain the sovereignty and independence of each and every one of them; to maintain the integrity of their respective territories; to ensure in them their dominion and seigniorage; and to disallow that undue offenses or insults be inflicted with impunity against any one of them. (Peru. Archivo Diplomático del Peru II, 1938, p. 302)

Similarly emphatic statements asserting the sovereign rights of the region's states appeared in each of the episodes under consideration. Of course, each episode's historical context shaped the specific principles of sovereignty that were elaborated. For example, in 1856, when William Walker came to lead liberal forces in Nicaragua's civil war and when fears were high that the United States was supporting Walker's filibuster, the Latin American diplomats reaffirmed the principle of non-intervention in another's civil wars.

Recognition

A third theme that resonates throughout the documents relating to congress diplomacy involves gaining recognition and respect from outside powers. In 1825, Simón Bolívar argued that although Spanish American unity was important to prevail in the wars for independence against Spain, appearances mattered most. The image of the new republics meeting in a congress was as valuable to the identity and survival of the new states as whatever military force they could muster, if not more so. As Bolívar wrote in 1825 to Francisco de Paula Santander, the Vice President of Colombia, the congress in Panama, "must serve us at least for the first ten or twelve years of our infancy, even though it should dissolve forever following that period. It is my feeling that we will live on for centuries if we can survive the first dozen years of childhood. First impressions last forever" (quoted in Lecuna & Bierck, 1951, pp. 461–462).

The desire for respect by creating a spectacle of unity and strength was clearly articulated again in an 1848 foreign policy statement by Colombia. After outlining a "series of alarming acts" carried out by European powers against South American states, Foreign Minister Manuel Ancizar protested that "the European governments do not see in us moral entities worthy of benevolence and respect but as markets and nothing more than markets for the consumption of manufactures." The only solution would be an American congress gathered in Washington, which "would produce a notable sensation in Europe" (Peru. Archivo Diplomático del Peru II, 1938, pp. 210–211). The diplomatic correspondence from later congresses continued to reveal a concern for appearances and for gaining recognition and respect from outside powers threatening aggressions against the young states.

Relationship/Outreach

The congresses provided valuable opportunities for the young states to escape their international isolation and foment important international ties within the region and with the rest of the world. They also provided opportunities to try to coordinate certain foreign policy positions beyond security issues. By the 1840s, the congresses produced several treaties aimed at improving commercial relations, coordinating customs rates, and facilitating postal correspondence in the region. The promise of such new channels and increased communication was apparently widely seen as a key to national development and stability. The region's diplomats often expressed an interest in institutionalizing this interaction by creating "faithful organs" or "authorized and expert agents" to facilitate communications within the region (Peru. Archivo Diplomático del Peru II, 1938, p. 208). There is also a clear awareness expressed in the diplomatic writings of the need to overcome the region's foreign policy isolation by developing stronger ties with the rest of the world through a multilateral diplomacy.

Lawmaking

A fifth theme centers on the desire of the Latin American states to embrace a uniform code of law to guide and facilitate their foreign relations. The role of Latin American states in contributing to the development of international legal principles in the 19th-century was important, even if this role is rarely acknowledged today. In addition to defending principles of sovereignty, the congress movement also defended the principle of neutral rights, upheld the principle of *uti possidetis* (that Latin American states would recognize the territorial borders inherited at the time of independence from colonial rule), asserted the principle of nonuse of one state's territory to destabilize its neighbor, and helped developed other legal codes relating to political asylum, extradition rules, and commerce.

It is important to note that the various treaties produced at these congresses failed to achieve much ratification success, but it was not for lack of trying to negotiate such matters. The diplomats did their part even if the unstable national political scenes prevented timely ratifications. Nevertheless, and despite such political setbacks, the treaties produced at the regional congresses in 1826, 1848, 1856, and 1865 all created a record that was often invoked in later congresses. If the legal status of the various treaties was ambiguous or weak, their moral status apparently was not, and the treaties continued to provide a model for action in subsequent congresses and crises. Overall, the congress movement thus made many important contributions to the development of international legal principles and rules for the region.

Conflict Resolution

Closely associated with the interest in developing an American system of international law, the congress movement became increasingly interested in creating innovative and viable mechanisms for conflict resolution. Indeed, the very nature of the congress movement centered on a genuine desire of a number of Latin American states to avoid war with outside powers and find nonmilitary solutions to conflicts involving such powers. As with the turn to international law, such a desire may have been based in a realistic recognition that the young republics were too weak to prevail militarily against greater powers. Yet the diplomatic correspondence of the 19th-century suggests that the congress movement produced increasingly sophisticated ideas for developing peaceful methods of conflict resolution for the region, both vis-à-vis outside powers and among Latin American states.

In 1826, the Peruvian delegate to the Congress of Panama, Manuel Lorenzo de Vidaurre, urged the Congress to find a way to "avoid war by reducing everything to mediations" (United States Senate, 1890, p. 105). By the 1840s, Latin American diplomats actively sought more innovative means of both resolving and preventing military conflicts in the region than with a confederal army. The Congress of Lima of 1847 was called to create a new defensive confederation against great power aggressions against Ecuador and Mexico. But the diplomats meeting in 1847 and 1848 went further. They tried to institutionalize the congress by requiring regular meetings and expanding the congress's powers to include the roles of agreement-maker, interpreter of agreements, mediator and arbiter in any future conflicts between confederates (see e.g., 1848 Treaty of Confederation, Article 21, in Peru. Archivo Diplomático del Peru II, 1938).

The Continental Treaty of 1856 went even further by requiring signatories not to rush into war without first presenting their positions diplomatically and exhausting all peaceful means of resolving differences (Article 19). The treaty also spelled out the mechanism by which a congress would be convened to offer its mediation in differences arising between confederates, who were obliged to accept the mediation (Article 21, in Peru. Archivo Diplomático del Peru, 1938). The idea that an international congress should serve as a mechanism of regional conflict resolution was apparently gaining ground at the time. The simultaneous Latin American diplomatic legation meetings in Washington, DC, also posited the need for an institutionalized congress to serve as a forum for the peaceful discussion of disputes, to maintain harmony in the region, and to resolve conflicts involving a confederate and a foreign power (Osma to Foreign Ministry, March 3, 1856, in Peru. Archivo Diplomático del Peru II, 1938).

By the 1860s, the confederation among Latin American republics was discussed as a "system of perpetual peace in the new world" by pamphleteers like Medinaceli (1862). Moreover, in invitations to the Second Lima Congress of 1864–1865, the Peruvian foreign minister specified that one of the proposed congress's objective was to abolish war irrevocably, "substituting it with arbitration as the only way to accommodate all the lack of information and reasons for disagreement between some of the South American republics. Our good standing, our well-being, and our common happiness demand the adoption of this method, on which the hopes of America are concentrated" (in Peru. Archivo Diplomático del Peru II, 1938, pp. 341–342).

To meet this objective, the congress negotiated and signed the Treaty on the Conservation of Peace between the Contracting American States, which both provided for arbitration and outlined states' responsibilities for preventing war, such as not allowing political exiles or emigres to use border territories to attack their home government, stopping the trafficking of arms, troops and war *matériel*, and generally preventing one's territory from being used to wage war on a neighbor (in Peru. Archivo Diplomático del Peru, 1938). This arbitration treaty makes clear the growing Latin American concern for clarifying and codifying methods for reducing or preventing the chances for military conflict at a time when border conflicts were indeed heating up. The Treaty on the Conservation of Peace suggests a real interest on the part of Latin American diplomats to find innovative and viable regional mechanisms for the peaceful settlement of disputes, but the lack of ratifications suggested it was an effort somewhat ahead of its time. However, by the 1880s, arbitration was becoming a widely used mechanism to resolve bilateral disputes in the region, and the idea of creating regional machinery to resolve conflict and maintain peace began to interest the United States as well.

Leadership

At least two factors appear to have been necessary for the successful holding of a congress. The first depended on the actual or imminent intervention or use of force by an extraregional power against a Latin American state. The second factor depended on the interest and/or ability of at least two or more leading states to sponsor and support the holding of a congress in response to such a threat. The positions of the governments of Peru, Colombia, and Chile were the most significant in determining whether a congress would be held, and the cooperation of two or more of these leading states was needed to get a successful, united response to a foreign threat.

CONTEMPORARY LATIN AMERICAN DIPLOMACY AND THE CENTRAL AMERICAN PEACE PROCESS OF THE 1980S

There have been many cases of multilateral cooperation among Latin American states since the congress movement, but the diplomacy that gave rise to the Central American peace process of the 1980s provides a particularly important case showing the persistence of a regional diplomatic style of conflict resolution that arose in the last century. The Central American peace process began to emerge in 1982 as several Latin American countries became alarmed at the escalation of war in Central America and the role of extraregional powers in the growing regional violence. In January 1983, Mexico, Venezuela, Colombia, and Panama, each with significant political interests and commercial ties in Central America, gathered on the Panamanian island of Contadora to discuss their deepening concerns. Out of this first meeting, the Contadora Group was formed and the first phase of the Central American peace process was born.

The Contadora phase of the peace process lasted from January 1983 to the summer of 1987. This phase centered on the efforts of the Contadora Group states to create a framework for the five Central American states to discuss their differences directly and to negotiate a peace agreement aimed at diffusing the region's indigenous and interstate tensions. This Contadora mediation effort included nine joint meetings of foreign ministers from the four Contadora states and the five Central American countries, plus another foreign ministers meeting that included the four additional Contadora Support Group states that joined the mediation effort after 1985 (Argentina, Brazil, Peru, and Uruguay). This phase of the peace process also included numerous lower level meetings of the technical experts who developed several drafts of a regional peace agreement (Contadora Act, 1987). Throughout its four and a half years, the Contadora peace process overcame serious obstacles thrown in its way, primarily (if not exclusively) by the Reagan administration. Although the Central American states did not make peace during this phase of the peace process, the Contadora Group did succeed in keeping the Central Americans talking to each other, despite Washington's divisive pressures and growing military buildups. To the extent that the talks continued and an expanded region-wide war (or U. S. intervention) was averted, the mediation during the Contadora phase was a success. The Contadora Group's mediation sought to create the diplomatic framework and political space in which the Central American states could find their own solutions to their problems (Meyer, 1992).

The second phase of the Central American peace process emerged from the Contadora phase and overlapped with it. Beginning in the winter of 1986 with the inaugurations of new presidents in Guatemala and Costa Rica, the Central Americans moved through the political space opened by Contadora and began to build their own framework for peace. In May 1986, the five Central American presidents held their first summit meeting ever in the town of Esquipulas, Guatemala, and agreed to meet again the following year. By August 1987, through the leadership of Presidents Oscar Arias Sánchez (Costa Rica) and Vinicio Cerezo (Guatemala), the five Central American presidents were able to find a language and a formula for reconciliation. "The Esquipulas II Procedure for a Firm and Lasting Peace in Central America" was signed on August 7, 1987, and set in motion a difficult yet focused plan for cease fires, national reconciliations, and democratization in the region. An unprecedented series of presidential summits and ongoing meetings of the region's foreign ministers and diplomats, along with important diplomatic help from the Contadora Group and the United Nations' Secretary-General's office, kept the Esquipulas phase of the peace process alive.

The Central American peace process shares an important contextual characteristic with the 19th-century congress movement. The initial meeting of the Contadora group's foreign ministers in 1983 was triggered by a widely shared perception of a serious regional security threat originating from an extraregional source. It was not the civil wars per se in Nicaragua, El Salvador, or Guatemala that compelled the Contadora Group to act. Rather, the escalation and internationalization of the region's civil wars by military aid from outside powers as well as growing fears of a U. S. military invasion in the region united the Contadora Group. Washington's tough cold-war rhetoric, its growing military aid programs to El Salvador and Honduras, and its less than covert role in training and arming the Nicaraguan *contras* based in Honduras represented a serious deterioration of regional security. With regional interests to protect, the Contadora Group acted to check the militarization of the region by initiating its mediation effort (Meyer, in press).

The Contadora Group's diplomatic response shows several thematic similarities with its 19th-century predecessors. First, the Contadora Group sought to enhance regional security through diplomatic unity. The Contadora states practiced a concerted diplomacy in Central America to ensure their common security interests in the region, namely, an end to costly wars that threatened to escalate and drag them in, the return of refugees, the reinvigoration of regional trade, and so on. The Contadora Group also urged the Central Americans to see that their own security also rested with a regional vision and regional unity, not with the interests of outside powers. This idea was expressed in numerous Contadora documents stressing the need for the Central Americans to find "regional solutions to regional problems," meaning that Latin American unity in the peace process could find an indigenous solution to the region's problems (Contadora Group, 1987). This idea was also manifested in the Contadora Group's numerous reminders that the causes for Central America's upheavals were primarily indigenous, and that it was wrong for outsiders to inject the East–West conflict into the region's problems.

A second similarity between the Central American peace process and the 19th-century congress movement is the concern for sovereignty. The Contadora Group seemed to focus on the nonintervention and noninterference principles, stressing the obligation of states to stay out of each other's affairs and underscoring the 19th-century principle of the nonuse of a state's territory to overthrow its neighbor. The Esquipulas phase also stressed these principles of sovereignty; however, it differed by adding the duty of the Central American states to promote internal democratization (Procedimiento para establecer la paz firme y durada en centroamérica, 1987). This represented an important difference both from Contadora, which was silent on the issue of democratization, and from the 19th-century diplomats, who were sensitive about political litmus tests for governments.

A third common theme is related to the politics of recognition. Like their 19th-century counterparts, the Contadora Group's diplomacy depended on an image of unity to create an impression of strength in regional and international affairs. Coming together and standing as a united group of states in the face of outside threats, speaking with a common voice to the rest of the world, rejecting militarization and the East–West rhetoric: This is the image the Contadora Group sought to project. When the Contadora Support Group joined the original Contadora Group in the summer of 1985, a poignant moral tone was added to the common call for peace in Central America due to the recent return to civilian rule in the Support Group countries. Together, the eight leading Latin American states posed a weighty image of diplomatic unity against further militarization by the U. S. of the region's conflicts.

Fourth, as in the congress movement, the Central American peace process also provided the various states with the opportunities to increase their channels of communication with each other. In addition to Central America, the Contadora Group and the Support Group states soon found themselves stepping up their regional contacts and coordinating their foreign policies on other issues, most notably the debt crisis. More importantly, the numerous meetings of the technical groups who worked on the Contadora Act as well as the Esquipulas II Procedure created new channels of contact between states and more personal contacts between diplomats (A. Bendaña, personal communication, June 8, 1990; L. G. Solís, personal communication, January 14, 1991; J. L. Talavera, personal communication, June 4, 1990). This may have been the most important contribution of the Contadora phase of the peace process. As the Esquipulas phase of the peace process emerged, the Central American states built on their newly expanded contacts and instituted new channels of communication by holding several presidential summit meetings between 1986 and 1990 and by supporting more face-to-face meetings of foreign ministers and other diplomats responsible for finding a formula for peace.

Although the diplomats involved in the Central American peace process did not seek to develop new codes of law for Latin America, they, like their 19th-century counterparts, did seek to uphold respect for international law and legal principles, a fifth point of similarity. Moreover, they explicitly invoked existing international codes of law to give authority to their diplomatic work.

A sixth point of similarity involves conflict resolution. The Central American peace process was aimed first at preventing further militarization of the region's interstate conflicts and then at finding a viable means for their peaceful resolution. The institutionalized mechanisms of conflict resolution in the Organization of American States (OAS) were stalemated given the serious policy and power differences between the United States and the Central Americans. The Contadora Group and the Central Americans had to create new mechanisms, or a new framework outside of the OAS, for mediation and conflict resolution. As in the past, Latin American diplomats found a workable means to do so.

The peace process evolved from an initial call for peace by the Contadora Group to an active and effective mediation effort. The Contadora Group manifested many of the techniques Pruitt and Rubin (1986) identified as effective third-party intervention and problem solving. The various meetings in this phase of the peace process produced many useful diplomatic documents identifying and defining issues, structuring the diplomatic agenda, and searching for some overarching formula or framework to keep the Central Americans talking with each other. The Contadora Group succeeded in helping the Central Americans find their own solution. In the Esquipulas phase, the Central American states built a new framework for peace on the foundations laid by the Contadora Group. As Pruitt and Rubin (1986, p. 166) noted, an "effective third party is the one who becomes involved only when needed and who is so successful at helping the principals find a settlement and develop a working relationship with each other that they no longer need or want his or her services."

A final similarity between the Central American peace process and the 19th-century congress movement centers on the leadership of the most active states in the peace process. Mexico, Venezuela, and Colombia were the leading Contadora Group states and brought important leverage in dealing with the Central Americans. For example, Mexico was seen as sympathetic to Nicaragua, leading the latter to stay involved in the process. Venezuela's ruling Christian democratic party had a special relationship with Salvadoran President Napoleón Duarte, ensuring his government's involvement. Colombia's President Belisario Betancur was seen as a trusted broker by all and proved crucial to getting the peace process moving in the first place. These complementary strengths helped keep the lines of communication open, despite difficult obstacles. The leaders of the Contadora phase of the peace process needed each other. Their interests, commitment, and strengths led them to cooperate in keeping the mediation effort alive. After the Central Americans agreed to the Esquipulas II Procedure, they still faced difficulties in implementing the agreement, but with time and continued support from the Contadora Group and the United Nations, the internal peace processes within Nicaragua and El Salvador got under way.

The Central American peace process of the 1980s was rooted in a long history of Latin American diplomatic cooperation as a response to violent interstate conflict. In both the 19th-century and the 1980s, Latin American states responded to military and security threats from outside powers with a concerted and coordinated diplomacy. This diplomatic style is cooperative and defensive but nonmilitary in nature. It seeks to defend the sovereignty and integrity of fellow Latin American states through the presentation of a united image or voice deserving of respect. It develops increased channels of communication and interaction between states. It identifies legal principles and upholds rulegoverned behavior between states. Most remarkably, with the right leadership, it creates viable if temporary mechanisms for mediation and conflict resolution. Since Manuel Lorenzo de Vidaurre's day, Latin American diplomats may not have avoided war by reducing everything to mediations, but they have come rather close.

ACKNOWLEDGMENTS

I would like to thank Stella Villagran, Gladys Ingram, Beverly Warthon-Lake, and Jean Craigwell, all at the Columbus Memorial Library at the OAS, for helping me find the texts that form the backbone of this study and for so generously sharing their workspace with me for a week in June 1994. I would also like to thank Alejandro Bendaña, former Vice-Minister and Spokesperson for the Nicaraguan Foreign Ministry, Luís Guillermo Solís, former Chief of Staff of the Costa Rican Ministry of Foreign Affairs, and José León Talavera, former Nicaraguan Vice Minister of Foreign Relations, for graceously granting me interviews. All translations from Spanish are my own.

REFERENCES

Contadora Act. (1987). Acta de Contadora para la paz y la cooperación en Centroamérica [The Contadora Act for Peace and Cooperation in Central America]. In Heraldo Muñoz, (Ed.), *Las políticas exteriores de América Latina y el Caribe: Continuidad en la crisis. Anuario de políticas exteriores latinoamericanos 1986* (pp. 614–639). Buenos Aires: Grupo Editor Latinoamericano, Colección PROSPEL.

Contadora Group. (1987). (Mensaje de Caraballeda para la paz, la seguridad, y la democracia en América Central, [The Caraballeda message for peace, security, and democracy in Central America]. In H. Muñoz (Ed.), *Las Políticas exteriores de América Latina y el Caribe: Continuidad en la crisis. Anuario de políticas exteriores latinoamericanos 1986* (pp. 610–613). Buenos Aires: Grupo Editor Latinoamericano, Colección PROSPEL.

Gobierno de Venezuela. *Documentos Históricos del Congreso Anfictiónico de Panama* [Historical documents of the Panama Congress]. (1976). Oficina Central de Información, Dirrección de Publicaciones. Caracas: Editorial Genesis.

Lecuna, V., & Bierck Jr., H. A. (Eds.). *Selected writings of Bolívar*. New York: Banco de Venezuela and The Colonial Press.

Medinaceli, B. (1862). *Proyecto de confederación de las repúblicas Latino-Americanas, o sea sistema de Paz Perpetúa en el Nuevo Mundo* [Project of confederation of the Latin American republics, or a system of perpetual peace in the new world]. Sucre, Bolivia: Tipografía de Pedro España.

México. Secretaria de Estado y del Despacho de Relaciones Exteriores. 1897. *Congreso Americano Convocado por el Gobierno de la República del Ecuador e Instalación de la Junta de Delegados al*

Congreso Internacional Americano, México, 1896. Actas y Resoluciones de la Junta [American congress convened by the government of the republic of Ecuador and the installation of the group of the delegates to the International American Congress, Mexico, 1896]. México: Salvador Gutiérrez, Impresor.

Meyer, M. K. (in press). Security as diplomacy: Comparing interests, capabilities, and contributions of selected states to the Central American peace process. *New Political Science.*

Meyer, M. K. (1992). Latin American diplomacy and the Central American peace process: The contadora and esquipulas II cases. *Dissertation Abstracts International, 53* (08), 2099A. (University Microfilms No. AAD93-15947)

Perú. Archivo Diplomático del Perú, II. (1938). *Congresos Americanos de Lima. Recopilación de Documentos Precedida de Prólogo por Alberto Ulloa. Tomo I* [American Congress of Lima. Compilation of documents preceded by a prologue by Alberto Ulloa]. Lima: Imp. Torres Aguirre.

Peru. Ministerio de Relaciones Exteriores. (1942). *Archivo Diplomático Peruano. El Congreso de Panama de 1826. Documentación Inédita* [Peruvian diplomatic archive. The congress of Panama of 1826. Unedited documentation]. Lima: Ministro de Relaciones Exteriores del Perú.

Peru. Secretaria de Relaciones Exteriores. (1867). *Correspondencia Diplomática Relativa al Congreso Americano* [Diplomatic correspondence relative to the American Congress]. Lima: Imprenta del Estado, por J. Enrique del Campo.

Procedimiento para establecer la paz firme y duradera en Centroamérica [Procedure for establishing a firm and lasting peace in Central America]. (1987). In H. Muñoz (Ed.), *Las Políticas exteriores de América Latina y el Caribe: Un balance de esperanzas. Anuario de políticas exteriores latinoamericanas 1987* (Anexo, 4, pp. 427–432). Buenos Aires: Grupo Editor Latinoamericano, Colección PROSPEL.

Pruitt, D. G., & J. Z. Rubin. (1986). *Social conflict: Escalation, stalemate, and settlement* (1st ed.). New York: Random House.

United States Senate. (1890). 51st Congress. First Session. *International American Conference. Reports of Committees and Discussions Thereon. Vol. IV. Historical Appendix. The Congress of 1826, at Panama, and Subsequent Movements toward a Conference of American Nations.* Washington, DC: U. S. Government Printing Office.

Zubieta, P. A. (1912). *Congresos de Panama y Tacubaya. Breves Datos para la Historia Diplomática de Colombia* [Congress of Panama and Tacubaya: Facts for the Diplomatic History of Columbia]. Bogotá: Imprenta Nacional.

16

Nonviolent Conflict Resolution and Civic Culture: The Case of Czechoslovakia

Martina Klicperová
Czech Academy of Sciences

Ivo K. Feierabend
C. Richard Hofstetter
San Diego State University

This chapter provides a description of the Czechoslovakian nonviolent Velvet Revolution in 1989. Specific features of the Czechoslovak democratic experience are discussed, such as civility, civic culture, and civic patriotism. Examples from Czechoslovak conflict resolution history, such as the aftermath of the Munich agreement, Nazi occupation, the Stalinist terror, the Prague Spring, the Velvet Revolution, and the Velvet Divorce, are analyzed within the conceptual framework of Black (1993). The authors find support for the Pax Democratica thesis, that is, there is a link between democracy and peace.

—*The Editors*

The creation of Czechoslovakia in 1918 was a challenging experiment in transforming differing parts of the Habsburg monarchy into a modern democracy. The experiment lasted from 1918 until 1992 when Czechoslovakia split into two independent states, the Czech Republic and the Slovak Republic. During these 74 years, Czechoslovakia went through political conflicts that could have been dealt with by use of force but were not. This chapter analyzes the Czechoslovak propensity toward peaceful conflict resolution, civic culture, and democracy (for a more detailed analysis see Klicperová, Feierabend, & Hofstetter, 1995).

A NONVIOLENT VELVET REVOLUTION

After World War II, Czechoslovakia became a Soviet satellite until the Velvet Revolution toppled the communist regime. The Velvet Revolution started on November 17, 1989, when a peaceful student demonstration was brutally suppressed. Against expectations, students did not surrender but instead united in a resistance movement. They went on strike and were joined by actors, playwrights, and dissidents, and the revolutionary Civic Forum was founded. Together they started to communicate with other citizens, triggering an avalanche of meetings and demonstrations that included hundreds of thousands of participants. Finally, a general strike convinced the communist government to share power: A multiparty government was appointed, the Federal Assembly elected Václav Havel as President, and democratic elections were scheduled for 1990.

During the November 17, 1989 approved demonstration, the prodemocratic speeches were on the brink of the impermissible (e.g., "better to die than to live without freedom"), but the march to the center of Prague that followed was unlawful. After the crowd reached the city center, it was blocked by armored vehicles that threatened to run over the demonstrators (just 6 months after the Tiananmen Square massacre, this was a frightening experience). An eyewitness reported: "A horrible pressure started, the crowd began to wave, we tried to stop that by shouting 'keep calm' [klid] and by holding hands. The students tried to form groups taking women and children to the middle so they could protect them by their own bodies although they themselves were getting many blows. It was admirable how people mutually tried to cope with the situation and keep calm" (Srnec & Netík, 1990, p. 11, translation by Klicperová).

The violent police action shocked the participants, injured some of the students, and dispersed them. However, the students soon congregated and declared an occupational strike. Students formulated their demands, organized an information network with other schools and centers outside Prague, verified rumors, obtained legal consultations, managed logistics, and contacted the media (focusing on foreign TV that was covering at least some Czechoslovak territory while domestic TV was still being censored). The movement spread further—the people were encouraged to initiate their own civic forums at workplaces and to take part in the general strike. During this time, remarkably, people behaved in a most civil manner.

It also must be noted that the general strike in support of the nontotalitarian opposition was meant as a 2-hour demonstration. As Havel stressed, "We do not want to ruin our economy. On the contrary, we want it to function better!" Many people even made up the lost working hours. The strike had a very orderly, dignified, even a merry character and was considered a valid referendum because approximately 70% of the citizens participated.

The Velvet Revolution was explicitly nonviolent from the very beginning. At the November 17th demonstration, students asked for a dialogue and carried banners with the inscription, "Nonviolence." Later, after being stopped by the police, they chanted "We do not want violence," "We don't want another China," "Gandhi," "We have empty hands" (with hands raised above heads), and even "We love you!"

There were no threats, physical attacks, throwing of objects or demolition of property on the part of demonstrators. Young women in the first rows handed flowers to the riot policemen. A song, "We Shall Overcome"—a hymn of nonviolent protest—was sung (in Czech) before the national anthems. When the tension rose and there was a threat of an attack, the crowd sat on the ground.

The movement stressed its humanism by its symbols: Civic Forum logo (Občanské Forum in Czech) had a smiling face built into the letter O; the Slovak counterpart of civic forum bore name Public Against Violence; posters of Havel held his quotation "Love must win over lies and hate." Not even symbolic aggression was involved. At one point a person came to a demonstration holding a shovel (not the threatening symbol of gallows) with the inscription "For Štěpán" (the Prague Communist Party Secretary), suggesting that he should quit politics and work, for a change. In Olomouc, rather than destroying the huge statue of Lenin, people covered it with children's balloons and the inscription, "Fly away."

"A nonviolent revolution is a creative process," claimed journalist Michal Horáček (1990, p. 5). Literature (including drama and songs) provided a unique medium for disclosing suppressed feelings and for giving moral support. Humor was used as a creative coping mechanism. "There are people here!" shouted someone in the November 17th crowd facing the brutal police, quoting a famous sentence from Jaroslav Hašek's The Good Soldier Schweik, the title character of which shouted these words on the battlefield of the World War I (Horáček, 1990, p. 7).

Later during the struggle, there were other satirical events. People brought big paper boxes and walled in governmental buildings so that the comrades could get the message of how isolated they were. On Saint Nicholas day (when mischievous Czech kids receive "presents" of coal and potatoes instead of candy and fruit) people brought coal and potatoes to the communist president. A similar nonviolent message was given later on when a student repainted a Soviet tank (symbol of the still-present Soviet occupying army) pink.

The objective of the Velvet Revolution was dialogue and the aim was democracy. The means of accomplishing democracy were no less democratic than the goal. First, it was necessary to develop a general national discussion, starting at schools and theaters, and after they became too crowded, the dialogues spilled over to the main square in Prague, the Václavské Square. When even that was not large enough, the meetings were called to the vast Letná area. Faithful to the name of the organizing body (the Civic Forum movement) the daily meetings indeed became a forum of direct democracy.

Cultural patterns together with the institutions of civil society may have a crucial significance for the choice of violent or nonviolent conflict-resolution strategy. A general statement could be drawn for Czechoslovakia that, when left alone, without interference from abroad, the country had a tendency to install a democratic political system. (That proved true in 1918, 1968, and again in 1989.) Its presidents, Masaryk and Havel, were inspired democratic leaders who enjoyed respect and popular admiration. Deference toward democratic political leaders (Feierabend, Hofstetter, Huie, Klicperová, & Lautenschlager, 1993) seem to dominate Czech political culture. The support given to democratically elected politicians is noteworthy. According to the *Budování státu [nation building] (1990–1995)*, since the Velvet Revolution, the top five or six governmental office holders have enjoyed continuous popularity and trust of the majority of the Czech nation.

PEACE, DEMOCRACY, AND CZECHOSLOVAKIA

In general, the Czechoslovak democratic experience exhibits a peculiar blend of peaceful conflict resolution, civility, civic culture, and civic patriotism, and these traits were all present during the Velvet Revolution. Our current aim is to reflect on the Czechoslovak case in the light of democratic theory. The link that binds democracy and peace is widely explored in political science at the present time. The empirical findings seem less in dispute than the theoretical underpinnings that try to explain the relationship (Merritt & Zinnes, 1991; Poe & Tate, 1994). Among the many hypotheses of the Pax Democratica thesis, let us choose one that thus far, has not been applied in the literature on democracy. Nonetheless, it is capable of a parsimonious explanation that is compatible with other hypotheses and is broad enough to embrace the ambiguous case of Czechoslovakia. (After all, the country has spent most of its political life under dictatorships.) This is the theoretical construct of Black (1993).

Black (1993) classifies the forms of conflict management into several categories: *self-help* (which is a unilateral handling of grievance by aggression), *avoidance, negotiation, toleration* (needing little or no aggression), and *settlement.* Self-help is further subdivided into *vengeance, discipline,* and *rebellion,* whereas settlement is "the handling of a grievance by a nonpartisan third party" (Black 1993, p. 85). Third-party intervention is further categorized as: *friendly pacification* (carrying no aggression), *mediation, arbitration, adjudication,* and *repressive pacification* (in order of increasing authoritativeness). Another concept related to the aggressive form of conflict resolution is *moralism,* rather unusually defined as "a tendency to treat people as enemies" (Black 1993, p. 144). Moralism "features formalism and decisiveness . . . the tendency to create and apply explicit rules" of right and wrong by the aggressive means or coerciveness and punitiveness (Black 1993, p. 145).

Although Black does not say so, we suggest that most of the aggressive forms of conflict management fit the pattern of autocratic regimes, whereas the nonaggressive forms fit democracies. Empirical evidence in political science sustains this hunch, including an apparently incontestable general law of political science; perhaps the only one where thus far there is no exception to it, to wit: Modern democracies do not make war on each other. Instead, they prefer peaceful conflict resolution (Small & Singer, 1976; Rummel, 1983; Russett, 1993; Singer & Wildavsky, 1993).

Corollaries (perhaps less universal) follow from this nonviolent propensity of democracies. Democracies exemplify less violence—less killing in wars in which they participate—than do autocracies (Rummel, 1994b, p. 6). For democracies, their mutual hostilities short of war are much less frequent than those among autocracies (Rummel, 1983). In their internal politics democracies use an incomparably lower level of coercive or violent force (Feierabend, Nesvold, & Feierabend, 1970), relying instead on peaceful conflict resolution.

In the same vein, the less democratic and the more autocratic the government, the more violence and aggression is expended in all the directions of the political field. Consequently, totalitarian regimes are the most brutal offenders (Rummel, 1994a, p. 3). It also seems that the more stable the democracy, the less the manifestations of violence, coerciveness, and aggression (Russett, 1993, p. 35). For example, the very stable democratic regime of New Zealand during 1955 to 1961 did not experience any event at all that qualified as a case of internal political aggression (Feierabend & Feierabend, 1966, p. 138).

Black furthermore postulated that, "*Conflict management is isomorphic with its social field,*" recapitulates and intensifies its larger environment (1993, p. 91, italics in original). Such a social field or environment is shaped by social distance–closeness among other variables. In a simplified version of his thesis, social distance is more likely to produce the aggressive kinds of conflict resolution: discipline, rebellion, repressive pacification, and moralism. Social closeness instigates the nonaggressive forms: negotiation, tolerance, and friendly pacification.

Social distance–closeness subsumes vertical distance–closeness, which corresponds to inequality–equality of status. Thus, given the hypothesis of social distance, it is less likely for a child to discipline an adult than vice versa and easier for equal partners to negotiate, because superiors command and inferiors obey. In addition to the vertical social distance–closeness, there is horizontal distance–closeness, which includes relational distance–closeness that distinguishes between strangers and intimates, and cultural distance–closeness, that is the heterogeneity–homogeneity of culture. Hence, it is assumed that it is more difficult to kill a friend and a compatriot than a stranger and an ethnic enemy.

Let us orient Czechoslovakia's conflict events in Black's typology: The aftermath of the Munich agreement is the case of repressive pacification. The expulsion of the Sudeten Germans after World War II was vengeance. The years of Nazi occupation and Stalinist terror together with the milder autocracy of the post-Stalinist era qualify under the label of discipline, relying on moralism with coerciveness and punitiveness of ideological totalitarianism. The years of the First Republic were the least involved in the aggressive nexus. Negotiation, toleration, and peaceful settlement prevailed in the democratic political system. The Prague Spring and reaction to the August Warsaw Pact invasion in 1968 qualify as mass nonviolent rebellions. The 10 days of the Velvet Revolution combined the astonishingly civil mass protest in the streets (which qualifies as a rebellion) and negotiation, symbolized by the picture in which the dissident Havel, now the president, shakes hands over the negotiating table with Communist Premier Adamec. "Negotiation is the handling of a grievance by joint decision" (Black, 1993, p. 83), and that negotiation happened. The dissidents, including the hundreds of thousands in the streets who equalized the status of the negotiators, got the revolution and the old elite structures got the "velvet" rather than the vengeance. The subsequent Velvet Divorce between the Czechs and the Slovaks, creating separate statehoods, is a case of avoidance.

Let us now orient the essentials of democracy in Black's scheme. What is it in the democratic political system that fosters social proximity in the vertical as well as in the horizontal sense, and with it the peaceful forms of conflict resolution? The enumerations of democratic traits always include popular sovereignty and almost always individual and civil rights, tolerance of opposition, and their corollaries (Dahl, 1971, 1989; Čermák, 1992; Sartori, 1987; Friedrich, 1950).

Vertical proximity is fostered in the equality of political citizenship, in which popular sovereignty calls for "one person, one vote," in which freely contested elections may replace one set of officeholders with another, and in which the opposition can become the governing party. Distance between the governors and the governed is diminished by the democratic authority pattern through which political elites are not sovereign but depend on the electorate. Autocracies deny these aspects of popular sovereignty, thereby maximizing the distance between the power status of the political elites and nonelites. Vertical distance is also diminished by civil, individual and minority rights, provided there is equal protection before the law.

The granting of popular sovereignty and civil rights alone, however, is not enough to guarantee a stable democratic polity. It is the national political culture that may do so by providing for cultural and relational closeness among the citizens. The potentially unruly and excitable master of democracy, the *demos*, must conduct itself responsibly. A robust civic culture provides for the homogeneity of democratic political culture, and civic patriotism promotes the homogeneity of the national culture, thus fostering horizontal closeness.

These two cultures, together with popular sovereignty and civil rights are the most likely to create civility, which includes tolerance rather than bigotry, respect for law and the rights of others, and most fundamentally, peace rather than aggression among the citizenry, that is to say, Black's nonviolent forms of conflict management. If conflict management is isomorphic with its social field, as Black held, then it can also be said that civility and civic culture are isomorphic with democracy.

These qualities in all likelihood recreate and reinforce each other, just as one weakened may diminish the other. Just as, for example, the exercise of the democratic system may reinforce civic culture and civility, so civic culture or civic patriotism may resuscitate democracy. It could also be argued that, in small nations such as Czechoslovakia, when democracy is taken away because of external pressure, civic culture and civility may survive, and, given a chance, it will reappear as it did in Czechoslovakia in 1968 and 1989. Such an expectation corresponds to the notion of culture as an enduring rather than an ephemeral set of attitudes.

Whereas civic culture and civility are postulated as the guarantors of the stability of the democratic political system, exclusive ethnic nationalism is highly disruptive. The explosion of nationalism in the former multinational states—especially in Yugoslavia—is a tragic example of such dynamics. On the other hand, liberal nationalism or civic patriotism (also called civicism) appears to be a powerful cement of the stable (civil) democratic polity (Brass, 1991; Tamir, 1993). This is because the civic culture and civility constitute an essential portion of the national identity above and beyond purely cultural elements of ethnic nationalism. In Black's terms, the *homogeneity* of political and national culture combined narrows the cultural and relational distance, thereby fostering peace and nonviolent conflict resolution.

The nationals of the civic culture tend to symbolize their nationality in terms of freedom or democracy, rather than just language, religion, or the arts, literature or music. In other words, the political legitimacy of the democratic regime is reinforced by the sense of national identity of its citizens. Such civic patriotism is likely to act as an energizer of political democracy. The democrat and the patriot are one and the same. In the Czechoslovak case some extraordinary personalities of civic patriotism became national heroes and martyrs such as Jan Palach and Jan Zajíc.

The Velvet Revolution is a good example of civic patriotism. It was a protest against the old regime, but, even more, it was the call for democracy combined in a poignant, even sacred moment in the life of the nation when this "*imagined community*" (Anderson, 1992) came fully alive in a mass encounter and peak experience, for example, with the brotherly caring behavior of the crowd, the exemplar of civility, and the aesthetic and moral attributes of a national cultural event of the first magnitude.

The very name *Czechoslovakia* connoted the aspiration toward civic patriotism on the part of Czechoslovaks. Czechoslovak political identity embraced both the Czech and the Slovak nation, certainly during the First Republic (1918–1938). There were indications that such ambition was succeeding. One could suppose success was prevented by the abrupt interruption of the democratic enterprise by Nazi and Communist rule. That the Slovaks parted company with the Czechs in 1992 is witness to the ethnic nationalism that prevailed in the end but certainly against a considerable resistance of Czechoslovak sentiment in both nations. That the establishment of two independent states turned out to be the Velvet Divorce rather than the murderous struggle of the Balkans, may be, in part, the legacy of the Czechoslovak civicism.

An element of civic patriotism seemed present in Czech political tradition, or at least was clear during the Czech National Awakening. This tradition relied on Czech intellectuals, including students, but above all, it was T. G. Masaryk, the revered founder of Czechoslovakia who (by the end of the 19th century) clearly enunciated the tenets of democracy and linked them with the legacy of Czech history, the idea of Czech nationalism, and later with the idea of the Czechoslovak nation (Masaryk, 1971; Opat, 1990; Čapek, 1990). Philosophically, he made democracy part of his notion of humanism and the pursuit of truth. Both concepts stem from tradition that span the time from the Protestant reformer Jan Hus (1369–1415) and J. A. Comenius (1592–1670) to T. G. Masaryk (1850–1937) and still is reiterated by Václav Havel in his admonition "to live in truth" (Havel, 1991). The official presidential flag carries the inscription "The Truth Prevails." In the Czech lexicon truth and humanism are powerful symbols of the democratic creed.

In Czechoslovak history, we witness a series of manifestations of the obedient civic culture: the civility of the crowds during the Prague Spring and the Velvet Revolution, the observed discipline of the nation at the time of Munich (people determined to fight for their freedom yielded to president Beneš's decision to surrender), the behavior during the Second Republic in 1938–1939 (L. K. Feierabend, 1994) and waiting in vain for a president's appeal for resistance against the Communist putsch of 1948. All are of the same cloth. Altogether, the Czechs seemed to adore their leaders and rely on them more than they did on themselves, provided these leaders had impeccable democratic credentials.

Such a deferential culture, together with a postulated degree of civic patriotism should be assumed to be highly supportive of a stable democracy and especially appropriate for times of crisis. And equally so it should foster peaceful conflict resolution. A recent study of Czech students at Charles University in Prague by the authors (Klicperová, Feierabend, & Hofstetter, 1995) is highly suggestive of the remarkable continuation of such a political culture. The study focuses on cognitive structures of organized views or schemata that facilitate processing of new information in the context of what is known, provide meaning to current experiences and aid in evaluating experiences (Conover & Feldman, 1984; Taylor & Crocker, 1981). To summarize the findings, no schema (with the exception of one minor schema of alienation) expresses either anticivic or antidemocratic culture, whereas the robust civic culture (Almond & Verba, 1989) predominates in nearly half of the 95 students in the sample.

CONCLUDING REMARKS

We may conclude that the nonviolent conflict resolution in Czechoslovakia's internal and international affairs confirms the nexus that links peace to structural and cultural traits generally referred to as political democracy. The *Pax Democratica* thesis is confirmed in modern Czechoslovak history and so is its opposite: Whenever democracy was extinguished in the country, however involuntarily, discipline or vengeance followed, to use Black's terms. Furthermore, the Velvet Revolution as well as the empirical finding about the Czech students is witness of the resilience of the civic culture and civility.

The demise of the Soviet system left behind no doubt about the pernicious character of autocracies, especially their totalitarian and Soviet offshoots. Horowitz (Rummel, 1994a, p. xiii) spoke of the "need to revise our sense of the depth of the horrors committed by communist regimes on ordinary humanity," whereas the Nazi horrors have been apprehended for close to half a century. Singer and Wildavsky (1993) refer to "Zones of Peace" governed by democracies and "Zones of Turmoil" ruled by nondemocratic systems.

The Czechoslovaks in their modern history lived in both of these zones, in democracy and totalitarianism, and with them experienced both the virtues and glory as well as the pain and shame of the 20th century. Yet, in retrospect it would seem obvious that the democratic culture of peaceful conflict resolution is not always glorious. In 1938, the Munich appeasement did not serve the Czechs well, nor the Europeans, nor anybody else. The tragedy of World War II soon followed. Munich was just the most dramatic and the least honorable of the democratic peaceful resolutions in the chain of conciliatory events. Later at Yalta and Potsdam again the acquiescence of Western democracies to a dictator's demands, as well as the conciliatory complicity of the Czechoslovak democratic leadership with the Czechoslovak communists, led Czechoslovakia into the vengeance against the Sudeten Germans (Rummel, 1994a, pp. 304–310) and immediately after that into the full blown Soviet-type totalitarianism.

Again today (so far without the benefit of hindsight but with the experience of the past) one may well wonder about the wisdom of the belated intervention of the NATO forces in the Balkans and the tardy invasion of Haiti by American troops to shelter democracy; the tolerance of "ethnic cleansing" on the part of democratic powers whether it takes place in Europe, Africa, or elsewhere. Some measure of democratic "moralism," a term of opprobrium as used by Black, instead of blind democratic tolerance and civility, perhaps should be put on the democratic wish list for the next century.

ACKNOWLEDGMENTS

This research was supported by the International Research and Exchanges Board to Drs. Feierabend and Klicperová, with funds provided by the U. S. Department of State and the National Endowment for the Humanities. None of these organizations is responsible for the views expressed. The authors also gratefully acknowledge the support of the Grant Agency of the Czech Academy of Sciences, Prague, the Czech Republic, grant No. A8025504, "Psychological Analysis of the Manifestations of Civic Culture (Moral Aspects)," Biophysica Foundation, La Jolla, California and the Department of Political Science at San Diego State University.

REFERENCES

Almond, G. A., & Verba, S. (1989). *The civiv culture.* Newbury Park, CA: Sage Publications.
Anderson, B. (1992). *Imagined communities: Reflections on the origin and spread of nationalism.* London: Verso.
Black, D. (1993). *The social structure of right and wrong.* San Diego, CA: Academic.
Brass, P. R. (1991). *Ethnicity and nationalism: Theory and comparison.* New Delhi: Sage Publications.
Budování státu: Přehledy české a slovenské politiky (1990–1995) [Nation Building: Digest of Czech and Slovak politics]. (Vol. I–V). Brno: Mezinárodní politologický ústav Právnické Fakulty Masarykovy univerzity.
Čapek, K. (1990). *Hovory s T. G. Masarykem. Spisy XX.* [Talks with T. G. Masaryk. Works XX] Praha: Československý spisovatel.
Cermák, V. (1992). *Otazka demokracie* [Question of Democracy]. Praha: Academia.
Conover, P. J., & Feldman, S. (1984). How people organize the political world: A schematic model. *American Journal of Political Science, 98,* 95–126.
Dahl, R. (1971). *Polyarchy: Participation and opposition.* New Haven: Yale University Press.
Dahl, R. A. (1989). *Democracy and its critics.* New Haven, CT: Yale University Press.
Feierabend, I. K., & Feierabend, R. L. (1966). Aggressive behaviors within politics, 1948-1962: A cross-national study. *Journal of Conflict Resolution, 10,* 249–271.

Feierabend, I. K., Hofstetter, C. R., Huie, C. J., Klicperová, M., & Lautenschlager, D. (1993). Democracy, civic culture and the post-communist condition in the Czech Republic: A pilot study using q-methodology. In V. Dvořáková & E. Voráček (Eds.), *The legacy of the past as a factor of the transformation process of post communist countries of Central Europe* (pp. 281–314). Praha: Vysoká škola ekonomická.

Feierabend, I. K., Nesvold, B. A., & Feierabend, R. L. (1970). Political coerciveness and turmoil: A cross-national inquiry. *Law and Society Review, 5,* 93–118.

Feierabend, L. K. (1994). *Politické vzpomínky I* [Political memories I]. Brno: Atlantis.

Friedrich, C. J. (1950). *Constitutional government and democracy: Theory and practice in Europe and America.* (Rev. ed.). Boston, MA: Ginn Publishers.

Havel, V. (1991). The power of the powerless. In P. Wilson (Ed.), *Václav Havel: Open letters, Selected Prose 1965–1990* (pp. 125–214). London: Faber and Faber.

Horáček, M. (1990). *Jak pukaly ledy* [How the ice was breaking]. Praha: Ex libris.

Klicperová, M., Feierabend, I. K., & Hofstetter, C. R. (1995). Peaceful conflict resolution in Czechoslovakia. *Bulletin PsÚ, 2,* 1–46.

Masaryk, T. G. (1971). *Humanistic ideals.* Lewisburg, PA: Bucknell University Press.

Masaryk, T. G. (1990). *Česká otázka* [The Czech question]. Praha: Svoboda.

Merritt, R. L., & Zinnes, D. (1991). Democracies and war. In A. Inkeles (Ed.), *On measuring democracy: Its consequences and concomitant,* (pp. 207–234). New Brunswick, NJ: Transaction Publishers.

Opat, J. (1990). *Filozof a politik T. G. Masaryk. 1882–1893. (Příspěvek k životopisu)* [T. G. Masaryk—philosopher and politician (A contribution to his biography)]. Praha: Melantrich.

Poe, S. C.. & Tate, C. N. (1994). Regression of human rights to personal integrity in the 1980's: A global analysis. *American Political Science Review, 88,* 853–872.

Rummel, R. J. (1983). Libertarianism and international violence. *Journal of Conflict Resolution. 27,* 7–71.

Rummel, R. J. (1994a). *Death by government: Genocide and mass murder since 1900.* New Brunswick, NJ: Transaction Publishers.

Rummel, R. J. (1994b). Power, genocide and mass murder. *Journal of Peace Research, 31,* 1–10.

Russett, B. (1993). *Governing the democratic peace.* Princeton, NJ: Princeton University Press.

Sartori, G. (1987). *The theory of democracy revisited.* Chatham, NJ: Chatham House.

Singer, M., & Wildavsky, A. (1993). *The Real World Order: Zones of Peace/Zones of Turmoil.* Chatham, NJ: Chatham House.

Small, M., & Singer, J. D. (1976). The war proneness of democratic regimes. *Jerusalem Journal of International Relations, 1,* 50–69.

Srnec, J., & Netík, K. (1990). *Znalecký posudek z oboru psychologie* [Expert psychological testimony]. Praha: Vojenská obvodová prokuratura.

Tamir, J. (1993). *Liberal nationalism.* Princeton, NJ: Princeton University Press.

Taylor, S. E., & Crocker, J. (1981). Schematic bases of social information processing. In T. E. Higgins, P. C. Herman, & M. P. Zanna (Eds.), *Social Cognition* (pp. 89–134). Hillsdale, NJ: Lawrence Erlbaum Associates.

Part V

Socialization
for Conflict Resolution

In this section, we turn to the investigation of how conflict resolution may be enhanced in adolescents. The chapters are written by social and developmental psychologists, and their focus is on the socialization process. It is worth noting that, from a theoretical point of view, the authors describe the learning process in cognitive terms: What children learn are cognitive scripts about appropriate behavior in conflict situations.

The first chapter, by Österman and her colleagues, explores the development of skills of conflict resolution—dyadic, constructive conflict resolution as well as third-party interventions in conflicts between others. The authors present a large cross-cultural study including data from four countries—Italy, Israel, Finland, and Poland—and they provide findings pertaining to sex differences and developmental trends in conflict resolution. These findings are analyzed in the light of metacognitive theory, which provides a valuable framework for understanding the development of conflict-resolution skills.

The second chapter, by Guerra and her colleagues, describes a program aiming toward the prevention and mitigation of aggression among inner-city youth in Chicago. What makes their program special is the fact that it considers multiple contexts in which aggression is learned: the classroom, school, peer group, family, and community. Any program, they claim, that is not targeting multiple contexts, is doomed to failure, because children are exposed to and learn conflict scripts in many situations. Both cultural aspects and individual learning histories are important factors to take into consideration. The community context is particularly important in the work with inner-city youth, because environmental conditions are extreme.

The third chapter in this section, by Olweus, describes another well-established intervention program, targeting bully–victim problems in school settings. This particular program claims extraordinary success, and it has been copied and implemented in a number of other countries, including England, Canada, Australia, and Sweden, among others. Bullying is a specific, asymmetric kind of aggression, in which a child is powerless against continuous harassment by one or more of his or her peers. Based on solid research, Olweus provides the reader with a concise summary of how aggressive reaction patterns develop in children: too little love and care, lack of warmth and involvement, and too much permissiveness from primary caretakers for aggressive behavior.

17

Sex Differences in Styles of Conflict Resolution: A Developmental and Cross-Cultural Study with Data From Finland, Israel, Italy, and Poland

Karin Österman
Kaj Björkqvist
Åbo Akademi University

Kirsti M. J. Lagerspetz
University of Turku
with

Simha F. Landau
New Hebrew University

Adam Fraczek
Polish Academy of Sciences

Concetta Pastorelli
University of Rome

This chapter describes a cross-cultural study of spontaneous nonviolent conflict resolution in adolescents of three age groups: 8, 11, and 15 years of age, in Finland, Israel, Italy, and Poland (n = 2094). The participants' behavior in conflict situations was measured with peer-estimation techniques. Although cultural variation was found, girls, across nations and age groups, tended to make use of dyadic constructive conflict resolution and third-party intervention more than boys. Developmental trends were also found, revealing that the highest frequency in interpersonal conflict resolution was reported to occur at age 11, when adolescents reach the metacognitive stage of mutual perspective-taking (Flavell, 1979; Selman, 1980).

—The Editors

Interpersonal conflict resolution among children is a rapidly growing research area. The term conflict resolution refers here to strategies by which individuals attempt to solve conflicts in nonaggressive manners. In the present study, three ways of resolving conflicts were investigated in adolescents of three age groups (8, 11, and 15 years of age), in Finland, Israel, Italy, and Poland. Variation dependent on age, sex, and ethnic group was studied.

CONFLICT RESOLUTION SKILLS IMPROVE WITH AGE

Research on the development of conflict resolution skills during childhood and adolescence shows that the ability to solve conflicts improves with age. Kolominskii and Zhiznevskii (1992) investigated resolution of conflict during play in very young children. They found that the most frequently applied method in the resolution of disputes with peers used by 1- to 3-year-olds was some form of physical influence, whereas 3- to 4-year-olds relied more on verbal influence. In 1- to 3-year-olds, conflicts were most often resolved unfavorably. The help of adults was most useful for resolution among 3- to 4-year-olds, whereas for 4- to 5-year-olds, resolution occurred independently during the course of play—that is, not until that age are children able to solve conflicts during play without the intervention of elders.

Conflict resolution skills consistently improve during adolescence. For instance, Leyva and Furth (1986) studied the understanding of societal conflict and its resolution in 11- to 17-year-old adolescents. They found an increase in frequency of constructive compromise with age. Accordingly, it seems likely that conflict resolution skills are related to social intelligence.

THE DEVELOPMENT OF SOCIAL INTELLIGENCE
AND METACOGNITION

Developmental psychologists have presented a variety of sequential theories that may be relevant for the understanding of how conflict resolution skills develop. The ability to solve conflicts peacefully is obviously dependent on social skills, which in turn are based on social perception as well as social intelligence.

Flavell's (1979; see also Flavell, Fry, Wright, & Jarvis, 1968) theory of the development of metacognition is of particular importance. *Metacognition* means knowing about cognition; that is, knowing about thinking, one's own as well as that of others. Flavell et al. (1968) described experiments designed to explore metacognitive development. Not surprisingly, children's metacognitive skills increase with age. Three levels were identified. A child is categorized as being at level A if he or she does show awareness of the fact that there is a motive behind the opponent's choice but does not show awareness of the possibility that the other participant might also be cognizant of his or her motives or strategies. At level B, the child has reached the awareness that the other may be reciprocally cognizant; "he or she knows that the other child knows that he or she knows." As the child makes a decision on the basis of his or her attributing thoughts and motives to the other, the child also sees that the other is capable of similar attribution. At level C, metacognition goes even one step further. The child is now able to abstractly step outside the dyad and realize that both opponents can simultaneously take into consideration their own as well as the other's motives *and* perspective; "I know that you know that I know that you know."

Without the ability to take a mutual level B, or, even better, a level C metacognitive perspective, it is difficult to attain durable conflict resolution between two parties or individuals without a mediator. It is questionable whether all adults are able to operate at level C, as defined by Flavell's scheme.

It is worth noting also that nonhuman primates are, to at least some extent, capable of metacognition, which is a prerequisite of both conflict resolution and indirect aggression. Byrne and Whiten (1987, 1988) found that chimpanzees were able to perform tactical deception by faking nonverbal communication, thereby concealing their motivation from other chimpanzees.

Selman (1980) proposed a sequence of five developmental levels in children's understanding and perception of their social environment. These levels of social cognition are based on the ability of perspective taking, and Selman defined them in accordance with the child's concepts of persons and relations. At level 0 (ages 3–6), the child's concepts of persons is undifferentiated, and the child's concepts of relations are egocentric. At level 1 (age 5–9), the child's concepts of persons have become differentiated. The child can distinguish between intentional and unintentional acts. The child's concepts of relations are, however, still subjective and seen in a unilateral way, there is no reciprocity. At level 2 (ages 7–12), the child's concepts of persons is self-reflective. The child is now able to step mentally outside himself or herself and to take a second-person perspective on his or her own thoughts and actions, and the child realizes that others can do so as well. The child's concepts of relations have reached the level of reciprocity. Level 3 (ages 10–15) is characterized by the ability to take a third-person and mutual perspective. This critical conceptual advance implies that the child is now able to step outside not only of his or her own immediate perspective, but also outside the dyadic interaction he or she is involved in. At level 4 (ages 12 to adult), the individual is able to take in-depth and societal–symbolic perspective. He or she can now abstract multiple mutual perspectives to a totality of societal, conventional, legal, and moral perspectives.

CONFLICT RESOLUTION AND PEER RELATIONS

The use of constructive conflict resolution is applied more among friends than with acquaintances. Newcomb and Bagwell (1995) found that friendships compared with nonfriend relations were characterized by more frequent conflict resolution. Conciliatory gestures have been found to be used more often with friends than with acquaintances (Vespo & Caplan, 1993). Bryant (1992) found that socially preferred children were identified by peers as more likely to use a calm approach to resolve conflicts, and less likely to use either an anger retaliation approach or an avoidance approach. It is also likely that conflict resolution is more applied with same-sex peers: Sackin and Thelen (1984) found in an observational study of 5-year-old children that conciliatory behaviors were offered more frequently to children of the same sex.

SEX DIFFERENCES IN CONFLICT RESOLUTION BEHAVIOR IN CHILDREN

There are several studies indicating that girls are better at conflict resolution than boys. Miller, Danaher, and Forbes (1986) explored differences in conflict resolution strategies in 5- and 7-year-olds. The results showed that once in a conflict situation, boys tended to use threat and physical force significantly more often, whereas girls tended to attempt to mitigate conflicts significantly more often, especially when interacting with other girls. Ohbuchi and Yamamoto (1990) also obtained results that implied a higher level of resolution skills in conflicts for girls. Hay, Zahn-Waxler, Cummings, and Iannotti (1992) found that girls in general recommended more socialized tactics than boys did, when interviewed about solutions to peer conflicts.

METHOD

Three styles of nonaggressive conflict resolution (constructive resolution, intervening as a third part in a conflict between others, and withdrawal) were investigated among adolescents of three age groups (8, 11, and 15 years of age) in Finland, Israel, Italy, and Poland ($n = 2094$), by help of both peer- and self-rating techniques. Data from ethnic subgroups in Finland (Finnish and Swedish speakers) and in Israel (secular and religious Israelis) were included. The distribution within the sample is presented in Table 17.1.

Peer Estimations

Peer-estimation techniques were used in order to map conflict resolution behavior among school children. The study was conducted in connection with a larger cross-cultural project investigating sex differences and developmental trends in aggressive behavior (the results on aggressive conflict behavior have been presented elsewhere: Österman, Björkqvist, Lagerspetz, Kaukiainen, Huesmann, & Fraczek, 1994; Österman, et al. 1996).

Each child estimated the conflict resolution behavior of every child (including himself or herself) in the class. The peer estimated scores within this particular contest are based on estimations made by pupils of the same sex only, because within-sex conflicts are more common than between-sex conflicts in the school environment (Björkqvist & Niemelä, 1992; Lagerspetz & Björkqvist, 1994). The question posed to every child was, "How does he/she behave when in conflict?" The instrument had closed-ended alternatives. The participants were instructed to

TABLE 17.1

Number of Peer Estimated Subjects From the Six Ethnic Groups Included in the Study

	Girls	Boys
Finland, Turku		
Finnish-speaking (Finn)	162	150
Swedish-speaking (FiSw)	126	118
Israel, Jerusalem		
Secular (IsrS)	163	172
Religious (IsrR)	139	156
Italy, Rome (Ital)	122	157
Poland, Warsaw, and Morag (Pol)	313	316
Total	1,025	1,069

estimate how frequent this behavior was on a 5-point scale ranging from 0 (*never*) to 4 (*very often*).

Three types of conflict resolution behavior were studied: constructive conflict resolution, intervention of a third party in conflicts between others, and withdrawal from a conflict situation. Constructive conflict resolution was measured with three items: "solves problems by trying to talk," "finds peaceful solutions," and "manages to calm down the situation." Withdrawal was measured with two items: "goes away," "gives in." Third-party intervention was measured with one item, "helps others who get teased."

Although the summed variables consisted of few items, they had reasonable internal consistency: The α-scores of constructive conflict resolution varied between .73 and .94 in the different samples. The correlations between the two items measuring withdrawal varied between .59 and .83 in Finland and Israel. In Poland and Italy they were below .50 but still significant.

RESULTS

The data were analyzed by use of multivariate analysis of variance (MANOVA). The results are presented in Table 17.2 and Fig. 17.1 and summarized in the following pages. Significant univariate group differences were pinpointed with Scheffé's contrast.

Effect of Sex

Girls were estimated by their peers to use constructive conflict resolution techniques and third-party intervention more than boys. According to the multivariate analysis, they also withdrew from conflicts more often than boys did, but this effect was accounted for by the Finnish-speaking sample.

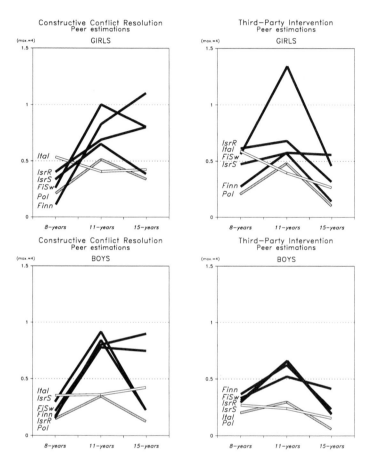

FIG. 17.1.   Three styles of conflict resolution (constructive conflict resolution, third-party intervention, and withdrawal) in children of three age groups (8-, 11-, and 15-years of age) in four countries: Italy (*Ital*), Israel with secular (*IsrS*) and religious (*IsrR*) subgroups, Poland (*Pol*), and Finland with a Finnish-Speaking (*Finn*) and a Swedish-Speaking (*FiSw*) subgroup. The top three graphs present data for girls, and the lower three graphs give data for boys.

Effect of Age Group

Both sexes used conflict resolution most at the age of 11, probably a reflection of the circumstance that peer group conflicts are most frequent in this period and the fact that aggressive behavior has a peak at age 11 (Björkqvist, Lagerspetz, & Kaukiainen, 1992; Österman et al., 1996).

Effect of Ethnic Group

Finnish and Israeli children used (according to peer estimations) more constructive conflict resolution behavior than Polish and Italian children. The Swedish-speaking

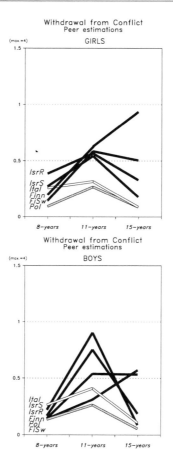

Fig. 17.1 *cont.*

sample in Finland used significantly more third-party intervention than others. The Finnish-speaking sample withdrew significantly more from conflicts than others. The Polish children used less of all types of conflict resolution behavior than others.

Notable Interactions

Constructive conflict resolution and withdrawal were still frequent at age 15 among Finnish children, which was not the case in the other countries studied. Religious Israeli girls used constructive conflict resolution significantly more than others at age 15.

DISCUSSION

Age trends in regard to conflict resolution in the different countries were almost identical. Thus, although cultural variation appeared, similarities across countries and ethnic groups in respect to developmental trends was a more important finding

TABLE 17.2
F- and *p*-Values of a 2 x 3 x 6 (Sex x Age Group x Ethnic Group)
MANOVA of Three Styles of Conflict Resolution

	F	df	p <
Main Effect of Sex			
Multivariate analysis	23.91	3.2056	.001
Univariate test			
Constructive conflict resolution	31.53	1.2058	.001
Third-party intervention	69.03	"	.001
Withdrawal from conflict	4.70	"	.05
Main Effect of Age Group			
Multivariate analysis	141.66	6.4114	.001
Univariate test			
Constructive ronflict resolution	192.69	2.2058	.001
Third-party intervention	127.94	"	.001
Withdrawal from conflict	172.59	"	.001
Main Effect of Ethnic Group			
Multivariate Analysis	33.44	15.6174	.001
Univariate test			
Constructive conflict resolution	59.78	5.2058	.001
Third-party intervention	44.68	"	.001
Withdrawal from conflict	77.99	"	.001

Note. All multivariate 2-way and 3-way interactions were significant at the .001 level.

than cultural variation (see *F*-values in Table 17.2). Children who live in different countries and belong to various ethnic groups still are members of the same human species, and their cognitive development follows similar patterns. Cognitive development provides the possibilities for resolving of conflicts, whereas culture affects they way in which it appears.

Peer-estimated conflict resolution behavior showed a peak at age 11. In Österman et al. (1996) peer-estimated aggression scores were also higher at age 11 than at ages 8 or 15. At age 11, children are entering Level 3, according to Selman's (1980) stage theory: They are now getting able to take a third-person mutual perspective. They are becoming able to analyze not only the dyadic interaction they are involved in, but they are also able to mentally step outside it, and analyze it from a third-person perspective. According to Flavell's (1979) theory about metacognitive development, children are becoming reciprocally cognizant. They are not only able to analyze other children's motives, but they are also aware of the fact that other children can analyze their motives.

The development of metacognition affects not only conflict resolution skills but it also facilitates the prevention of conflicts. With increasing age, adolescents learn how to solve their conflicts, and how to stay out of them as well. This fact may explain why conflict resolution behavior does not continuously increase by age, conflicts are instead likely to be prevented before they become overt.

A distinct finding of the present study was that girls, across nations and ethnic subgroups, were estimated by their peers to use constructive conflict resolution and third-party intervention more than boys.

We have suggested that conflict resolution skills are closely related to social intelligence. Cohn (1991) found that girls mature faster than boys. According to him, adolescent girls achieve developmental milestones earlier than boys, but he also found that the difference declines with age. This fact may favor girls as compared to boys, when conflict resolution is required—at least during adolescence. Gire and Carment (1993) have shown that females may have an advantage over males also during adulthood, as far as conflict resolution skills are concerned.

Girls' better capacity to analyze social situations may be used to escalate conflicts also, not merely to resolve them. Girls have been found to use indirect aggression more than boys (e.g., Lagerspetz, Björkqvist, & Peltonen, 1988; Björkqvist, Österman, & Kaukiainen, 1992; Björkqvist, Lagerspetz, & Kaukiainen, 1992; Österman et al., 1996). A similar finding has been made by Goodwin (1990), who reports that girls used stories about an absent party to restructure alignments of their peer group, not only for the current interaction, but also for the future. Girls used "he-said-she-said" constructions to instigate future confrontations. Boys, on the other hand, confronted one another directly, whereas girls discussed grievances as a kind of indirect aggression.

One possible explanation for the female advantage in conflict resolution skills would be that it is due to higher verbal intelligence. There are indeed studies indicating that such a sex difference exists (e.g. Cohen, Levy, & McShane, 1989; Knowles & Nixon, 1989; Kramer, Delis, & Daniel, 1988; Shucard & Shucard, 1990; Taylor, Smith, & Iron, 1990). On the other hand, a recent review by Hyde (1990) shows that sex differences in verbal skills are not so clear as previously thought, and, in some verbal areas, males may even score better than females.

As far as nonverbal communication is concerned, however, females have a clear advantage over males. The meta-analysis by Hyde (1990) states that gender differences in nonverbal communication are larger than in other areas. Nonverbal skills constitute an important part of social intelligence, and the fact that females are more involved in conflict resolution behavior could partly be explained by their skills in decoding and encoding nonverbal signals. Women, across cultures, are more skilled than men in both the interpreting (decoding) and the sending (encoding) of nonverbal signals (Brody & Hall, 1993; Custrini & Feldman, 1989; Giovannini

& Ricci-Bitti, 1981; Hall, 1978, 1984, 1987, 1990; Hall & Briton, 1993; Hall & Halberstadt, 1986; Stier & Hall, 1984).

Another explanation would be based on experience and learning. Females are generally smaller in size and have lesser physical strength than males. Björkqvist, Österman, and Lagerspetz (1994) suggested the principle of the effect–danger ratio: When in conflict, the individual estimates both the effect and the danger of different conflict strategies, and chooses an optimal ratio. Accordingly, females might learn that overt, direct aggressive behavior does not pay in their case. Instead they learn to use constructive conflict resolution, or, alternatively, indirect aggression, because both are forms of social manipulation and do not require physical strength. For example, Gire and Carment (1993) found that women showed a greater preference for negotiation where men showed a greater tendency to use threats.

It should be stressed that the fact that females display more conflict resolution behavior does not imply that they are not aggressive: Female aggression only takes different forms, and is used in somewhat different situations than male aggression (Björkqvist & Niemelä, 1992). Whatever the reason may be, females seem to be better at, or at least to rely more on, conflict resolution behavior than males.

A frequent stereotype in film and literature is the female who goes between two fighting males and manages to stop them, whereas a third male would only escalate the fight. Females' capacities as conflict resolvers have been little realized in Western culture. In the Kimberley tribe in Northwest Australia, however, as women age, they wield more power and authority. Among them, it used to be the older women who took the initiative in settling disputes (Kaberry, 1939).

Males and females tend to analyze conflicts somewhat differently. Watson and Kasten (1989) observed gender differences in negotiating behavior, and found that women were less effective negotiators than men in situations where the negotiation process was viewed as a competitive win–lose game rather than a problem-solving endeavor seeking resolution at no sacrifice to continuing relationships. The female concern for the relationship is also central in the findings of Miller (1991). The development of women's scripts depended on whether the offending party apologized or not, whereas men's scripts depended more on the offended party's initiation of conflict.

Weingarten and Douvan (1985) found systematic differences by gender in style and approach to mediation. Female mediators were comprehensive and attempted to get to underlying problems in contrast to males, whose style was characterized as short-term and task-oriented. Wall and Dewhurst (1991) found that women used more formulations that attempted to clarify what a disputant said, whereas male mediators used more formulations designed to control and direct the meditation. They also found that when disputes were resolved, parties expressed greater satisfaction with the process with women mediators than with men. Maxwell and Maxwell (1989) showed that agreements mediated by men were more likely to be broken, whereas those mediated by women were more likely to last.

Conclusively, findings indicate that females are good mediators and that they also tend to view conflict resolution from a slightly different perspective than males. Stamato (1992) warns about the fact that centers for negotiation training neglect this difference, and as a result, women adopt a more "masculine" style of communication. Thus import aspects of mediation techniques may be lost. Accordingly, we suggest that it could be beneficial if women, to a greater extent than now, would mediate also in higher-level political disputes.

REFERENCES

Björkqvist, K., Lagerspetz, K. M. J., & Kaukiainen, A. (1992). Do girls manipulate and boys fight? *Aggressive Behavior, 18,* 117–127.

Björkqvist, K., & Niemelä, P. (1992). New trends in the study of female aggression. In K. Björkqvist & P. Niemelä (Eds.), *Of mice and women: Aspects of female aggression* (pp. 3–16). San Diego, CA: Academic.

Björkqvist, K., Österman, K., & Kaukiainen, A. (1992). The development of direct and indirect aggressive strategies in males and females. In K. Björkqvist & P. Niemelä (Eds.), *Of mice and women: Aspects of female aggression* (pp. 51 64). San Diego, CA: Academic.

Björkqvist, K., Österman, K., & Lagerspetz, K. M. J. (1994). Sex differences in covert aggression among adults. *Aggressive Behavior, 20,* 27–33.

Brody, L. R., & Hall, J. A. (1993). Gender and emotion. In M. Lewis & J. M. Haviland (Eds.), *Handbook of emotions* (pp. 447–460). New York: Guilford.

Bryant, B. K. (1992). Conflict resolution strategies in relation to children's peer relations. *Journal of Applied Developmental Psychology, 13,* 35–50.

Byrne, R., & Whiten, A. (1987). The thinking primate's guide to deception. *New Scientist, 116,* 54–56.

Byrne, R., & Whiten, A. (Eds.). (1988). *Machiavellian intelligence: Social expertise and the evolution of intellect in monkeys, apes, and humans.* Oxford, England: Clarendon.

Cohen, H., Levy, J. J., & McShane, D. (1989). Hemispheric specialization for speech and non-verbal stimuli in Chinese and French Canadian subjects. *Neuropsychologia, 27,* 241–245.

Cohn, L. D. (1991). Sex differences in the course of personality development: A meta-analysis. *Psychological Bulletin, 109,* 252–266.

Custrini, R. J., & Feldman, R. S. (1989). Children's social competence and nonverbal encoding and decoding of emotions. *Journal of Clinical Child Psychology, 18,* 336–342.

Flavell, J. H. (1979). Metacognitive development and cognitive monitoring: A new area of cognitive development inquiry. *American Psychologist, 34,* 906–911.

Flavell, J. H., Fry, C., Wright, J., & Jarvis, P. (1968). *The development of role-taking and communication skills in children.* New York: Wiley.

Gire, J. T., & Carment, D. W. (1993). Dealing with disputes: The influence of individualism-collectivism. *Journal of Social Psychology, 133,* 81–95.

Goodwin, M. H. (1990). Tactical uses of stories: Participation frameworks within girls' and boys' disputes. *Discourse Processes, 13,* 33–71.

Giovannini, D., & Ricci-Bitti, P. E. (1981). Culture and sex effect in recognizing emotions by facial and gestural cues. *Italian Journal of Psychology, 8,* 95–102.

Hall, J. A. (1978). Gender effects in decoding nonverbal cues. *Psychological Bulletin, 85,* 845–857.

Hall, J. A. (1984). *Nonverbal sex differences: Communication accuracy and expressive style.* Baltimore, MD: John Hopkins University Press.

Hall, J. A. (1987). On explaining gender differences: The case of nonverbal communication. In P. Shaver & C. Hendrick (Eds.), *Sex and gender. Review of personality and social psychology* (Vol. 7, pp. 177–200). Newbury Park, CA: Sage.

Hall, J. A. (1990). *Nonverbal sex differences: Accuracy of communication and expressive style.* Baltimore, MD: John Hopkins University Press.

Hall, J. A., & Briton, N. J. (1993). Gender, nonverbal behavior, and expectations. In P. D. Blanck (Ed.), *Interpersonal expectations: Theory, research, and applications. Studies in emotional and social interaction* (pp. 276–295). New York: Cambridge University Press.

Hall, J. A., & Halberstadt, A. G. (1986). Smiling and gazing. In J. S. Hyde & M. C. Linn (Eds.), *The psychology of gender: Advances through meta-analysis* (pp. 136–158). Baltimore, MD: John Hopkins University Press.

Hay, D. F., Zahn-Waxler, C., Cummings, E. M., & Iannotti, R. J. (1992). Young children's views about conflict with peers: A comparison of the daughters and sons of depressed and well women. *Journal of Child Psychology and Psychiatry and Allied Disciplines, 33,* 669–683.

Hyde, J. S. (1990). Meta-analysis and the psychology of gender differences. *Signs, 16,* 55–73.

Kaberry, P. M. (1939). *Aboriginal woman: Sacred and profane.* London: Routledge and Kegan Paul.

Kramer, J. H., Delis, D. C., & Daniel, M. H. (1988). Sex differences in verbal learning. *Journal of Clinical Psychology, 44,* 907–915.

Knowles, A. D., & Nixon, M. C. (1989). Children's comprehension of expressive states depicted in a television cartoon. *Australian Journal of Psychology; 41,* 17–24.

Kolominskii, I. L., & Zhiznevskii, B. P. (1992). A sociopsychological analysis of conflicts among children during play. *Journal of Russian and East European Psychology, 30,* 72–86.

Lagerspetz, K. M. J., & Björkqvist, K. (1994). Indirect aggression in boys and girls. In L. R. Huesmann (Ed.), *Aggressive behavior: Current perspectives* (pp. 131–150). New York: Plenum.

Lagerspetz, K. M. J., Björkqvist, K., & Peltonen, T. (1988). Is indirect aggression typical of females? *Aggressive Behavior, 14,* 403–414.

Leyva, F. A., & Furth, H. G. (1986). Compromise formation in social conflicts: The influence of age, issue, and interpersonal context. *Journal of Youth and Adolescence, 15,* 441–452.

Maxwell, J., & Maxwell, D. (1989, February). *Male and female mediation styles and their effectiveness.* Paper presented at the National Conference on Peacemaking and Conflict Resolution, Montreal, Quebec.

Miller, J. B. (1991). Women's and men's scripts for interpersonal conflict. *Psychology of Women Quarterly, 15,* 15–29.

Miller, P. M., Danaher, D. L., & Forbes, D. (1986). Sex-related strategies for coping with interpersonal conflict in children aged five and seven. *Developmental Psychology, 22,* 543–548.

Newcomb, A. F., & Bagwell, C. L. (1995). Children's friendship relations: A meta-analytical review. *Psychological Bulletin, 117,* 306–347.

Ohbuchi, K. I., & Yamamoto, I. (1990). The power strategies of Japanese children in interpersonal conflict: Effects of age, gender, and target. *Journal of Genetic Psychology, 15,* 349–360.

Österman, K., Björkqvist, K., Lagerspetz, K. M. J., Kaukiainen, A., Huesmann, R. L., & Fraczek, A. (1994). Peer and self estimated aggression in 8-year old children from five ethnic groups. *Aggressive Behavior, 20,* 411–428.

Österman, K., Björkqvist, K., Lagerspetz, K. M. J., with Kaukiainen, A., Landau, S. F., Fraczek, A., & Caprara, G. V. (1996). *Cross-cultural evidence of female indirect aggression.* Manuscript submitted for publication.

Sackin, S., & Thelen, E. (1984). An ethological study of peaceful associative outcomes to conflict in preschool children. *Child Development, 55,* 1098–1102.

Selman, R. L. (1980). *The growth of interpersonal understanding. Developmental and clinical analyses.* New York: Academic.

Shucard, J. L., & Shucard, D. W. (1990). Auditory evoked potentials and hand preference in 6-month-old infants: Possible gender-related differences in cerebral organization. *Developmental Psychology, 26,* 923–930.

Stamato, L. (1992). Voice, place, and process: Research on gender, negotiation, and conflict resolution. *Mediation Quarterly, 4,* 375–386.

Stier, D. S., & Hall, J. A. (1984). Gender differences in touch: An empirical and theoretical review. *Journal of Personality and Social Psychology, 47,* 440–459.

Taylor, M. J., Smith, M. L., & Iron, K. S. (1990). Event-related potential of sex differences in verbal and nonverbal memory tasks. *Neuropsychologia, 28,* 691–705.

Wall, V. D., & Dewhurst, M. L. (1991). Mediator gender: Communication differences in resolved and unresolved mediations. *Mediation Quarterly, 9,* 63–85.

Watson, C., & Kasten, B. (1989). Separate strengths? How men and women negotiate. *CNCR Working Paper Series.* Newark, NJ: Rutgers University.

Weingarten, H. R., & Douvan, E. (1985). Male and female visions of mediation. *Negotiation Journal, 4,* 349–358.

Vespo, J. E., & Caplan, M. (1993). Preschooler's differential conflict behavior with friends and acquaintances. *Early Education and Development, 4,* 45–53.

18

A Cognitive–Ecological Approach to the Prevention and Mitigation of Violence and Aggression in Inner-City Youth

Nancy G. Guerra
University of Illinois at Chicago

Leonard D. Eron
L. Rowell Huesmann
University of Michigan

Patrick Tolan
Richard Van Acker
University of Illinois at Chicago

This chapter describes a large-scale cognitive–ecological intervention program aiming at reducing aggressive behavior among inner-city youth in Chicago. Until recently, few studies of the learning of aggression and violence have included consideration of the multiple contexts in which these behaviors are learned. These contexts include the classroom, school, peer group, family, and community. In working with inner-city children, understanding the community context is of particular relevance, because of the extreme environmental conditions that often exist there. It is important that intervention programs with inner-city youth take into account the interaction between environmental hazards, such as poverty and exposure to violence, and personal risk factors, such as individual learning histories. Existing research suggests that the developing child learns cognitive scripts and information-processing techniques that are adaptive for the child's environmental context, and that these, in turn, influence aggressive behavior.

—The Editors

There has been increasing concern in the United States about the rise in both the number and the seriousness of violent crimes committed by young persons. It appears that this problem is most acute among urban, lower-class minority youth living in the inner city (Elliot & Ageton, 1980), particularly young African-American males. At the same time, because of the early onset of this pattern of behavior in development and its relative intractability once established (Eron, 1987; Olweus, 1979), there has been an increasing emphasis on early prevention and intervention.

Intervention programs conducted in inner-city schools and communities that are aimed at teaching children alternative ways of behaving and solving interpersonal problems are doomed to failure if they do not take into account the extreme and persistent environmental constraints such as violence, hopelessness, and limited social resources that surround these children 24 hours a day. It is naive of investigators to believe that they can change the attitudes and behavior of young people growing up under these conditions with any type of brief, single-focus program, such as public service announcements, classroom management strategies for teachers, or a few weekly lectures and exercises designed to change children's social skills or cognitions about aggression. In order to effect behavioral change, a more complex and sustained approach, carried out more frequently over a number of years and affecting several psychosocial contexts and settings of development, is necessary.

We have engaged in preventive intervention programs in both the inner city of Chicago, its suburbs and other communities (Dubow, Huesmann, & Eron, 1988; Guerra & Slaby, 1990). These programs were based on principles derived from social learning theory, studies of social cognitions, and recently developed information-processing models of social behavior. These interventions were designed to mitigate the aggressive behavior of young children growing up in these areas by changing their cognitions. We believe that information-processing models of social behavior provide a viable basis for intervening with school children because they emphasize the central role of cognitive structures that are learned, and thus are potentially modifiable, through direct intervention. When working with inner-city children, we have found it necessary to alter the language, the examples, and the content of both our assessment and intervention procedures from those used with suburban, middle-class children to make them culturally sensitive and relevant to this specific environment. We have also found it necessary to extend the contexts of concern from the individual child to the classroom, peer group, and family, because cognitive factors are learned and maintained through both direct instruction, reinforcement, and observation of models across these different contexts. Such a focus on the different settings and contexts for social learning is also consistent with an ecological perspective on prevention that we have adopted, whereby the dynamic interaction of individual and environmental characteristics in determining behavior is emphasized (Lorion, Tolan, & Wahler, 1987; Seidman, 1991; Van Acker & Valenti, 1989).

In this chapter, we review research and theory linking the development of information-processing styles and cognitions to aggression, describe how this development is influenced by relevant social contexts, and discuss how the environment in which inner-city children develop affects the learning and maintenance of aggressive behavior. We then describe a large-scale program designed to prevent antisocial behavior in high-risk inner-city children. This approach extends our focus toward an integration of individual and contextual factors relevant to the development of antisocial behavior in inner-city children. Thus, an attempt is made to examine how those individual cognitive processes that are precursors to aggressive and violent behavior can be modified directly and by influencing the varied contexts of development.

THE ETIOLOGY OF AGGRESSIVE BEHAVIOR

Violent human behavior is multiply determined. The factors involved range from genetics, neuroanatomy, endocrinology, and physiology, through exogenous substances and firearms, to peer, gang, family, and community influences. There has been a plethora of research on each of these factors. However, none of these factors by itself can explain much of the variance in the extent or intensity of violent behavior in the population, much less predict who will engage in such behavior. Only when there is a convergence of a number of variables does aggressive or violent behavior occur (Eron, 1982; Huesmann & Eron, 1984; Loeber & Tolan, 1993).

However, aggressive behavior does not routinely occur even when these factors do converge. The individual most likely to behave aggressively and violently is one who has been programmed to respond in this way through previous experience and learning (Eron, 1982). Individuals with given genetic, neurological, and physical endowment and living under circumstances that put them at risk for violence still vary in their likelihood of behaving violently. Aggressive behavior must somehow have been learned in the past (although not necessarily performed) and incorporated into the individuals' repertoire of responses before it can be elicited by some external situation or stimulation from within the individual. In addition, alternative prosocial behaviors must not have been learned, or, at least, not learned as well as the aggressive behavior.

How is aggression learned? A number of different learning theories of aggression were proposed in the 1970s by Bandura (1973), Berkowitz (1974), Eron, Walder, & Lefkowitz (1971), Patterson (1976), and others. More recently, researchers have introduced learning models based on current thinking in cognitive psychology (Berkowitz, 1984; Dodge, 1986; Huesmann, 1982b, 1986, 1988; Huesmann & Eron, 1984; Guerra & Slaby, 1990). The various learning theories have differed in terms of exactly what is learned—specific behaviors, cue-behavior connections, response biases, beliefs, or scripts. In all cases, though, learning is hypothesized to occur both as a result of one's own behaviors and as a result of viewing how others behave.

It is hypothesized that the developing child's learning and response-generation processes are influenced by the emerging cognitive system. The child must ultimately make sense of his or her social world through some type of cognitive appraisal (e.g., Bandura, 1986; Bowlby, 1969). Therefore, to understand the development of habitual (learned) aggressive behavior, one needs to examine the operation of the child's cognitive system in the presence of the environmental and characteristic factors that promote aggressive behavior.

The specific conditions that have been shown empirically to be most conducive to the learning and maintenance of aggression are those in which the child is reinforced for his or her own aggression (e.g., Patterson, 1976, 1986), is provided many opportunities to observe aggression (e.g., Bandura, 1979; Eron, Huesmann, Lefkowitz, & Walder, 1972), is given few opportunities to develop positive affective social bonds with others (e.g., Hawkins & Weis, 1985), and is the object of aggression (e.g., Dodge, Bates, & Petit, 1990). Although these conditions can exist in all settings, they are more likely in the inner-city environment with its extreme economic and social deprivation (McLoyd, 1990). Thus, this environment increases the general level of risk for all children growing up there. In this country at this time, African-American, Hispanic, and other minority group members disproportionately grow up in such environments, placing inner-city minority children at highest risk for developing habitual aggressive and violent behavior.

However, even within this high-risk environment, not all children grow up to be aggressive and violent (Huesmann & Eron, 1992). Although more violent crimes are committed by inner-city youth (Elliot & Ageton, 1980), it is still only a small percentage of these children who will ultimately display serious and chronic antisocial behavior. It is our hypothesis that the various causal factors that have been implicated in the development of aggression in the general population are also relevant for inner-city children. We believe that the convergence of the previously mentioned learning conditions with constitutional factors, abetted by the high level of environmental hazards, produces cognitive structures and processes that predispose some children to aggressive and violent behavior. But what we must constantly bear in mind is that the environmental hazards loom very large. Not only do they increase general population risk but they also exacerbate individual differences.

Some early work in the area of information-processing and aggression was derived from an interpersonal cognitive problem-solving model that emphasized the relation between aggressive behavior and deficits in information-processing skills including means–ends thinking, generating solutions, and generating consequences (Shure & Spivack, 1976; Spivack & Shure, 1974). Intervention programs derived from this model have yielded equivocal results. Although some studies have demonstrated short-term cognitive and behavioral gains with elementary school children (e.g., Camp & Bash, 1981), studies with urban minority populations have been less successful, particularly when the primary focus has been on teaching children to generate alternative solutions (Weissberg et al., 1981). More recently, several researchers have demonstrated relations between aggressive behavior and deficits in searching for cues (Dodge & Newman, 1981), generating nonaggressive solutions (Richard & Dodge, 1982), and generating consequences (Guerra, 1989; Guerra & Slaby, 1989). Additionally, recent research has consistently identified a tendency of aggressive children to overattribute hostile intentions to others in ambiguous situations (Dodge & Frame, 1982; Dodge, Price, Bachorowkski, &

Newman, 1990; Slaby & Guerra, 1988), and to attribute social failure to controllable causes (Guerra, Huesmann, & Zelli, 1990).

Drawing on this literature, Dodge (1986) described a model emphasizing the importance of defective information-processing skills in the development of aggression. Aggressive children are viewed as possessing diminished abilities for generating and selecting behaviors and defective processes for interpreting others' behaviors. Enduring attributional biases toward perceiving hostility promote the stability of aggression across situations. Berkowitz (1988), on the other hand, has emphasized the importance of enduring cognitive associations in explaining stable aggressive behavior. Aggression is an aversively stimulated behavior. An aversive event produces negative affect that cues a variety of behavioral tendencies. The strongest tendency dominates, and, if aggressive behavior occurs, the emotional experience is then interpreted as anger. Thus, the behavior results from an automatic cognitive process but the attributions about it result from a controlled cognitive process (Shiffrin & Schneider, 1977).

Hypotheses about the relation between social beliefs and antisocial behavior come from both the sociological and social learning traditions. For example, sociologists have linked delinquent behavior among inner-city youth to an adherence to lower-class rules and norms, or "focal concerns" (Miller, 1958), a separate set of subcultural norms (Cohen, 1955), a set of beliefs that "neutralize" the consequences of delinquent activity (Sykes & Matza, 1957), or a weakening of moral beliefs (Hirschi, 1969). Similarly, social learning theorists suggested a relation between aggressive behavior and three specific classes of beliefs: self-efficacy beliefs, normative beliefs about the acceptability of aggression, and response-outcome expectancies. Aggressive children were found to be more likely than their less aggressive peers to believe that they are able to perform aggressive behaviors (Perry, Perry, & Rasmussen, 1986), that aggression is legitimate and acceptable (Huesmann, Guerra, Miller, & Zelli, 1992; Slaby & Guerra, 1988), that violent TV shows reflect real life (Huesmann, 1982b; Huesmann & Eron, 1986), and that aggression results in positive outcomes for self, including tangible rewards (Perry et al., 1986) and increased status and self-esteem (Bandura, 1973; Slaby & Guerra, 1988), while negative consequences for others are minimized (Guerra, 1989; Slaby & Guerra, 1988). Bandura (1986) has argued that these beliefs are utilized by each individual as part of an internal self-regulating process that controls behavior.

Turning to the literature on cognitive schemata, a *schema* is a cognitive structure that represents organized generic prior knowledge and guides how people encode, store, and retrieve information (Rumelhart, Lindsay, & Norman, 1972). This organized prior knowledge enables individuals to function in a complex social world (Fiske & Taylor, 1984; Huesmann, 1982a). Although there are several types of cognitive schemata, Huesmann (1982b, 1986, 1988) has hypothesized that habitual aggressive behavior is associated with *event schemata*, or scripts (Abelson, 1976), that call for aggressive responses. A script suggests what events are to happen in the environment, how the person should behave in response to these events, and what the likely outcomes of those behaviors would be. Scripts may be used to guide behavior in a controlled manner, producing seemingly reflective behavior, or, after they are well learned, in an automatic manner generating seemingly impulsive behavior (Shiffrin & Schneider, 1977).

According to Huesmann (1988), individuals differ markedly both in terms of the range of different types of scripts they have available, as well as the specific content of their most utilized scripts. For example, aggressive children who are less skilled at processing social information probably have more aggressive scripts available and rely on these aggressive scripts more frequently than children more skilled in processing social information. Therefore, during the course of social interaction, aggressive children can be expected to be more likely to rely on these aggressive scripts. Furthermore, to the extent that a child's environment is characterized by randomness, disorder, and emotional distress, he or she is also more likely to rely on very well-learned scripts in order to keep the information-processing load within his or her capabilities during this chaos. This is because automatic cognitive processing dominates controlled processing under conditions of high stress (Huesmann, 1988). Although these environmental factors are not unique to the inner city, they are clearly a reality for almost all children growing up there (Kotlowitz, 1991).

In summary, this view of the development of aggression has been theoretically grounded in behavioral and cognitive psychology. It is believed that interventions directed at changing cognitions of high-risk inner-city youth should address both information-processing skills and cognitive content. In addition to modifying children's beliefs, it is important to promote the development of cognitive structures, particularly cognitive scripts, that include viable and effective prosocial responses and promote consideration of the consequences of one's action for self and others. Earlier intervention efforts focused on changing specific beliefs and information-processing skills. More recently, these cognitive factors have been elaborated and incorporated into a model designed to promote the development of prosocial, effective scripts or "action plans" in response to everyday social tasks children face. This emphasis is particularly relevant when working with inner-city children, whose very survival may depend on quick access to appropriate scripts, yet whose environment promotes the development primarily of aggressive scripts with limited long-term adaptability.

THE METROPOLITAN AREA CHILD STUDY

The Metropolitan Area Child Study is a large-scale, long-range program in which interventions are being conducted in 16 urban schools with the same subjects over 2-year periods and in a variety of contexts. Within these schools, the initial Cohort 1 sample consisted of 1,935 permission children who were in grades 2, 3, and 5 in the fall of 1992. From this sample, 945 children were identified as at risk for later aggression based on teacher aggression ratings on the Child Behavior Checklist (Achenbach, 1978) and peer nominations of aggression (Eron et al., 1971). By 1996, four new cohorts will have been added. School and subject selection procedures were detailed elsewhere (Guerra, Huesmann, Tolan, Van Acker, & Eron, 1995).

Some subjects receive the early-treatment program only (during grades 2 and 3), some receive the late-treatment only (during grades 5 and 6), and some receive both early and late treatments. All subjects are followed for a number of years to determine the long-range effects of these efforts at preventing the emergence of antisocial aggression and violence.

In this project, there is an evaluation of the efficacy of three intervention procedures that represent extensions in systems involved and dose applied of a multidimensional, social information-processing treatment model. The strategy for preventing the emergence of serious antisocial behavior in inner-city high-risk children is to modify the individual child's cognitive system and relevant aspects of those contextual systems that have been shown empirically to be most influential in the learning of antisocial behavior and at the same time that are also amenable to change. These contextual systems are the classroom and school environment, the antisocial peer group, and the family (Hawkins & Lam, 1987; Loeber & Dishion, 1983; Lorion, et al., 1987; Tolan, Cromwell, & Braswell, 1986). This new emphasis represents a shift from an individual model focused primarily on cognitive factors to an ecological model that emphasizes the dynamic interaction of individual and environmental factors (Cairns, 1979; Hawkins & Weis, 1985; Lorion et al., 1987; Patterson, 1982).

An important but basically unanswered question is how much intervention in which domains is necessary to prevent or mitigate aggression in the highest-risk portion of this population. To address this question, an additive model of program evaluation has been adopted, wherein we begin with the most cost-effective and least intrusive method of intervention (i.e., general enhancement, classroom-based training), and add components that represent more costly and more intrusive targeted treatments focused on identified high-risk children and their families. All subjects (with the exception of a no treatment control condition) are included in the general enhancement classroom-based program. This program consists of 40 cognitive lessons (50–60 minutes per lesson) conducted weekly by teachers over the course of 2 years (20 lessons per year) during regular classroom hours (including all students). These teachers also participate in 30 hours of teacher training during the first year of intervention and in monthly reviews and supervision during the second year of intervention.

At a second level, a large group of subjects who are identified as being at high risk for developing aggressive behavior have been divided into two additional treatment groups. Both of these groups also receive more intensive cognitive and behavioral training in small groups of high-risk children in addition to the general enhancement noted in the previous paragraph. These groups are led by graduate students in clinical psychology and meet once a week for a total of 28 weeks over the course of the 2-year intervention period. At a third level one of these groups of subjects also receives 22 sessions of small group family training during the second year of the program. In this regard, it is important to examine the extent to which corresponding behavioral gains justify the social and economic costs of identifying children as high-risk, and the expenditure of resources necessary to involve multiple systems in treatment programs. This focus also addresses the concern over whether prevention programs should single out high-risk children for special attention, or whether they should be limited to general enhancement programs for all children (Hawkins & Lam, 1987).

At each of the three levels of intervention, we are ultimately concerned with changing the child's cognitive system in order to change his or her behavior. Drawing on recent social-cognitive research, five primary areas of cognitive change have been identified that are related to the development of antisocial behavior and that are also important for children living in the inner-city environment. They are: (1) self understanding; (2) self and others; (3) moral beliefs; (4) sense of control; and (5) social-problem-solving and prosocial action plans (scripts). These five areas are presented as programmatic themes in the classroom curriculum (*Yes I Can*). The small-group training primarily emphasizes social-problem solving and prosocial action plans (and emphasizes lessons from the second year of the classroom *Yes I Can* training). Thus, the small-group format provides an opportunity for children to generate and practice their action plans in a more intimate setting. In addition, the family intervention also emphasizes change in these five cognitive components.

The self-understanding component focuses on increasing the complexity of children's self definitions and fostering the development of skills in labeling feelings and emotions. The developmental literature suggests that children progress from conceptions of self based on physical attributes and activities towards conceptions of self based on psychological dimensions (Damon & Hart, 1982). To the extent that antisocial behavior is related to a "developmental lag" in such skills (e.g., Chandler, 1973), age-appropriate activities focused on self understanding should promote the normative development of such competencies and mitigate the development of antisocial behavior. In addition, increasing self-awareness has been shown to decrease deindividuation (Ickes, Layden, & Barnes, 1978), and deindividuation has been associated with a willingness to commit aggressive and antisocial acts (Zimbardo, 1970).

The self-and-others component focuses on increasing children's awareness that they are part of a social context that includes classmates, friends, family, and culture. In this regard, we are attempting to teach children that it is important to belong to social groups, but that it is also necessary to distinguish social groups that are helpful from social groups that are hurtful (e.g., violent gangs), and to develop ties or bonds with helpful groups. There is a large literature linking deficits in "attachment" or "bonding" to prosocial groups with aggression and delinquency (Hawkins & Lam, 1987). In addition, although children are taught to identify with specific social groups, they are also taught to understand that there are many similarities across social groups. Thus, the attempt is made simultaneously to increase students' perceptions of similarity to "out groups," since aggressive behavior can also be facilitated by in group–out group biases (Zimbardo, 1970). This emphasis on self in context is relevant for African-American children since it builds on the shared cultural value of communalism (Jagers & Boykin, 1989).

The third component focuses on normative beliefs. Children are trained to consider the consequences of aggressive and prosocial actions on self and others. In addition, this component involves challenging children's beliefs about aggression as an acceptable behavior, and fostering the development of prosocial standards for behavior. A variety of studies have revealed a relation between antisocial behavior and deficits in several components of moral development, including lack of concern over moral consequences of harmful behaviors (Nucci, Guerra, & Lee, 1991; Guerra, 1989), and endorsement of aggressive behavioral standards (Huesmann, Guerra, Miller, & Zelli, 1992). This component is particularly critical in the inner-city environment where children witness violent actions regularly. Because challenging normative beliefs about aggression is difficult in an environment where violence is so ubiquitous, the focus is primarily on changing beliefs about its acceptability. In a previous intervention with inner-city children (Huesmann et al., 1989), it was possible to change these beliefs. In addition, there is a focus on modifying children's beliefs about the desirability of acting like aggressive television characters, because change in this belief was most predictive of decreases in aggression in a previous study (Huesmann, Eron, Klein, Brice, & Fisher, 1983).

The fourth component focuses on children's sense of control. Specifically, this component emphasizes teaching children to differentiate controllable from uncontrollable events, develop prosocial strategies for gaining control, increase general feelings of hopefulness in social interaction, and decrease attributions of hostile intent to others following negative outcomes of ambiguous intent (hostile bias). There is an emerging literature linking aggressive behavior with difficulties in differentiating controllable and uncontrollable events, a heightened sense of control over seemingly random events, and the endorsement of aggressive strategies for gaining control (Guerra, Huesmann, & Crawshaw, 1994). There is also a substantial literature that has demonstrated a relation between hostile bias and the development of aggressive behavior (Dodge, 1986; Slaby & Guerra, 1988).

The fifth component, social problem solving and prosocial action plans (scripts), provides children with opportunities to develop and rehearse specific prosocial and effective microscripts for common social tasks. Two major types of social interaction of relevance to aggression are included: peer relations and conflict resolution. These broad categories have been further divided into six major areas of interest: initiating social interaction, maintaining social interaction, developing social relationships, understanding ambiguity, solving interpersonal conflicts, and dealing with rejection and victimization. These areas of intervention were derived from a related study of common "social tasks" generated by inner-city children, teachers, and clinicians (Asher, Guerra, & Tolan, 1992). There is a large literature linking aggressive behavior with immature social-problem-solving skills (Dodge, 1986; Slaby & Guerra, 1988) as well as with aggressive behavioral scripts (Huesmann, 1988). Consistent with most social-problem-solving interventions, the aim is to teach children a three-step model.

1. Wait (calm down and attend to cues).
2. Think (generate solutions and consider consequences).
3. Act (utilize an effective behavioral response involving communication or cooperation).

However, by having children write and rehearse specific scripts (using both predetermined and student-generated scenarios), it is expected that the automaticity of such responding will increase.

General Enhancement Classroom Training for All Students

The Yes I Can program is intended specifically to address the five components just outlined. Separate training programs have been developed for the different grade levels, and each program is tailorèd to match the children's developmental level. During the first year of intervention, the themes of self-understanding, self and others, and moral beliefs are targeted. The intent is to increase children's motivation to behave prosocially rather than aggressively by increasing their ability to understand self and others and by decreasing their endorsement of the acceptability of aggression in social interactions. During the second year of intervention, the themes of sense of control and prosocial action plans are targeted in order to provide children with cognitive and behavioral repertoires for use in daily social interactions.

Small-Group Training for High-Risk Youth

At the second level of intervention, identified high-risk children are targeted for the small group training (one hour per week for 12 weeks during the first year of intervention and for 16 weeks during the second year of intervention). The small-group training provides a more intimate setting (6 children per group) for reviewing the classroom lessons and for practicing (through modeling and role play) specific action plans (during the second intervention year). As mentioned previously, the second year of the Yes I Can training follows a social problem-solving format with an emphasis on developing action plans for specific social tasks in the areas of peer relations and conflict resolution. Based on ratings of frequency of social tasks by children, teachers, and clinicians (Asher, Guerra, & Tolan, 1992), it has been possible to identify six general categories of social tasks of relevance for urban children: initiating social interaction, maintaining social interaction, developing social relationships, understanding ambiguity, solving interpersonal conflicts, and dealing with rejection and victimization.

Family Training for High-Risk Youth

At the third and most intensive level of intervention, the families of high-risk children become involved. Like the other two interventions, this is a multiunit, multifactor program. However, at the family level, the emphasis moves from information-processing theory to a social transaction perspective. This theoretical focus is more aligned with family systems theory (Tolan & Mitchell, 1989; Tolan et al., 1986), although it is expected that changes in family functioning will alter the conditions for the learning of aggression and thus ultimately influence the child's cognitive system.

The family-relations training component consists of a 22-week program that provides skill building, communication enhancement, and support-network building activities to address three primary components and several subcomponents of family functioning that have been found to relate to serious antisocial behavior. These are: (1) parent management methods, including inconsistent discipline style (Loeber & Stouthamer-Loeber, 1987, Patterson, 1982), reliance on coercion and poor behavior management skills (Patterson, 1982), and low monitoring (Loeber & Dishion, 1983); (2) emotional atmosphere of the systemic organization, including low emotional cohesion (Olson & Barnes, 1985; Tolan, 1988), negative emotional atmosphere and low emotional congruity between members (Tolan et al., 1986); and (3) poor family problem-solving and coping skills, including "defensiveness" in family interactions (Reiss, 1981), divergence and disagreement about values and inefficient use of family resources when facing a problem (Tolan et al., 1986), and deviant shared values (Loeber & Stouthamer-Loeber, 1987). Thus, it is expected that several aspects of family organization and collective functioning will be modified. This group of subjects receives the most intensive and extensive form of intervention, focused on individual cognitive factors, classroom and school environment, peer group influences, and family functioning.

CONCLUSION

A multidimensional program aimed at preventing the emergence of antisocial behavior in inner-city youth by changing their cognitions has been described. Focusing on the child's cognitions as the critical locus of change holds promise for long-term generalized effects. However, because these cognitions are learned and maintained in multiple settings, the conditions for the learning of aggression present in at least some of these settings must also be altered. The need for a comprehensive, cognitive–ecological approach is most critical in inner-city communities, where the environmental risk factors are so extreme that they place entire populations of children at risk and can exacerbate the impact of individual risk factors.

The ineffectiveness of unidimensional, single-focus programs has been pointed out in a review article by Kazdin (1987). The research design described here plans and evaluates the differential benefits of extending the intervention beyond the general classroom enhancement level to include the antisocial peer group and the family. Given the importance of multiple contexts in the development of aggression, it is expected that the most intrusive, costly, and extensive intervention will be more effective for all children because it permits it to have an impact both on the child and his or her ecology of development. It is expected that unless the context can be shifted, few lasting effects on the children will be found. However, it is also expected that unless cognitive change in the child occurs, the effects of environmental change will not be sustained. The influence on outcome is mutual, dynamic, and summative.

ACKNOWLEDGMENT

This research was supported by grant #MH 48034 from the National Institutes of Mental Health.

REFERENCES

Abelson, R. P. (1976). Script processing in attitude formation and decision making. In J. S. Carroll & J. W. Payne (Eds.), *Cognition and social behavior* (pp. 33–46). Hillsdale, NJ: Lawrence Erlbaum Associates.

Achenbach, T. M. (1978). The child behavior profile: I. Boys aged 6–11. *Journal of Consulting and Clinical Psychology, 46*, 478–488.

Asher, S., Guerra, N. G., & Tolan, P.H. (1992). *Children's social tasks.* Unpublished manuscript.

Bandura, A. (1973). *Aggression: A social learning analysis.* Englewood Cliffs, NJ: Prentice-Hall.

Bandura, A. (1979). Psychological mechanisms of aggression. In M. Von Cranach, K. Foppa, W. LePenies, & D. Ploog (Eds.), *Human ethology: Claims and limits of a new discipline* (pp. 316–356). London: Cambridge University Press.

Bandura, A. (1986). *Social foundations of thought and action: A social cognitive theory.* Englewood Cliffs, NJ: Prentice-Hall.

Berkowitz, L. (1974). Some determinants of impulsive aggression: The role of mediated associations with reinforcements for aggression. *Psychological Review, 81*, 165–176.

Berkowitz, L. (1984). Some effects of thoughts on anti and prosocial influences of media events: A cognitive neoassociation analysis. *Psychological Bulletin, 95*, 410–427.

Berkowitz, L. (1988). Frustrations, appraisals, and aversively stimulated aggression. *Aggressive Behavior, 14*, 3–12.

Bowlby, J. (1969). *Attachment and loss: Vol 1: Attachment.* New York: Basic Books.

Camp, B. W., & Bash, M. A. S. (1981). *Think aloud: Increasing social and cognitive skills—A problem-solving program for children.* Champaign, IL: Research Press.

Cairns, R. B. (1979). *Social development: The origins and plasticity of interactions.* San Francisco, CA: Jossey-Bass.

Chandler, M. (1973). Egocentrism and antisocial behavior: The assessment and training of social perspective-taking skills. *Developmental Psychology, 9*, 326–332.

Cohen, A. (1955). *Delinquent boys.* New York: The Free Press.

Damon, W., & Hart, D. (1982). The development of self-understanding from infancy to adolescence. *Child Development, 53*, 841–864.

Dodge K. A. (1986). A social information-processing model of social competence in children. In M. Perlmutter (Ed.), *Minnesota symposium on child psychology* (Vol. 18, pp. 77–125). Hillsdale, NJ: Lawrence Erlbaum Associates.

Dodge, K. A., Bates, J. E., & Petit, G. S. (1990). Mechanisms in the cycle of violence. *Science, 250*, 1678–1683.

Dodge, K. A., & Frame, C. M. (1982). Social cognitive biases and deficits in aggressive boys. *Child Development, 53*, 620–635.

Dodge, K. A., & Newman, J. P. (1981). Biased decision-making processes in aggressive boys. *Journal of Abnormal Psychology, 90*, 375–379.

Dodge, K. A., Price, J. M., Bachorowski, J., & Newman, J. P. (1990). Hostile attributional biases in severely aggressive adolescents. *Journal of Abnormal Psychology, 99*, 385–392.

DuBow, E., Huesmann, L. R., & Eron, L. D. (1988). Mitigating aggression and promoting prosocial behavior in aggressive elementary school boys. *Behavior Research and Therapy*, 577–581.

Elliot, D. S., & Ageton, S. A. (1980). Reconciling race and class differences in self-reported and official estimates of delinquency. *American Sociological Review, 45*, 95–110.

Eron, L. D. (1982). Parent–child interaction, television violence, and aggression of children. *American Psychologist, 37,* 197–211.

Eron, L. D. (1987). The development of aggressive behavior from the perspective of a developing behaviorism. *American Psychologist, 42,* 435–442.

Eron, L. D., Huesmann, L. R., Lefkowitz, M. M., & Walder, L. O. (1972). Does television violence cause aggression? *American Psychologist, 27,* 253–263.

Eron, L. D., Walder, L. O., & Lefkowitz, M. M. (1971). *The learning of aggression in children.* Boston, MA: Little, Brown.

Fiske, S. T., & Taylor, S. E. (1984). *Social cognition.* Reading, MA: Addison-Wesley.

Guerra, N. G. (1989). Consequential thinking and self-reported delinquency in high school youth. *Criminal Justice and Behavior, 16,* 440–454.

Guerra, N. G., Huesmann, L. R., & Crawshaw, V. (1994). *Desire for control, control strategies, and childhood aggression.* Manuscript submitted for publication.

Guerra, N. G., Huesmann, L. R., Tolan, P. H., Van Acker, R., & Eron, L. D. (1995). Environmental stress and individual beliefs as correlates of economic disadvantage and aggression: Implications for preventive interventions among inner-city children. *Journal of Consulting and Clinical Psychology, 63,* 518–528.

Guerra, N. G., Huesmann, L. R., & Zelli, A. (1990). Attributions for social failure and aggression in incarcerated delinquent youth. *Journal of Abnormal Child Psychology, 18,* 342–355.

Guerra, N. G., & Slaby, R. G. (1989). Evaluative factors in social–problem–solving by aggressive boys. *Journal of Abnormal Child Psychology, 17,* 277–289.

Guerra, N. G., & Slaby, R. G. (1990). Cognitive mediators of aggression in adolescent offenders: 2. Intervention. *Developmental Psychology, 26,* 269–277.

Hawkins, J. D., & Lam, T. (1987). Teacher practices, social development, and delinquency. In J. D. Burchard & S. N. Burchard (Eds.), *Prevention of delinquent behavior* (pp. 241–274). Newbury Park, CA: Sage.

Hawkins, J. D., & Weis, J. G. (1985). The social development model: An integrated approach to delinquencyprevention.xQÿÿ , 73–97.

Hirschi, T. (1969). *Causes of delinquency.* Berkeley, CA: University of California Press.

Huesmann, L. R. (1982a). Information-processing models of behavior. In N. Hirschberg and L. Humphreys (Eds.). *Multivariate applications in the social sciences* (261–288). Hillsdale, NJ: Lawrence Erlbaum Associates.

Huesmann, L. R. (1982b). Television violence and aggressive behavior. In D. Pearl, L. Bouthilet, & J. Lazar (Eds), *Television and behavior: Ten years of programs and implications for the 80's* (pp. 126–237). Washington, DC: U.S. Government Printing Office.

Huesmann, L. R. (1986). Psychological processes promoting the relation between exposure to media violence and aggressive behavior by the viewer. *Journal of Social Issues, 42,* 125–139.

Huesmann, L. R. (1988). An information-processing model for the development of aggression. *Aggressive Behavior, 14,* 13–24.

Huesmann, L. R., & Eron, L. D. (1984). Cognitive processes and the persistence of aggressive behavior. *Aggressive Behavior, 10,* 243–251.

Huesmann, L. R., & Eron, L. D. (1986). *Television and the aggressive child: A cross national comparison.* Hillsdale, NJ: Lawrence Erlbaum Associates.

Huesmann, L. R., & Eron, L. D. (1992). Childhood aggression and adult criminality. In J. McCord (Ed.), Advances in criminological theory: Crime facts, fictions and theory. (pp. 137–156). New Brunswick, NJ: Transaction Publishers.

Huesmann, L. R., Eron, L. D., Klein, R. Brice, P., & Fisher, P. (1983). Mitigating the initiation of aggressive behaviors by changing children's attitudes about media violence. *Journal of Personality and Social Psychology, 44,* 899–910.

Huesmann, L. R., Guerra, N. G., Eron, L. D., Miller, L. S., Zelli, A., Wroblewska, J., & Adami, P. (1991). Mitigating the development of aggression in young children by changing their cognitions. *Aggressive Behavior, 17,* 75–76.

Huesmann, L. R., Guerra, N. G., Miller, L. S., & Zelli, A. (1992). The role of social norms in the development of aggressive behavior. In A. Fraczek & H. Zumkley (Eds.), *Socialization and aggression* (pp. 139–151). New York: Springer-Verlag.

Ickes, W., Layden, M. A., & Barnes, R. D. (1978). Objective self awareness and individuation: An empirical link. *Journal of Personality, 46,* 146–161.

Jagers, R. J., & Boykin, A. W. (1989). Family characteristics and psychosocial orientations among African-American students. In A. Harrison (Ed.), *The twelfth conference on empirical research in black psychology*. Washington, DC: National Institutes of Mental Health.

Kazdin, A. (1987). Treatment of antisocial behavior in children: Current status and future directions. *Psychological Bulletin, 102,* 187–203.

Kotlowitz, A. (1991). *There are no children here.* New York: Doubleday.

Loeber, R., & Dishion, T. J. (1983). Early predictors of male delinquency: A review. *Psychological Bulletin, 94,* 68–99.

Loeber, R., & Stouthamer-Loeber, M. (1987). Prediction. In H. C. Quay (Ed.), *Handbook of juvenile delinquency* (pp. 325–382). New York: Wiley.

Loeber, R., & Tolan, P. H. (1993). Conduct disorders. In P. H. Tolan & B. Cohler (Eds.), *Handbook of clinical research and practices with adolescents* (pp. 307–332). New York: Wiley.

Lorion, R. P., Tolan, P. H. & Wahler, R. G. (1987). Prevention. In H. C. Quay (Ed.), *Handbook of juvenile delinquency* (pp. 383–416). New York: Wiley.

McLoyd, V. (1990). The impact of economic hardship on black families and children: Psychological distress, parenting, and socioemotional development. *Child Development, 61,* 311–346.

Miller, W. (1958). Lower class culture as a generating milieu of gang delinquency. *Journal of Social Issues, 14,* 5–19.

Nucci, L., Guerra, N., & Lee, J. (1991). Adolescent judgments of the personal, prudential, and normative aspects of drug usage. *Developmental Psychology, 27,* 841–848.

Olson, D. H., & Barnes, H. F. (1985). Parent adolescent communication and the circumplex model. *Child Development, 56,* 438–447.

Olweus, D. (1979). The stability of aggressive reaction patterns in human males: A review. *Psychological Bulletin, 85,* 852–875.

Patterson, G. R. (1976). The aggressive child: Victim and architect of a coercive system. In L. A. Hamerlynck, J. C. Handy, & E. J. Mash (Eds.), *Behavior modification and families: Theory and research* (Vol 1, pp. 267–316). New York: Bruner/Mazel.

Patterson, G. R. (1982). *Coercive family process.* Eugene, OR: Castalia.

Patterson, G. R. (1986). Performance models for anti-social boys. *American Psychologist, 41,* 432–444.

Perry, D. G., Perry, L. C., & Rasmussen, P. (1986). Cognitive social learning mediators of aggression. *Child Development, 57,* 700–711.

Reiss, D. (1981). *The family's construction of reality.* Cambridge, MA: Harvard University Press.

Richard, B., & Dodge, K. A. (1982). Social maladjustment and problem-solving in school-aged children. *Journal of Consulting and Clinical Psychology, 42,* 789–793.

Rumelhart, D. E., Lindsay, P. H., & Norman, D. A. (1972). A process model for long-term memory. In E. Tulving & W. Donaldson (Eds.), *Organization of memory.* New York: Academic Press.

Seidman, E. (1991). Growing up the hard way: Pathways of urban adolescents. *American Journal of Community Psychology, 19,* 173–205.

Shiffrin, R. M., & Schneider, W. (1977). Controlled and automatic human information-processing: II. Perceptual learning, automatic attending, and general theory. *Psychological Review, 84,* 127–190.

Shure, M. B., & Spivack, G. (1976). Problem-solving techniques in childrearing. San Francisco, CA: Jossey-Bass.

Slaby, R. G., & Guerra, N. G. (1988). Cognitive mediators of aggression in adolescent offenders: 1. Assessment. *Developmental Psychology, 24,* 580–588.

Spivack, G., & Shure, M. B. (1974). *Social adjustment of young children.* San Francisco, CA: Jossey-Bass.

Sykes, G. H., & Matza, D. (1957). Techniques of neutralization: A theory of delinquency. *American Sociological Review, 22*, 664–670.

Tolan, P. H. (1988). Socioeconomic, family, and social stress correlates of adolescents' antisocial and delinquent behavior. *Journal of Abnormal Child Psychology, 17*, 317–332.

Tolan, P. H., Cromwell, R. E., & Brasswell, M. (1986). The application of family therapy to juvenile delinquency: A critical review of the literature. *Family Process, 25*, 619–649.

Tolan, P. H., & Mitchell, M. E. (1989). Families and antisocial and delinquent behavior. *Journal of Psychotherapy and the Family, 6*, 29–48.

Van Acker, R., & Valenti, S. S. (1989). Perception of social affordances by children with mild handicapping conditions: Implications for social skills research and training. *Ecological Psychology, 1*, 383–405.

Weissberg, R. P., Gesten, E. L., Rapkin, B. D., Cowen, E. L., Davidson, E., Flores de Apodaca, R., & McKim, B. J. (1981). Evaluation of a social-problem-solving training program for suburban and inner-city third-grade children. *Journal of Consulting and Clinical Psychology, 49*, 251.

Zimbardo, P. G. (1970). The human choice: Individuation, reason, and order versus deindividuation, impulse, and chaos. In W. J. Arnold & D. Levine (Eds.), *Nebraska Symposium on Motivation*. Lincoln: University of Nebraska Press.

19

Tackling Peer Victimization with a School-Based Intervention Program

Dan Olweus
University of Bergen

This chapter describes the effects of a school-based intervention program against bully–victim problems in Norwegian schools. Bullying in schools has received great attention in Scandinavia. Bullying is characterized by an asymmetric power relationship, in which the victim is being harassed, and exposed, repeatedly and over time, to negative actions by the bully or bullies. The victim has difficulty defending himself or herself and is somewhat helpless. The intervention program has proven to be effective, with marked reductions, by 50% or more, in bully–victim problems; it is now being implemented in a number of other countries.
—The Editors

For two years, Johnny, a quiet 13-year-old, was a human plaything for some of his classmates. The teenagers badgered Johnny for money, forced him to swallow weeds and drink milk mixed with detergent, beat him up in the rest room and tied a string around his neck, leading him around as a "pet." When Johnny's torturers were interrogated about the bullying, they said they pursued their victim because it was fun (newspaper clipping presented in Olweus, 1993a, p. 7).

Bullying among schoolchildren is certainly a very old phenomenon. The fact that some children are frequently and systematically harassed and attacked by other children has been described in literary works, and many adults have personal experience of it from their own school days. Though many are acquainted with the bully–victim problem, it was not until fairly recently—in the early 1970s—that the phenomenon was made the object of more systematic research (Olweus, 1973a, 1978). For a number of years, these efforts were largely confined to Scandinavia. In the 1980s and early 1990s, however, bullying among schoolchildren has attracted attention also in other countries such as Japan, Great Britain, the Netherlands, Australia, Canada, and the United States. There are now clear indications of an increasing societal as well as research interest into bully–victim problems in several parts of the world.

WHAT IS MEANT BY *BULLYING*?

I define *bullying* or *victimization* in the following general way (see, e.g., Olweus, 1993a): A student is being bullied or victimized when he or she is exposed, repeatedly and over time, to negative actions on the part of one or more other students. A *negative action* is the intentional injury or discomfort inflicted on another—basically what is implied in the definition of aggressive behavior (Olweus, 1973b). Negative actions can be carried out by physical contact, by words, or in other ways, such as making faces or dirty gestures, and by intentionally excluding from a group.

Proper use of the term *bullying* also implies that there is imbalance in strength (an asymmetric power relationship): The student who is exposed to the negative actions has difficulty in defending himself or herself and is somewhat helpless against the student or students who harass. One might add that the bullying behavior often occurs without apparent provocation.

Bullying can be carried out by a single individual—the bully—or by a group. The target of bullying can also be a single individual—the victim—or a group. In the context of school bullying, the target usually is a single student. Data from our study in Bergen, Norway (Olweus, 1991, 1993a), indicate that, in the majority of cases, the victim is harassed by a group of two or three students. A considerable proportion of the victims, some 35% to 40%, report, however, that they are mainly bullied by one student (Olweus, 1988).

The definition given above makes it clear that bullying can be considered a form of abuse, and I sometimes use the term *peer abuse* as a label for the phenomenon. What sets it apart from other forms of abuse, such as child abuse, and wife abuse is the context in which it occurs and the relationship characteristics of the interacting parties. It is useful to distinguish between *direct bullying and victimization*—with relatively open attacks on the victim—and *indirect bullying and victimization* in the form of social isolation and intentional exclusion from a group.

BASIC FACTS ABOUT BULLY–VICTIM PROBLEMS

Prevalence

On the basis of a survey of more than 130,000 Norwegian students with my Bully–Victim Questionnaire (Olweus & Smith, in press), it is estimated that some 15% of the students in elementary and secondary or junior high schools (grades

1–9, roughly corresponding to ages 7–16) in Norway were involved in bully–victim problems with some regularity (in the autumn of 1983) either as bullies or victims (Olweus, 1985, 1987, 1991, 1993a). This percentage represents 1 student out of 7, or 84,000 students. Approximately 9%, or 52,000 students, were victims, 7%, or and 41,000 students, bullied other students (see Figs. 19.1 and 19.2). Some 9,000 students were both victim and bully (1.6% of the total of 568,000 students or 17% of the victims). A total of some 5% of the students were involved in more serious bullying problems (as bullies or victims or bully and victim), occurring about once a week or more frequently. Because the prevalence questions in the questionnaire refer to only part of the autumn term, there is little doubt that the figures presented actually underestimate the number of students involved in such problems during a whole year.

It is apparent, then, that bullying is a considerable problem in Norwegian schools; in fact, it is a problem that affects a very large number of students. Data from other countries (in large measure collected with the Bully–Victim Questionnaire), such as Sweden (Olweus, 1992b), Finland (Lagerspetz, Björkqvist, Berts, & King, 1982), Great Britain (Smith, 1991; Whitney & Smith, 1993), the United States (Perry, Kusel & Perry, 1988), Canada (Ziegler & Rosenstein-Manner, 1991), The Netherlands (Haeselager & van Lieshout, 1992; Junger, 1990), Japan (Hirano, 1992), Ireland (O'Moore & Brendan, 1989), Spain (Ruiz, 1992), and Australia (Rigby & Slee, 1991) indicate that this problem certainly exists outside Norway and with similar or even higher prevalence rates.

Many more boys than girls bully others, and a relatively large percentage of girls report that they are mainly bullied by boys. Also, there is a somewhat higher percentage of boys who are victims of bullying. Although direct bullying is thus a

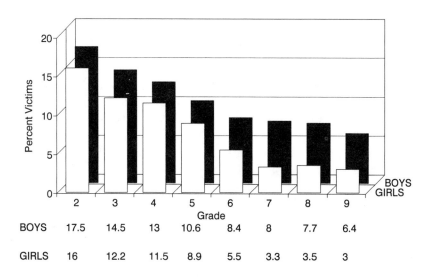

FIG. 19.1. Percentage of students in different grades who reported being bullied.

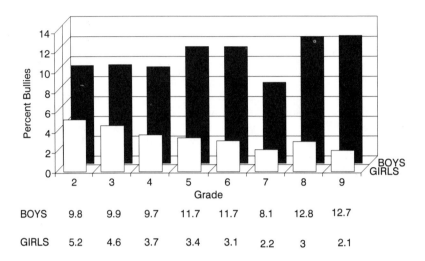

FIG. 19.2. Percentage of students in different grades who reported having bullied other students (*n* for boys = 42,324; *n* for girls = 40,877).

greater problem among boys, there occurs a good deal of bullying among girls as well. Bullying with physical means is less common among girls, however; girls typically use more subtle and indirect ways of harassment such as slandering, spreading of rumors, intentional exclusion from the group, and manipulation of friendship relations (e.g., depriving a girl of her "best friend"). Such forms of bullying may be more difficult to detect for adults. We have also found that it is the younger and weaker students who are most exposed to bullying. Although most bullying occurs among students at the same grade level, a good deal of bullying is also carried out by older students toward younger ones (more details about bullying in different grades and among boys and girls are given in Olweus, 1993a).

There is a good deal of evidence to indicate that the behavior patterns involved in bully–victim problems are fairly stable over time: This means that being a bully or a victim is something that is likely to continue for substantial periods of time, unless systematic efforts (from adults) are made to change the situation (Olweus, 1977, 1978).

Three Common Myths about Bullying

One common view holds that bully–victim problems are a consequence of large classes or schools: The larger the class or the school, the higher the level of bully–victim problem is. Closer analysis of this hypothesis, making use of the Norwegian survey data from more than 700 schools and several thousand classes (with great variations in size) resulted in the conclusion that the size of the class or the school appears to be of negligible importance for the relative frequency or level of bully–victim problems in the class or the school (Olweus, 1993a).

A second myth that has been commonly maintained is that bullying is a consequence of competition and striving for grades in school. More specifically, it has been argued that the aggressive behavior of the bullies toward their environment can be explained as a reaction to failures and frustrations in school. This hypothesis also failed to receive support from detailed analyses of (longitudinal) data: Though there was an association (of moderate magnitude) between aggressive behavior and poor grades, there was nothing in the results to suggest that the behavior of the aggressive boys was a consequence of poor grades and failure in school (Olweus, 1983).

Third, a widely held view is that victimization is caused by external deviations. It is argued that students who are fat or red-haired, wear glasses, or speak with an unusual dialect, and so on, are particularly likely to become victims of bullying. This explanation is quite common among students. This hypothesis received no support in empirical analyses (Olweus, 1978). It was concluded that external deviations play a much smaller role in the origin of bully–victim problems than generally assumed (see also Junger, 1990). In spite of the lack of empirical support for this hypothesis, it seems still to enjoy considerable popularity. Some probable reasons why this is so have been advanced, and the interested reader is referred to this discussion (Olweus, 1978, 1993a).

These hypotheses have thus failed to receive support from empirical data. Accordingly, one must look for other factors to find the origins of these problems. The research evidence presented in Olweus (1993a) and summarized here clearly suggests that personality characteristics and typical reaction patterns, in combination with physical strength or weakness in the case of boys, are quite important for the development of these problems in individual students. At the same time, environmental factors such as the teachers' attitudes, routines, and behavior play a major role in determining the extent to which the problems will manifest themselves in a classroom or a school (see Olweus, 1993a).

What Characterizes Typical Victims?

A relatively clear picture of both the typical victims and the typical bullies has emerged from research (Olweus, 1973a, 1978, 1981, 1984; Björkqvist, Ekman & Lagerspetz, 1982; Boulton & Smith, 1994; Farrington, 1993; Lagerspetz et al., 1982; Perry, Kusel, & Perry, 1988). By and large, this picture seems to apply to both boys and girls, although it must be noted that clearly less research has so far been done on bullying among girls.

The typical victims are more anxious and insecure than students in general. Further, they are often cautious, sensitive, and quiet. When attacked by other students, they commonly react by crying (at least in the lower grades) and withdrawal. Also, victims suffer from low self-esteem, they have a negative view of themselves and their situation. They often look upon themselves as failures and feel stupid, ashamed, and unattractive.

The victims are lonely and abandoned at school. As a rule, they do not have a single good friend in their class. They are not aggressive or teasing in their behavior, and, accordingly, one cannot explain the bullying as a consequence of the victims themselves being provocative to their peers (see below). These children often have a negative attitude toward violence and use of violent means. If they are boys, they are likely to be physically weaker than other boys (Olweus, 1978).

I have labelled this type of victim the passive or submissive victim, as opposed to the far less common type described below. In summary, it seems that the behavior and attitude of the passive or submissive victims signal to others that they are insecure and worthless individuals who will not retaliate if they are attacked or insulted. A slightly different way of describing the passive or submissive victims is to say that they are characterized by an anxious or submissive reaction pattern combined (in the case of boys) with physical weakness.

In-depth interviews with parents of victimized boys indicate that these boys were already characterized by a certain cautiousness and sensitivity at an early age (Olweus, 1993b). Boys with such characteristics (perhaps combined with physical weakness) are likely to have had difficulty in asserting themselves in the peer group and may have been somewhat disliked by their age mates. There are thus good reasons to believe that these characteristics contributed to making them victims of bullying (see also Schwartz, Dodge, & Coie, 1993). At the same time, it is obvious that the repeated harassment by peers must have considerably increased their anxiety, insecurity, and generally negative evaluation of themselves.

There is also another, clearly smaller group of victims, the provocative victims, who are characterized by a combination of both anxious and aggressive reaction patterns. These students often have problems with concentration and behave in ways that may cause irritation and tension around them. Some of these students can be characterized as hyperactive. It is not uncommon that their behavior provokes many students in the class, thus resulting in negative reactions from a large part of, or even the entire class. The dynamics of bully–victim problems in a class with provocative victims differ in part from problems in a class with passive victims (Olweus, 1978).

A follow-up study of two groups of boys who had or had not been victimized by their peers in school showed that the former victims were much more likely to be depressed and had poorer self-esteem as young adults, at age 23 (Olweus, 1993b). The pattern of findings clearly suggested that this was a consequence of the earlier, persistent victimization which thus had left its scars on their minds.

What Characterizes the Typical Bullies?

A distinctive characteristic of the typical bullies is their aggression toward peers; this is implied in the definition of a bully. But bullies are often aggressive toward adults as well, both teachers and parents. Generally, bullies have a more positive attitude toward violence and use of violent means than students in general. Further, they are often characterized by impulsivity and strong needs to dominate others. They have little empathy with victims of bullying. If they are boys, they are likely to be physically stronger than boys in general and the victims, in particular.

A commonly held view among psychologists and psychiatrists is that individuals with an aggressive and tough behavior pattern are actually anxious and insecure "under the surface." The assumption that the bullies have an underlying insecurity has been tested in several of my own studies, also using indirect methods such as stress hormones (adrenaline and noradrenaline) and projective techniques. There was nothing in the results to support the common view, they rather pointed in the opposite direction: The bullies had unusually little anxiety and insecurity, or were roughly average on such dimensions (Olweus, 1981, 1984, 1986; see also Pulkkinen & Tremblay, 1992). They did not suffer from poor self-esteem.

These conclusions apply to the bullies as a group. The results do not imply that there cannot be individual bullies who are both aggressive and anxious. It should also be emphasized that there are students who participate in bullying but who do not usually take the initiative; these may be labelled *passive bullies, followers,* or *henchmen.* A group of passive bullies is likely to be fairly mixed and may also contain insecure and anxious students (Olweus, 1978).

Several studies have found bullies to be of average or slightly below average popularity (Björkqvist, et al., 1982; Lagerspetz, et al., 1982; Olweus, 1973a, 1978; Pulkkinen & Tremblay, 1992). Bullies are often surrounded by a small group of 2 to 3 peers who support them and who seem to like them (see also Cairns, Cairns, Neckerman, Gest & Gariépy, 1988). The popularity of the bullies decreases, however, in the higher grades and is considerably less than average in grade 9 (around age 16). Nevertheless, the bullies do not seem to reach the low level of popularity that characterizes the victims. In summary, the typical bullies can be described as having an aggressive reaction pattern combined (in the case of boys) with physical strength.

As regards the possible psychological sources underlying bullying behavior, the pattern of empirical findings suggests at least three partly interrelated motives (in particular for male bullies). First, the bullies have a strong need for power and dominance; they seem to enjoy being in control and subduing others. Second, as will be discussed shortly, the family conditions under which many bullies have been reared seem to contribute to a certain degree of hostility towards the environment; such feelings and impulses may make them derive satisfaction from inflicting injury and suffering upon other individuals. Finally, there is an instrumental component to their behavior. The bullies often coerce their victims to provide them with money, cigarettes, beer, and other things of value. In addition, it is obvious that aggressive behavior is in many situations rewarded in the form of prestige.

Bullying can also be viewed as a component of a more generally antisocial and rule-breaking (conduct-disordered) behavior pattern. From this perspective, it is natural to predict that youngsters who are aggressive and bully others run a clearly increased risk of later engaging in other problem behaviors such as criminality and alcohol abuse (e.g., Loeber & Dishion, 1983; Olweus, 1979). In my followup studies we have found strong support for this view. Approximately 60% of boys who were characterized as bullies in grades 6 through 9 had been convicted of at least one officially registered crime by the age of 24. Even more dramatically, as much as 35% to 40% of the former bullies had three or more convictions by this age, whereas this was true of only 10% of the boys in the control group (those who were neither bullies nor victims in grades 6–9). Thus, as young adults, the former school bullies had a fourfold increase in the level of relatively serious, recidivist criminality as documented in official crime records (Olweus, 1993a). It should be mentioned that the former victims had an average or somewhat below average level of criminality in young adulthood.

Development of an Aggressive Reaction Pattern

In light of the characterization of the bullies as having an aggressive reaction pattern–that is, they display aggressive behavior in many situations–it becomes important to examine the following question: What kind of rearing and other conditions during childhood are conducive to the development of an aggressive reaction pattern? Very briefly, the following four factors have turned out to be particularly important (based chiefly on my research with boys, Olweus 1980; see also Loeber & Stouthamer-Loeber, 1986):

1. The basic emotional attitude of the primary caretaker(s) toward the child during early years (usually the mother). A negative emotional attitude, characterized by lack of warmth and involvement, increases the risk that the child will later become aggressive and hostile toward others.
2. Permissiveness for aggressive behavior by the child. If the primary caretaker is generally permissive and tolerant without setting clear limits to aggressive behavior towards peers, siblings, and adults, the child's aggression level is likely to increase.
3. Use of power-assertive child-rearing methods such as physical punishment and violent emotional outbursts. Children of parents who make frequent use of these methods are likely to become more aggressive than the average child. Violence begets violence.

We can summarize these results by stating that too little love and care and too much freedom in childhood are conditions that contribute strongly to the development of an aggressive reaction pattern.

4. Finally, the temperament of the child, which is in part inherited. A child with an active and hot-headed temperament is more likely to develop into an aggressive youngster than a child with an ordinary or quieter temperament. The effect of this factor is less powerful than those of the first two conditions mentioned.

These factors can be assumed to be important for both younger and somewhat older children. It can be added that, for adolescents, the extent to which parents supervise the children's activities outside the school reasonably well (Patterson, 1986; Patterson & Stouthamer-Loeber, 1984) and check on what they are doing and with whom is also of great significance.

It should also be pointed out that the aggression levels of the boys participating in the analyses above were not related to the socioeconomic conditions of their families, which was measured in several different ways (Olweus, 1980). Similarly, there were no (or only very weak) relations between the four childhood factors discussed and the socioeconomic conditions of the family (Olweus, 1981).

A Question of Fundamental Democratic Rights

The victims of bullying form a large group of students who are to a great extent neglected by the school. We have shown that many of these youngsters are the targets of harassment for long periods of time, often for many years (Olweus, 1977, 1978). It does not require much imagination to understand what it is to go through the school years in a state of more or less permanent anxiety and insecurity and with poor self-esteem. It is not surprising that the victims' devaluation of themselves sometimes becomes so overwhelming that they see suicide as the only possible solution.

Bully–victim problems in school really concern some of our basic values and principles. For a long time, I have argued that it is a fundamental democratic right for a child to feel safe in school and to be spared the oppression and repeated, intentional humiliation of bullying. No student should be afraid of going to school for fear of being harassed or degraded, and no parent should need to worry about such things happening to his or her child!

It should be mentioned that the Swedish Parliament, following up on an earlier proposal of mine (from 1981), recently passed a school law containing formulations that are very similar to the ideas just expressed. The law also places responsibility for realization of these goals, including development of an intervention program against bullying for the individual, with the principal. Passing of a similar law is now being discussed in Norway, and there seems to be considerable political support for the idea.

EFFECTS OF A SCHOOL-BASED INTERVENTION PROGRAM

Against this background, it is appropriate to briefly describe the effects of the intervention program and related nationwide campaign against bully–victim problems in Norwegian schools. The major goals of the program were to reduce as much as possible existing bully–victim problems and to prevent the development of new problems. Evaluation of the effects of the intervention program was based on data from approximately 2,500 students originally belonging to 112 fourth to seventh grade classes (modal ages were 11–14 years at the start of the project) in 42 primary and secondary or junior high schools in Bergen, Norway. The subjects of the study were followed over a period of 2.5 years, from 1983 to 1985 (see e.g., Olweus, 1991, for details).

The main findings of the analyses can be summarized as follows:

1. There were marked reductions—by 50% or more—in bully–victim problems for the periods studied, with 8 and 20 months of intervention, respectively. By and large, these reductions were obtained for both direct bullying (in which the victim is exposed to relatively open attacks), for indirect bullying (in which the victim is isolated and excluded from the group, involuntary

loneliness), and for bullying others. The results generally applied to both boys and girls and to students from all grades studied (Fig. 19.3.).

2. There was no displacement of bullying from the school to the way to and from school. There were reductions or no change with regard to bully–victim problems on the way to and from school.

3. There were also clear reductions in general antisocial behavior such as vandalism, fighting, pilfering, drunkenness, and truancy (Fig. 19.4).

4. In addition, we could register marked improvement in various aspects of the social climate of the class: improved order and discipline, more positive social relationships, and a more positive attitude to schoolwork and the school. At the same time, there was an increase in student satisfaction with school life.

5. The intervention program not only affected already existing victimization problems; it also reduced considerably the number (and percentage) of new victims (Olweus, 1992a). The program had thus both primary and secondary prevention effects (Cowen, 1984).

Being Bullied (Direct & Indirect)

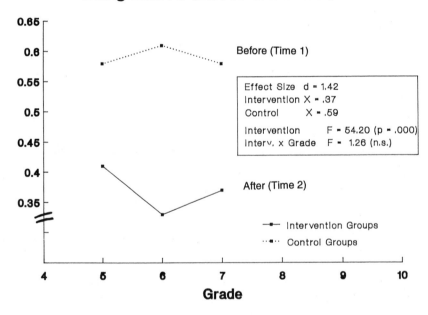

FIG. 19.3.   Effects of intervention program on being bullied (being exposed to direct as well as indirect bullying) for boys and girls combined. Upper curve (designated Before) shows baseline data (at Time 1, before intervention) for grades 5, 6, and 7 (or year 12, 13 and 14) cohorts, whereas the After curve displays data for corresponding cohorts (grades 4, 5, and 6, or years 11, 12 and 13) cohorts at Time 2 (one year later), after they had been exposed to the intervention program for 8 months.

Total Antisocial Behavior

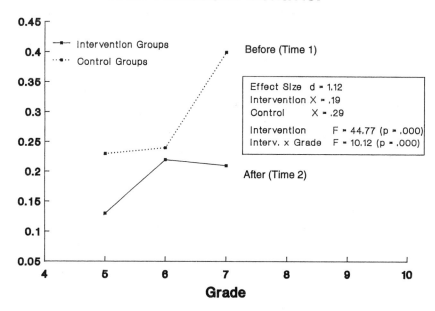

FIG. 19.4.   Effects of intervention program on Total Scale of Antisocial Behavior. See Fig. 19.3 for explanation.

In the majority of comparisons for which reductions were reported above, the differences between base line and intervention groups were significant or highly significant and with medium, large, or even very large effect sizes (*d*-values at the classroom level of more than 1.0 for several variables).

Detailed analyses of the quality of the data and the possibility of alternative interpretations of the findings led to the following general statements (Olweus, 1991): It is very difficult to explain the results obtained as a consequence of (a) underreporting by the students, (b) gradual changes in the students' attitudes to bully–victim problems, (c) repeated measurement, and (d) concomitant changes in other factors, including general time trends (Olweus, 1994). All in all, it was concluded that the changes in bully–victim problems and related behavior patterns were likely to be mainly a consequence of the intervention program and not of some other irrelevant factor. It was also noted that self-reports, which were implicated in most of these analyses, are probably the best data source for the purposes of this study. At the same time, largely parallel results were obtained for two peer-rating variables and for teacher ratings of bully–victim problems at the class level; for the teacher data, however, the effects were somewhat weaker.

Brief Comments

The reported effects of the intervention program must be considered very positive, particularly because many previous attempts to reduce aggressive and antisocial behavior systematically in preadolescents and adolescents were relatively unsuccessful (e.g., Dumas, 1989; Gottfredson, 1987; Kazdin, 1987).

The importance of the results is further accentuated by the fact that a highly disturbing increase in the prevalence of violence and other antisocial behavior has occurred in most industrialized societies in the last decades. In the Scandinavian countries, for instance, various forms of registered criminality have typically increased by 300% to 600% since the 1950s or 1960s (see e.g., Stortingsmelding nr. 23. 1991–1992, 1992, for the development in Norway). Similar changes have occurred in most Western industrialized societies.

As mentioned above, we estimated that approximately 80,000 students in Norwegian elementary and secondary or junior high schools were involved in bully–victim problems (in 1983). On the basis of the reported results the following conclusion can be drawn: If all elementary and secondary or junior high schools in Norway used the intervention program the way it was used in Bergen, the number of students involved in bully–victim problems would be reduced by 40,000 or more in a relatively short period. Effective use of the intervention program would also have a number of additional positive effects, including lower levels of vandalism, pilfering, and other antisocial behavior which would save society large amounts of money.

Basic Principles

The intervention program is built on a limited set of key principles derived chiefly from research on the development and modification of the problem behaviors concerned, in particular aggressive behavior. Thus it is important to try to create a school (and, ideally, also a home) environment characterized by warmth, positive interest, and involvement from adults, on one hand, and by firm limits to unacceptable behavior, on the other. Also, in cases of violations of limits and rules, nonhostile, nonphysical sanctions should be applied consistently. Implied in the latter two principles is a certain degree of monitoring and surveillance of the students' activities in and out of school (Patterson 1982, 1986). Finally, adults both at school and home are supposed to act as authorities, at least in some respects.

As regards the role of adults, the intervention program is based on an authoritative adult-child interaction or childrearing model (cf. e.g., Baumrind, 1967) in which the adults are encouraged to take responsibility for the children's total situation—not only their learning, but also their social relationships.

These principles were translated into a number of specific measures to be used at the school, class, and individual levels.[1] It is considered important to work on all of these levels, if possible (Olweus, 1993a).

With regard to implementation and execution, the program is mainly based on a utilization of the existing social environment: teachers and other school personnel, students, and parents. Non-mental-health professionals thus play a major role in the desired restructuring of the social environment. Experts such as school psychologists, counselors, and social workers serve important functions as planners and coordinators, in counseling teacher and parents (groups), and in handling more serious cases.

Additional Characteristics of the Intervention Program

Further understanding of the program can be gained from a brief description of the following four major subgoals:

1. Increasing awareness of the bully–victim problem and advancing knowledge about it includes dispelling some of the myths about it and its causes. Use of the Bully–Victim Questionnaire for an anonymous survey is an important step in obtaining more specific knowledge about the frequency and nature of the problems in the particular school.

2. Achieving active involvement on the part of teachers and parents implies, among other things, that the adults must recognize that it is their responsibility to control to a certain degree what goes on among the children and youngsters at school. One way of doing this is to provide adequate supervision during recess and lunch time. Further, the teachers are encouraged to intervene in possible bullying situations and give an absolutely clear message to the students: Bullying is not accepted in their schools. Teachers are also strongly advised to initiate serious talks with victims and bullies, and their parents, if a bully–victim problem has been identified in the class. Again, the basic message should be: We don't tolerate bullying in this school and will see to it that it comes to an end. Such an intervention on the part of the school must be followed up on regularly and closely supervised; otherwise the situation may easily become worse for the victim than it was before the intervention.

3. Developing clear rules against bullying such as: "We shall not bully other students"; "We shall try to help students who are bullied"; "We shall make it a point to include students who become easily left out" can serve as a basis for class discussions about what is meant by bullying behavior in concrete situations and what kind of sanctions should be used for students who break the rules. The behavior of the students in the class should be regularly related to these rules in class meetings (social hour). It is important that the teacher make consistent use of sanctions (some form of nonhostile, nonphysical punishment) in cases of rule violations, and also give generous praise when the rules have been followed.

4. Providing support and protection for the victims, for example, class rules against bullying, certainly support children who tend to be victimized. In addition, the teacher may enlist the help of neutral or well-adjusted students (the silent

---

[1]The updated "package" related to the intervention program consists of the Bully–Victim Questionnaire (Olweus & Smith, in press); a 20-minute video cassette showing scenes from the everyday lives of two bullied children (with English subtitles), and a copy of the book *Bullying at School—What We Know and What We Can Do* (Olweus, 1993a).

majority) to alleviate the situation of the victims in various ways. Also, teachers are encouraged to use their imagination to help victimized students to assert themselves in the class, to make them valuable in the eyes of their classmates. Parents of victims are exhorted to help their children develop new peer contacts and to teach them in detail (maybe with the help of the school psychologist or some similar person) how to make new acquaintances and to maintain a friendship relation.

Additional Comments

Possible reasons for the effectiveness of this nontraditional intervention approach have been discussed in some detail (Olweus, 1992a). They include a change of the opportunity-and-reward structures for bullying behavior (resulting in fewer opportunities and rewards for bullying). It is also generally emphasized that bully–victim problems can be seen as an excellent entry point for dealing with a variety of problems that plague today's schools. Furthermore, one can view the program from the perspective of planned organizational change (with quite specific goals) and in this way link it with the current lively work on school effectiveness and school improvement. It may also be pointed out that the program in many ways represents what is sometimes called "a whole-school policy approach to bullying" in the English literature. It consists of a set of routines, rules, and strategies of communication and action for dealing with existing and future bullying problems in the school.

This antibullying program is now in use or in the process of being implemented in a considerable number of schools in Europe and North America. Though so far there have been few research based attempts to evaluate the effects of the program beyond the study in Bergen, unsystematic information and reports indicate that the general approach is well received by the adults in the school community and that the program (with or without cultural adaptations or addition of culture-specific components) works well under varying cultural conditions including ethnic diversity. One additional large-scale evaluation of the basic approach containing most of the core elements of the program and with a research design similar to that of our study was made recently (Smith & Sharp, 1994). In this project, comprising 23 schools (with a good deal of ethnic diversity) in Sheffield, England, the results were quite positive (though fewer behavioral aspects were studied). It can be argued that the robustness and possible generalizability of the program is not really surprising, because the existing evidence seems to indicate that the factors and principles affecting the development and modification of aggressive, antisocial behavior are fairly similar across cultural contexts, at least within the Western industrialized part of the world.

FINAL WORDS

The basic message of our findings is quite clear: With a suitable intervention program, it is definitely possible to reduce dramatically bully–victim problems in school and related problem behaviors. This antibullying program can be implemented with relatively simple means and without major costs. Introduction of the program is likely to have a number of other positive effects as well.

ACKNOWLEDGMENTS

The research program reported on in this article was supported by grants from the William T. Grant Foundation, USA, and the Norwegian Research Council for Social Research (NAVF), and in earlier phases from the Swedish Delegation for Social Research (DSF) and the Norwegian Ministry of Education, assisttance from which is gratefully acknowledged.

REFERENCES

Baumrind, D. (1967). Child care practices anteceding three patterns of pre-school behavior. *Genetic Psychology Monographs, 75*, 43–88.

Björkqvist, K., Ekman, K., & Lagerspetz, K. (1982). Bullies and victims: Their ego picture, ideal ego picture and normative ego picture. *Scandinavian Journal of Psychology, 23*, 307–313.

Boulton, M. J., & Smith, P. K. (1994). Bully–victim problems among middle school children: Stability, self-perceived competence, and peer acceptance. *British Journal of Developmental Psychology, 12*, 315–329.

Cairns, R. B., Cairns, B. D., Neckerman, H. J., Gest, S. D., & Gariépy, J. L. (1988). Social networks and aggressive behavior: Peer support or peer rejection? *Developmental Psychology, 24*, 815–823.

Cowen, E. L. (1984). A general structural model for primary program development in mental health. *Personnel and Guidance Journal, 62*, 485–490.

Dumas, J. E. (1989). Treating antisocial behavior in children: Child and family approaches. *Clinical Psychology Review, 9*, 197–222.

Farrington, D. (1993). Understanding and preventing bullying. In M. Tonry (Ed.), *Crime and justice: A review of research* (vol. 17, pp. 348–458). Chicago: University of Chicago Press.

Gottfredson, G. D. (1987). Peer group interventions to reduce the risk of delinquent behavior: A selective review and a new evaluation. *Criminology, 25*, 671–714.

Haeselager, G. J. T., & van Lieshout, C.F.M. (1992, September). *Social and affective adjustment of self- and peer-reported victims and bullies.* Paper presented at the European Conference on Developmental Psychology, Seville, Spain.

Hirano, K. (1992, September). *Bullying and victimization in Japanese classrooms.* Paper presented at the European Conference on Developmental Psychology, Seville, Spain.

Junger, M. (1990). Intergroup bullying and racial harassment in the Netherlands. *Sociology and Social Research, 74*, 65–72.

Kazdin, A. E. (1987). Treatment of antisocial behavior in children: Current status and future directions. *Psychological Bulletin, 102*, 187–203.

Lagerspetz, K. M., Björkqvist, K., Berts, M., & King, E. (1982). Group aggression among school children in three schools. *Scandinavian Journal of Psychology, 23*, 45–52.

Loeber, R., & Dishion, T. (1983). Early predictors of male delinquency: A review. *Psychological Bulletin, 94*, 69–99.

Loeber, R., & Stouthamer-Loeber, M. (1986). Family factors as correlates and predictors of conduct problems and juvenile delinquency. In M. Tonry & N. Morris (Eds.), *Crime and justice* (Vol. 7, pp. 29–149). Chicago: University of Chicago Press.

Olweus, D. (1973a). *Hackkycklingar och översittare. Forskning om skolmobbning* [Bullies and victims. Research about school bullying]. Stockholm: Almqvist & Wicksell.

Olweus, D. (1973b). Personality and aggression. In J. K. Cole & D. D. Jensen (Eds.), *Nebraska Symposium on Motivation 1972.* Lincoln: University of Nebraska Press.

Olweus, D. (1977). Aggression and peer acceptance in adolescent boys: Two short-term longitudinal studies of ratings. *Child Development, 48*, 1301–1313.

Olweus, D. (1978). *Aggression in the schools. Bullies and whipping boys.* ... Washington, DC: Hemisphere.

Olweus, D. (1979). Stability of aggressive reaction patterns in males: A Review. *Psychological Bulletin, 86*, 852–875.

Olweus, D. (1980). Familial and temperamental determinants of aggressive behavior in adolescent boys: A causal analysis. *Developmental Psychology, 16*, 644–660.

Olweus, D. (1981). Bullying among school-boys. In N. Cantwell (Ed.), *Children and violence* (pp. 97–131). Stockholm: Akademilitteratur.

Olweus, D. (1983). Low school achievement and aggressive behavior in adolescent boys. In D. Magnusson, & V. Allen (Eds.), *Human development: An interactional perspective* (pp. 353–365). New York: Academic.

Olweus, D. (1984). Aggressors and their victims: Bullying at school. In N. Frude & H. Gault (Eds.), *Disruptive behavior in schools* (pp. 57–76). New York: Wiley.

Olweus, D. (1985). 80.000 barn er innblandet i mobbing. *Norsk Skoleblad, 2*, 18–23 (Oslo, Norway).

Olweus, D. (1986). Aggression and hormones: Behavioral relationship with testosterone and adrenaline. In D. Olweus, J. Block, & M. Radke-Yarrow (Eds.), *Development of antisocial and pro-social behavior* (pp. 51–72). New York: Academic.

Olweus, D. (1987). Bully–victim problems among schoolchildren. In J. P. Myklebust & R. Ommundsen (Eds.), *Psykologprofesjonen mot år 2000* (pp. 395–413). Oslo: Universitetsforlaget.

Olweus, D. (1988). Vad menar man med termen mobbning? *Psykologtidningen, 7*, 9–10.

Olweus, D. (1991). Bully–victim problems among schoolchildren: Basic facts and effects of a school based intervention program. In D. Pepler, & K. Rubin (Eds.), *The development and treatment of childhood aggression* (pp. 411–448). Hillsdale, N.J.: Lawrence Erlbaum Associates.

Olweus, D. (1992a). Bullying among schoolchildren: Intervention and prevention. In R. D. Peters, R. J. McMahon, V. L. Quincy (Eds.), *Aggression and violence throughout the life span* (pp. 100–125). Newbury Park, CA: Sage.

Olweus, D. (1992b). *Mobbning i skolan: Vad vi vet och vad vi kan göra* [Bullying at school: What we know and what we can do]. Stockholm: Almqvist & Wiksell.

Olweus, D. (1993a). *Bullying at school: What we know and what we can do.* Oxford, UK: Blackwell.

Olweus, D. (1993b). Victimization by peers: Antecedents and long-term outcomes. In K. H. Rubin & J. B. Asendorf (Eds.), *Social withdrawal, inhibition, and shyness in childhood* (pp. 315–342). Hillsdale, NJ: Lawrence Erlbaum Associates.

Olweus, D. (1994). Bullying at school: Long-term outcomes for the victims and an effective school-based intervention program. In L. R. Huesmann (Ed.), *Aggressive behavior: Current perspectives* (pp. 97–130). New York: Plenum.

Olweus, D., & Smith, P. K. (in press). *Manual for the Olweus Bully–Victim Questionnaire.* Oxford, UK: Blackwell.

O'Moore, M., & Brendan, H. (1989). Bullying in Dublin schools. *Irish Journal of Psychology, 10*, 426–441.

Patterson, G. R. (1982). *Coercive family process.* Eugene, Oregon: Castalia.

Patterson, G. R. (1986). Performance models for antisocial boys. *American Psychologist, 41*, 432–444.

Patterson, G. R., & Stouthamer-Loeber, M. (1984). The correlation of family management practices and delinquency. *Child Development, 55*, 1299–1307.

Perry, D. G., Kusel, S. J., & Perry, L. C. (1988). Victims of peer aggression. *Developmental Psychology, 24*, 807–814.

Pulkkinen, L., & Tremblay, R. E. (1992). Patterns of boys' social adjustment in two cultures and at different ages: A longitudinal perspective. *International Journal of Behavioral Development, 15*, 527–553.

Rigby, K., & Slee, P. (1991). Victims in school communities. *Journal of the Australasian Society of Victimology*, 25–31.

Ruiz, R. O. (1992, September). *Violence in schools. Problems of bullying and victimization in Spain.* Paper presented at the European Conference on Developmental Psychology, Seville, Spain.

Schwartz, D., Dodge, K., & Coie, J. (1993). The emergence of chronic peer victimization in boys' play groups. *Child Development, 64,* 1755–1772.

Smith, P. K. (1991). The silent nightmare: Bullying and victimization in school peer groups. *The Psychologist, 4,* 243–248.

Smith, P. K., & Sharp, S. (1994). *School bullying: Insights and perspectives.* Routledge.

Stortingsmelding nr. 23. 1991–1992. (1992). Om kriminalitetens bekjempande og forebygging [White paper on the combatting and prevention of criminality]. Oslo: Justis-og politidepartementet.

Whitney, I., & Smith, P. K. (1993). A survey of the nature and extent of bullying in junior/middle and secondary schools. *Educational Research, 35,* 3–25.

Ziegler, S., & Rosenstein-Manner, M. (1991). *Bullying at school: Toronto in an international context* (Rep. No. 196). Toronto: Toronto Board of Education, Research Services.

Part VI

Conclusions

This concluding section focuses on drawing lessons from the preceding chapters for dealing with conflict more productively and with less harm. Wiesel and Fry discuss the importance of preventing conflicts—a basic yet very important orientation. Investing resources in prevention can result in a tremendous bargain, not only in economic terms, but also in human and social dimensions. The price of conflict includes not only money, time, resources, and lives, but also the damaging effects on relationships, dissatisfaction with conflict outcomes, and recurrence of similar disputes in the future (Ury, Brett, & Goldberg, 1988). When people choose violence as an approach to conflict, the cost of the conflict can be monumental for themselves and others. The chapters in this book suggest that an array of options exist for dealing with conflict, including many nonviolent yet effective approaches.

In the concluding chapter, volume editors Björkqvist and Fry summarize and elaborate on general themes and principles from the previous chapters. Although the 20th century has witnessed incredible horror and bloodshed, it still does not follow that warfare is a necessary consequence of human nature. Cultural variation in styles of conflict resolution shows a continuum from nonviolent cultures to extremely violent ones, and it can be shown that aggression is not an innate drive. The editors emphasize cultural diversity and, particularly, the role of world view and the construction of scripts of behavior for styles of conflict resolution. The differences and similarities between dyadic negotiation and third-party intervention are analyzed, as well as the characteristics of effective mediation.

Björkqvist and Fry discuss some ideas derived from the chapters in this volume that have practical implications for reducing or preventing violence. Ideas include the importance of understanding a given culture's historiography of conflict (see chapter 11, this volume), the notion of supporting and harmonizing the peacemaking efforts of local citizens with higher-level institutional and governmental endeavors (see chapter 9, this volume), the application of the principle of redundancy, or overlapping dispute management procedures and mechanisms (see chapter 6, this volume), the importance of developing programs within the school and community to prevent the learning of aggressive behavior by children and, in contrast, to facilitate the learning of nonviolent, prosocial scripts for dealing with conflict (see chapters 18 and 19, this volume), the potential for providing positively-oriented organizations within the community as an alternative to youth gangs (see chapter 5, this volume) and the benefits of facilitating cross-ethic interaction and friendships (see chapter 13, this volume). Each of these ideas for reducing violence and various others discussed in the concluding chapter are derived from research reported in this volume. Human nature and social institutions show great variation. An overall conclusion based on the principles and examples explored in the foregoing chapters is that multiple alternatives to violence already exist, and others can be designed and implemented.

REFERENCES

Ury, W. L., Brett, J. M., & Goldberg, S. B. (1988). *Getting disputes resolved: Designing systems to cut the costs of conflict.* San Francisco: Jossey-Bass.

20

On Respecting Others and Preventing Hate: A Conversation with Elie Wiesel

Elie Wiesel
Boston University

Douglas P. Fry
Eckerd College

Dr. Elie Wiesel is the recipient of the 1986 Nobel Peace Prize and author of 37 books. During World War II, Dr. Wiesel and his family were imprisoned at Auschwitz and Buchenwald. His ordeal, including the loss of his family and the countless other acts of cruelty and inhumanity that Wiesel witnessed and experienced, is soberingly chronicled in his book, Night. Through The Elie Wiesel Foundation for Humanity, his teaching, writing, public speaking, and other activities, Dr. Wiesel continues to inspire others of all ages to abandon their indifference and work for a more just and peaceful world. In June of 1994, Dr. Wiesel met with Douglas P. Fry to discuss the nature of conflict and issues facing humanity today.

—*The Editors*

DPF: Perhaps a good place to begin is with a consideration of conflict resolution.

EW: Well, we all know that conflict resolution is a necessity, but whether it is a possibility, that is a different story. It has become an academic discipline, which is encouraging. Naturally, any person who has a sense of civilization must respond to the idea of conflict resolution.

The wiser path would be to prevent conflict and its escalation. The moment conflict erupts, it must be resolved peacefully and immediately. To resolve a conflict peacefully is a science: to bring the disputing parties together and to make them accept a certain technique. Very often today when we speak of conflict resolution, we speak actually about the containment of conflict, about not allowing it to go beyond civilized limits, not allowing it to spread over to other territories, into other domains. We are actually satisfied with little: We say, "okay, there is conflict, but at least let's contain it."

DPF: Conflict may be inherent in social life, but at least there are a variety of ways for dealing with it. You have mentioned prevention and containment, for example. Do you think conflict can be handled in other ways as well?

EW: If there is a redemptive dimension to conflict, it can be good—provided it is contained. Life and death go together. Being and nothingness are inseparable, as are silence and words. There would be no language without silence, without the tempo, the rhythm, the separation of one word and another. Art is conflict. Show me a creation without conflict, it's boring, be it a book, a theory, or a play. We *need* conflict, but the idea should be to give it a redemptive dimension. Again, if it is only artistic conflict, if it's only compositional, if it is only conflict of ideas, not of ideologies, it can be productive.

Ideologies are usually fixed, frozen. Only ideas move. A static idea is impossible. An idea by its nature must be in motion to transform itself. Not ideologies. Ideologies are forever the same. For communism to give up, it had to be given up totally. The same thing applies to Nazism. There are no compromises. They don't tolerate compromise, since they impose a total dictatorship, a total censorship, a total limit, an imprisonment onto others. Therefore, I think that ideas are worthier. Ideas are charming in the etymological sense, almost at the topological sense. We are charmed by the ideas. Enchanted.

DPF: As I read your book *Night*, I was deeply moved by passages such as:

> Never shall I forget that night, the first night in camp, which has turned my life into one long night, seven times cursed and seven times sealed. Never shall I forget that smoke. Never shall I forget the little faces of children, whose bodies I saw turned into wreaths of smoke beneath a silent blue sky. Never shall I forget those flames which consumed my faith forever.

You have said that there are lessons we must learn, and never forget, from the Holocaust, from World War II.

EW: Especially from the Nazi period, from the rise of Nazism. The lesson is don't give evil a second chance. Don't wait, fight it. Fight evil right away! In 1933, when Hitler sent his armies to occupy the Rhineland, had the rest of the world reacted immediately, had France simply mobilized, Hitler's armies would have staged a coup against him. There would have been no Hitler.

DPF: Now in this age of nuclear bombs and other extremely lethal types of weapons, do you have some thoughts as to how we might prevent the atrocities of a future "Hitler"?

EW: I think I would try to envisage a nuclear summit. We need an international police, a nuclear police. What Begin did in 1981, when the Israeli Air Force destroyed the Iraqi nuclear reactor Osirak, was called a surgical attack. At that time Begin was criticized all over the world, but he saved hundreds of thousands of lives: by using preventive strategy. Can you imagine Saddam Hussein with nuclear bombs? Therefore, what we need is a nuclear summit meeting to come up with some preventive measures, and enforcement strategies for saying to a nation, "unless you give up military nuclear weapons, we will take care of things."

DPF: International laws, with institutionalized mechanisms for enforcing these laws, would constitute an important step towards enhancing the common security of all nations on Earth. All communities—from hunting and gathering bands to today's emerging global community—require forms of social control for the good of the members.

Perhaps you could explain the goals and achievements of The Elie Wiesel Foundation for Humanity?

EW: The foundation is the domain of my wife, Marim, and acts on many levels. We have been building youth centers in Israel for young Ethiopian children immigrants. We organize many conferences, usually on a high level. The first was a conference for Nobel laureates "On the Threshold of the Twenty-First Century." The second project was to have seminars all over the world on the "Anatomy of Hate." We met in Oslo, Haifa, Boston, Moscow, Hiroshima, and so forth. In Moscow the meeting was attended by Gorbachev, Schmidt from Germany, and others. In Oslo, the participants included Mitterrand, Havel, Landsbergis—President of Lithuania—Mandela, and Jimmy Carter. The idea was to analyze, to explore hate: its genesis, texture, and mortal consequences. What is hate? How do you deal with hate? How do you find a remedy for hate?

I think this is *the* most important question facing society and this generation of ours. The 21st century is threatened by hate—attitudes of bigotry and prejudice. Ultimately it is hate that imperils our future.

What I have learned is that hate is like a cancer, spreading from limb to limb, or from person to person. Once hate is installed, it is too late. Like a cancer, it is almost impossible to eradicate. And, therefore, the easiest thing, the best, the most efficient method, is to prevent it. Once it is there, it is too late.

DPF: Do you really think that there is no way to deal with a hateful individual, once hate is established?

EW: How can you? The person who hates has set himself beyond language, beyond reason, beyond the will to resolve. Hate distorts the ability to reason, to imagine, to create, to remember, or to be generous. Conflict resolution is a way leading to generosity. I must realize that you have the same right to your beliefs as I have to mine. Although they are different, even in conflict, you and I must agree that we both are human beings. This is not possible for a person who is already invaded, dominated by hatred. A person who becomes a vehicle of hatred sees in me, not a human being, but a subhuman, a pariah.

DPF: You emphasize the importance of respecting other people—always seeing them as human beings and in that sense as equals. Could you elaborate on your ideas of how to respect others?

EW: First of all, we must see the other not as a stranger, but as a guest who came into my world from his or hers, just as I am a guest in his or her universe. And I see, therefore, in the other, someone who brings me a message from a distant land, from a strange culture, that I have never had access to. That person becomes my link to that world, and, therefore, my world emerges enriched. As for the respect I owe that person, it comes from all religious traditions. God created human beings alone. Why alone? So that nobody could say that, "according to my faith I am superior." The origin of the human species, the human consciousness, is the same for all of us. Therefore, I have no right to humiliate anyone. To me, the worst sin is humiliation. I cannot stand the person who needs to assert himself by humiliating others, be it a teacher toward students, or a writer to other writers, or a politician toward the voter. I find it intolerable. I understand that sometimes people defend themselves, but not in order to humiliate. Respect is the minimum that I would require from any group or any human being wishing to belong to a civilized community.

DPF: As an anthropologist, I've lived in Mexico and studied Zapotec culture. Zapotec people emphasize respect as one of their guiding principles. Benito Juarez, who was President of Mexico in the mid-1800s and a Zapotec Indian himself, said, "respect for the rights of others is peace." Today, Zapotec villagers regularly refer to their central belief in respect, and I think that regularly reaffirming this ideal can help keep violence in check. I also find this focus on respect to be a very interesting cultural difference from the U.S. where we don't emphasize thinking about others and our relationships in this way. Zapotec people also are more cooperative. Sometimes in the U.S., where we greatly value individualism and competition, we don't even see the possibilities of cooperating in our social interactions, to solve problems or to work together on a conflict.

EW: Yes. The belief in the necessity of winning a conflict is the beginning of all sorts of misfortune. Therefore, the mentality should be: "I don't have to win a conflict; I have to resolve it."

DPF: Do you think this realization is what finally has happened in South Africa and the Middle East?

EW: In both the Middle East and South Africa, neither side won. Peace won, and, therefore, humanity won. What is the beauty of conflict resolution? That because no one is losing, both are winning!

DPF: What type of role do you see for the U.N. or other international organizations in terms of bringing about conflict resolution?

EW: The U.N. is a beautiful dream, and as a dream I am for it. The specialized organizations I'm very much in favor of: the World Health Organization, the International Labor Organization, UNESCO, and UNICEF. They are crucial to our survival. The problem is that the U.N. represents a political forum for politically appointed people because everybody there represents a government.

The Secretary General has an important role to play. Former Secretary General Hammarskjöld played an essential role because he inspired. And his authority, therefore, was strong. The U.N. today is not doing what it should do: preventing conflicts from becoming larger and surely not from becoming battlefields where hundreds of thousands of people die. Somalia fizzed-out, and Rwanda was a scandal! A mark of shame. And then there is Bosnia. But then, the U.N. is not what many of us would have wanted it to be.

DPF: I'm wondering if you have a positive dream, or a positive vision of the future that you are willing to share.

EW: I would like to believe in the possibility of one human being helping one human being—it's enough—to create encounters other than in conflict. It doesn't have to be a national endeavor, a national phenomenon.

I would inaugurate compulsory courses of ethics for the armed forces. Just as I would like to have the same courses in all the universities, and at all the professional, law, and medical schools. That is the objective: to bring some morality, or at least the search for morality, into our society.

If I were utopian, I would say, abolish the armies and build more schools. One nation, Costa Rica, abolished the army. I'd actually limit the offensive weapons of powers, superpowers. I would limit all their intelligence agencies, because they are useless.

For centuries and generations we've been glorifying war. Why not glorify peace for once? The glorification of war is wrong. Even if a war is necessary, why glorify it? Why is the hero, the accepted hero, always a military hero? Why not a peace hero? The one who abolishes war?

DPF: We've had a few, of course, such as Gandhi and Martin Luther King, Jr. They were by no means passive in the face of injustice and hatred, but they chose other, effective paths besides violence. They modeled alternatives to violence, alternatives to war.

EW: In general though, we glorify the men who get medals, who get the medals of honor. Why not glorify something else? Why not give a medal to those who oppose and prevent war? Give *them* a medal of honor! Why don't we write poetry, drama, and plays about the triumph of peace instead of victory in war? All this means we need a totally new approach to many fundamental concepts in civilization, in this society.

DPF: I think we need a fundamental shift in values, parallel in a way to the remarkable change in thinking that has occurred regarding the institution of slavery. Obviously, slavery is no longer an acceptable institution in today's world, but for millennia it was. Likewise, I think humanity must evolve beyond its current acceptance and reliance on war—beyond, as you say, the glorification of war. We need a shift in cultural attitudes and also in the methods for handling international disputes effectively, without recourse to war. Anthropological evidence shows that not all cultures are violent and that some cultures do *not* engage in warfare. History shows that social institutions and cultural beliefs can change over time, as illustrated by the abolition of slavery. A shift away from war is possible, and necessary.

EW: A total shift. Of course, we know now that the next world war will be the last war. Both sides—or rather: many sides—will possess the ultimate weapon, they already have them, be it China, Russia, or America. It's a chain reaction. I am always angry when I read about the idea of a limited nuclear war. It's nonsense! If it's nuclear, it's all-out nuclear war. We have seen in the past that nations who have been pushed to the wall have used any weapons they had.

To this day, I don't understand why America used the atomic bomb in Nagasaki. There was no reason for that. In Hiroshima there may have been a reason, I understand, to save 50,000 lives—I have read all views of this issue. But why Nagasaki? Because it was there. That's all. If the U.S. had had two more, they too would have been used. Thus, we know that a nation that has the weapons will use them. That is why I am pessimistic. But I am also optimistic in believing that because of the danger, we will be alerted as to the consequences and will do something about it. There must be a total reevaluation of violence and the role of war in geopolitics. And, we must try to make peace seductive.

DPF: Do you think of American culture as being particularly violent?

EW: Look at television today. Nothing but violence on every level. Tourists are killed for money, just for the hell of it. Children killing children! They have security screening in elementary schools, in high schools. Ten-year-old children ought not go around with guns!

DPF: Have you heard of some of the peer mediation programs that have been started in the schools?

EW: Yes, I've heard of these. Whatever is mediation and resolution, I am for.

DPF: Some programs are having very positive results. In one case that I know of, a middle-school in Arizona, students were trained to help resolve disputes among their peers. Intentionally, some of the students selected as peer mediators were themselves problem students. When anthropologist Melissa McCormick evaluated the effects of this peer mediation program, she found that both officially reported and self-reported student aggression dropped by about 50% after the program was implemented. The peer mediators learned about conflict-resolution processes, thus increasing their skills for dealing with conflict, and other students learned that in times of difficulty, they could appeal to a helpful third party—the trained peers in this case—for help with their disputes. Another example of a successful intervention will appear in this book in a chapter by Dan Olweus as he describes reducing aggression in Norwegian schools.

In closing, let me ask you: What do you see as humanity's greatest challenge?

EW: Today, it is indifference. People are numb. When they see so much violence, they say, "Oh well, what can I do?" So much bloodshed: "What can I do?" So much suffering: "What can I do?" Indifference is not only a challenge, it is our greatest danger. Indifference is easy. You don't have to take any steps, any initiative. If you're not indifferent, it requires a commitment. You must send money to an organization. You must call up your congressman. You must write an op-ed piece and send it somewhere. You must do something! With indifference, you don't do anything. You just sit there in front of the television set, you eat your popcorn. For this generation, which is our generation, I think our problem—it's almost a metaphysical problem—is how to shake people out of indifference.

21

Conclusions:
Alternatives to Violence

Kaj Björkqvist
Åbo Akademi University

Douglas P. Fry
Eckerd College

In this chapter, the three major themes of the book, namely 1) the existence of alternatives to violence, 2) the critical role of culture, and 3) the search for conflict-resolution principles, are discussed in the light of the information provided in previous chapters. Although culture is critical in shaping the way individuals perceive and choose options for handling conflict, some general principles may still be identified. A variety of techniques, both at societal and individual levels, may be applied in order to avoid coercion and violence. By socialization into nonviolent conflict-resolution scripts of behavior, the emergence of violence can be prevented to a great extent. Finally, external conflict between individuals, groups, or nations cannot be seen as separated from their internal, intrapsychic representations. Lasting peace cannot be achieved by help of external control, but only by a change in attitude.

—*The Editors*

In this chapter, we consider certain implications that emerge from this collection of chapters. The implications relate to all three of the book's major themes, namely, (a) the existence of alternatives to violence, (b) the critical role of culture, and (c) the search for conflict resolution principles that may be applicable across cultures and conflict situations. Our search for connections and applications cannot be exhaustive, and we both hope and imagine that the reader will see other connections and derive additional conclusions as well.

VIOLENCE CAN BE AVOIDED

In this century, the world has experienced changes of thought and view, and of conduct and environment, so vast that hardly anyone could have imagined them beforehand. Despite the technical and economic development of our times, the fact remains that humankind has not as yet succeeded in creating a peaceful world and abolishing war. Perhaps partly as a consequence of development in other areas, the 20th century has witnessed more war casualties than any century before; it has experienced terrible genocide including the Holocaust and the invention of new and horrible means of torturing innocent victims. Our century has, in fact, seen unparalleled conflict and unprecedented evil. The two World Wars offer the lesson that "this must never happen again." However, the post-Cold War period has brought its own horrors: Rwanda, Bosnia, and Chechnya have in a painful manner reminded us of how easily the ghosts of the past, which we thought were long gone, can come alive again. This widespread suffering, this virtual bath in human blood, has put great shame on humanity, proving that we still need to regard seemingly small conflicts with deep respect. However small, conflicts may escalate and develop totally beyond our control. We need to have a humble attitude toward our ability (or inability) to resolve conflicts, not only on the interpersonal level, but also, and especially, on the ethnic and international levels.

In this light, the claims that the tendency toward warfare is not a built-in predisposition in human nature and that violence really can be avoided may appear as naive optimism. Yet, we still dare to suggest that this is really the case, and that the word can be more powerful than the sword. For humankind to abolish warfare, honest and deep reflection about the causes and process of conflict and about which factors lead either to escalation or resolution, is required.

Humankind has, during this century, created institutions with the sole purpose of avoiding warfare, the most important ones being the League of Nations after World War I and the United Nations after World War II. However, mere organizational and structural measures do not guarantee peace: Unless people develop a willingness to resolve conflicts by problem-solving methods rather than by attempts to win and suppress others, there cannot be lasting peace. Forced or repressive peace cannot substitute for peace by free will; compulsion is always inferior to volition. The best that peacekeeping forces can do, in the present state of human societal evolution, seems to be to act as kinds of international police; just as a police force cannot stop all crime, it can nevertheless prevent much crime. In the same way, at least at the present time, international organizations may not stop all wars, but they still may prevent many. They are, in our opinion, necessary and important.

External peace cannot be accomplished if war rages internally within people. As Wiesel suggested in his dialogue with Fry in the preceding chapter, hate is the worst problem. If people learn how not to hate their enemies, the problem is well on its way to being solved. A careful analysis of the situation can then lead to solutions. We have to unlearn hate.

In chapter 3, Björkqvist argued that aggression is not in itself an innate drive, functioning in accordance with the reservoir model. Aggressive behavior is learned.

Aggression is often habitual and to some extent justified by norms within a specific culture, and therefore, aggressive solutions to conflicts appear more frequently in some cultures than in others. Anthropological evidence of this circumstance is plentiful, and some is presented in this book. Examples of very aggressive cultures are the Bellona Islands (Kuschel, 1988, 1992) and the Yanomamö (e.g., Chagnon, 1992), while the Semai Senoi (Robarchek, 1979, 1994, and chapter 5 in this volume) and Upper Xingu peoples (Gregor, 1994) may be mentioned as examples of extremely peaceful—but not totally conflict-free—cultures (see chapter 1, this volume).

As cultures vary in their level of aggressiveness, so do people within each culture. Anger is an important precursor to aggressive approaches to conflict, and individual differences in anger-proneness may partly explain existing differences in aggressiveness. The main factors affecting the development of an aggressive personality are probably environmental rather than biological, a combination of the effect of repeated frustrations during one's life history coupled with the exposure to aggressive scripts, as will be discussed below. As Olweus stated in chapter 19 (this volume), too little love and care, and too much freedom (i.e., lack of clear behavioral norms) are conditions that contribute strongly to the development of an aggressive reaction pattern.

Björkqvist and Fry agree on the fact that aggression should not be regarded as an innate drive comparable to drives of hunger, thirst, and sex, but that aggression may serve as a means to fulfill other drives, whether learned or innate. We have, however, somewhat diverging opinions on whether humans have instincts that are likely to lure us more often into conflict than we would like. Mammalian species usually have territories or home ranges, and those living in groups form hierarchies. This is unquestionably true of some of our closest primate relatives: they show territorial behavior, and both males and females form same-sex hierarchies, which seem closely connected to sexual competition (Mason & Mendoza, 1993). Whereas Björkqvist finds it likely that humans also have innate tendencies towards territorial and hierarchical behavior, Fry does not. Whatever the case, we both conclude that humans can learn to deal with conflicts of these types in nonviolent ways. Conflicts as such may not be possible to avoid totally, but there is no reason to believe that humans cannot learn to employ nonviolent, problem-solving scripts of behavior.

CULTURE OF CONFLICT

Throughout the volume, we have seen how culture is critical in shaping the manner in which people perceive, evaluate, and choose options for dealing with conflict. Each society has its culture of conflict, to use Ross' (1993) term, which includes some options but excludes others. On the one hand, a number of general conflict strategies that occur across cultural situations can be identified (e.g., Black, 1984, 1993), while on the other hand, the cultural meaning of a specific conflict present in any given society should be analyzed within the context of that particular cultural environment. In other words, culturally comparative and culturally specific analyses of conflict can be viewed as complementary approaches rather than as mutually exclusive perspectives.

An awareness of the impact that culture has on conflict behavior has various implications. First, it allows for a consideration of how conflicting parties might be limiting their approaches to those found within their specific culture. Culturally grounded beliefs, terminology (also historiography, in Hjärpe's terms; see chapter 11), and norms must be considered as important aspects of understanding both intra- and intercultural conflicts. This cultural specificity is illustrated, for example, when Glazer (chapter 13) noted how New York African Americans and Jews bring heightened emotionality into their "competition of tears," when McCormick (chapter 10) discussed the "pass no remarks" avoidance approach of the Northern Irish, and when Olson (chapter 8) described the kava circle on Tonga as a means of resolving and reducing conflict.

It should be noted also that political life, at both national and international levels, has its own culture of conflict, with shared world views, assumptions, norms, and institutions. Perhaps the realization that the international political system is in some ways a culture of its own opens possibilities for developing innovations in political conflict resolution. As emphasized in the chapter by Fry and Fry (chapter 2), and as demonstrated by President Arias (chapter 14), alternative strategies for dealing with international conflict, other than muscle and force, do exist (e.g., the Arias Peace Plan).

Second, an appreciation of cultural influence on conflict and its resolution cautions against attempting quick applications of dispute resolution techniques developed in one cultural setting to another. As Avruch (1991) pointed out, such "cookbook" applications are problematic. Alternatively, a flexible and creative approach to praxis, grounded on more general principles, may be possible.

This possibility leads to a third implication, that a knowledge of conflict-resolution approaches used across a variety of cultures can be viewed as constituting a wealth of options and may lead to both practical and theoretical generalizations. Obviously, some approaches are so embedded in the specific world views and belief systems that they have virtually no transferability potential. On the other hand, awareness of the diversity of cultural approaches to conflict may lead to certain transcultural principles and fruitful, cross-cultural applications. We next consider some examples of more general principles for reducing violence, derivable from the chapters in the book.

WORLD VIEW, PLANS AND COGNITIVE SCRIPTS OF BEHAVIOR

It was suggested in some of the chapters (e.g., chapters 3, 4, 18, and 20) that there is something fundamentally wrong within our Western society in the way we relate to violence: Violent heroes are glorified in film, pseudo-Darwinian attitudes are augmented in politics and economy, and strength seems to be a virtue more highly evaluated than compassion and gentleness. The myth of the innate tendency towards warfare in humans is a typical example of this particular world view.

Cognitive psychology theories (e.g., Miller, Galanter, & Pribram, 1960; Schank & Abelson, 1977) point out that if we want to gain an understanding of human social motivation, we have to take into consideration the views people in a culture have of themselves in particular, of humans in general, and of their cosmology and world view, on a metalevel. Concepts such as world views, plans, and scripts of behavior have become increasingly popular in attempts to understand and explain human behavior and motivation. As an example, it is clear that the application of the notion that "might is right" will have a totally different impact on behavior than "do unto others. ... " World views state the truths and the meaning, plans formulate strategies for attaining goals people set for themselves, and their scripts of behavior give detailed directives on how to deal with specific situations. Views, normative beliefs, plans, and scripts—sometimes referred to as schemata—are developed by information processing, and the information obviously must be provided by the surrounding culture. It has become increasingly evident that behaviorist reinforcement theory is far too shallow to account for all the complexities of human motivation and social behavior. Individual behavior is governed by plans and scripts of behavior rather than by reward–punishment conditioning (a claim that does not imply that conditioning does not occur: It certainly does). Neither can human social behavior be explained only in terms of sociobiological, evolutionary-determined predispositions. Applications of cognitive motivation theory in the explanation of aggressive conflict behavior have been made by, for example, Huesmann and Eron (1986), Björkqvist and Österman (1992), and Björkqvist (in press). Chapter 18 by Guerra and her colleagues provides a detailed theoretical discussion on the development of both aggressive and prosocial scripts, including a review of relevant literature. One implication of their study is that to prevent violence, scripts of behavior need to be changed. These researchers are aiming to reduce aggression and increase prosocial problem solving in three social groupings: In the school overall, among higher-risk school children, and in the family setting. Olweus described, in chapter 19, great success in reducing and preventing bullying in schools. By paying greater attention to what scripts children are learning and being taught during socialization within home, school, community, and broader culture, it would be possible to prevent much of the misery caused by violence in society.

The culture of conflict of each society can be regarded as a network of scripts or schemata, providing models for how to deal with specific conflict situations. If this conception of human motivation is correct, more attention should be directed towards the understanding of world views, the internalization of normative beliefs, and the particular scripts for dealing with conflicts, provided within cultures.

COSMOLOGY AND CONFLICT

The importance of understanding world views is pointed out by Galtung in chapter 4 on conflict life cycles in Occident and Orient. He regards the monotheistic cultures of Christianity, Judaism, and Islam as one megacivilization and Eastern culture as another. These two megacivilizations differ widely in their cosmology, for instance in their conceptualization of time; such a seemingly irrelevant aspect may have wide implications for how people relate to conflict. The Western megacivilization regards time as bounded, having a beginning (genesis) and an end (apocalypsis-catharsis) whereas the Eastern megacivilization regards time as infinite. Galtung discussed implications this difference has on how conflicts are viewed; for a Westerner, conflicts are described in terms of being encased within finite time, having a clear beginning, an escalation, a climax, and an end, whereas the Easterner would regard conflict in cyclic terms. The cosmology will impose itself on us, demanding corresponding behavior and attitudes.

Another aspect of cosmology, or world view, is social in its nature: Westerners describe conflict in terms of individual actors, while Buddhists tend to apply a social-collective perspective. Galtung uses the knot–net metaphor: "Which is more real, the knots or the net?" Whereas the Westerner tends to conceive reality in terms of individual knots, the Easterner emphasizes the social net.

The amount of attention given to the individual in industrialized, Western culture may represent a recently derived anomaly when a holistic, cross-cultural perspective is adopted. Even though many cultures have been influenced by the West to various degrees, the emphasis on relationships and a conciliatory style in conflict resolution can be widely noted (e.g., Black, 1984, 1993; Nader, 1969; White, 1991). For example, conflict resolution among native Hawaiian families "is to restore harmonious relationships through prayer, discussion, apology, and forgiveness" (Shook & Ke'ala Kwan, 1991, p. 213). And with regard to Central America, Lederach (1991, p. 168) explained:

> Interpersonal conflict is perhaps a misnomer in this context. It leaves the impression that individual persons are in conflict. It fits Western conceptualization permitting focus on individuals and their issues, often in isolation from their network. In Central America issues and people, and therefore conflicts, are always viewed holistically, as embedded in the social network.

The parallel to Cook's emphasis (in chapter 7) on social network among native Margariteño culture is apparent.

These examples indicate the importance of world view. In his discussion of the historiography of Islam, Hjärpe (chapter 11) showed that although Islam and Christianity belong to the same megacivilization (in Galtung's terminology), Islam has its own world view. He suggested the application of a particular discipline, historiography, in understanding conflict and its resolution in other cultures. Hjärpe noted that the social scientist trying to grasp another culture works with a jigsaw puzzle in which most of the pieces are lacking. Only a fraction of previous history, forming the present-day world view and the vocabulary so closely attached to it, can be traced. With a better historiographical knowledge, leaders might better learn how to resolve conflicts instead of escalating them, as easily happens when politicians consider their image in the eyes of domestic voters as more important than whether a particular conflict is resolved peacefully or not. This type of historiographical knowledge would have been particularly useful during the Gulf crisis, and because much tension lies in Muslim–Christian–Jewish relations, a better understanding of the history of cultures in conflict is today more urgent than ever. In the Israeli–Palestinian peace talks, historiographical aspects have been recognized by both sides.

FORMAL AND INFORMAL CONFLICT RESOLUTION

Societies may deal successfully, or unsuccessfully, with interpersonal conflicts that unquestionably will occur. Each society develops forms, part of its particular culture of conflict, to deal with these. Olson (chapter 8) described kava drinking on the Tonga Islands as an informal and effective method. The kava drinking is to some extent ritualized and follows specific norms or rules, but it is not primarily thought of as a tension reducing activity by the Tongans themselves; accordingly, it should be considered an informal practice.

The *becharaa'* of the Semai, described by Robarchek (chapter 5) is, on the other hand, a formalized practice. When feelings are too intense or issues too important, and conflict cannot be avoided, the headman convenes a *becharaa'*, a dispute resolution process between the conflicting individuals, in which the whole community can partake. It is notable that the interdependence of all members of the community, and the need for maintaining unity and harmony, is stressed at the beginning and at the conclusion of the *becharaa'*. The marathon process can go on for days, and every conceivable argument, motive, and circumstance are carefully examined. The *becharaa'* continues until absolutely everything that can be said has been said. In that sense, it offers what Robarchek described as a total abreaction, a psychodynamic extinction of the conflict, not only socially, but also from within the psyches of the opponents. Robarchek points out that the *becharaa'* is only one component in a well-integrated system, operating on both psychodynamic and social levels, which helps explain why the Semai have managed to attain their high level of peacefulness. The Semai techniques may not be directly applicable in Western society, but we may certainly learn from them.

REINVENTING THE COMMUNITY NET

Robarchek gleaned from his work among the Semai an intriguing lesson for modern, complex societies suffering from violence: Make greater use of the positive aspects of community to prevent violence. In other words, to return to the knot–net metaphor discussed by Galtung; perhaps with creativity, modern complex societies might attempt to reinvent the net, at least to some degree, focusing on providing relational and community support for resolving disputes without violence. Glazer (chapter 13) provides a relevant example as she discusses the development of special interest friendships and programs such a Project C.U.R.E. which facilitate purposeful interaction across subgroup boundaries (see Rubin, Pruitt, & Kim, 1994, for a theoretical elaboration of the use of cross-cutting ties to mitigate intergroup conflict). The San Francisco Community Boards program, which makes available trained volunteer conciliators to help neighbors work out their problems, is another example of reinventing the net to resolve conflicts and enhance relationships within the community (Farnsworth & Kwong, 1984). Thus another implication from chapters such as Glazer's and Robarchek's involves focusing more attention on relationships during conflict resolution, and, by extension, on the maintenance of community, because this may have payoffs in reducing violence and promoting more effective resolution of disputes.

REDUNDANCY OF CONFLICT-RESOLUTION METHODS

Hollan (chapter 6) described how the Toraja have what he calls redundant controls, some internal and some external to the individual, which, when functioning together, are effective at keeping aggression at low levels. Although the cultural circumstances will vary, this principle of redundancy could be augmented in many settings from the interpersonal to the international levels of organization. Nordstrom (chapter 9) made a similar point about redundancy: Peace was more readily achieved in Mozambique, where local and national reconciliation efforts reinforced each other, working in concert, than in Sri Lanka where such a synergistic possibility went unnoticed. As Ury, Brett, and Goldberg (1988, p. 172) suggested, a good conflict-management system has a set of successive safety nets to halt conflict: "If one procedure fails, another is waiting."

PEOPLE POWER

Several chapters offer insights regarding conflict resolution, which might be referred to as "people power." People power appears particularly useful when there is an asymmetric power relationship, with a dictator or a dominating group oppressing the majority. Typical of this type of situation is that the dominating stratum does not admit being repressive, but claims instead that its power is legitimate and for the common good. Mohandas Gandhi can be regarded as the archetypal expert on how to use nonviolent resistance based on people power; Martin Luther King, Jr. was another, and their methods are well known and described in the literature on conflict resolution. Klicperová and her coauthors chronicled how the Czech and Slovak people succeeded in reestablishing democracy through nonviolent means during the Velvet Revolution. Recently, there have been several parallel cases of effective, nonviolent resistance to repressive governments. For instance, people power played a dramatic role in ousting dictators Pinochet from Chile and Marcos from the Philippines, as masses of unarmed civilians placed themselves in the front of riot police and army tanks. One lesson from the former Czechoslovakia and similar cases is that political oppression need not be met by violent rebellion; nonviolent, "velvet" tactics can be very effective.

"INTERNAL" AND EXTERNAL THIRD PARTIES

The literature on conflict resolution usually treats negotiation between two parties, without an intervening third party, as something categorically different from conflict resolution with the help of an intervening third party (be it in the role of mediator, arbitrator, judge, and so on; cf. Black, 1984). We suggest that this division is to some extent arbitrary: in fact, successful conflict resolution, with or without an external third party, requires some of the same psychological elements.

Conflict between two parties can be regarded as the "typical" conflict situation, because as has been shown (e.g., Höglund & Ulrich, 1972), a 3-party or, for that matter, an n-party conflict, tends to polarize into a two-party conflict. The war in Bosnia may be given as an example, in which two parties (Croats and Muslims) joined in order to withstand the Serbian force. Similar observations have been made also with respect to interpersonal conflict (Höglund & Ulrich, 1972).

Thus let us consider conflict between two parties. As Österman and her colleagues describe in chapter 17 on the development of conflict-resolution skills in adolescents, successful problem-solving cannot be attained until a certain level of metacognition has been achieved: that of mutual perspective-taking (Flavell, 1979; Selman, 1980). That is, not until both parties are able to "step outside" of their own restricted points of view, and, in a sense, take a third-party perspective to the situation, can conflict resolution be accomplished. A successful perspective has to be objective, with an emphatic understanding of the other party's needs, as well as of one's own. It can be regarded as taking an *internalized* third-party perspective.

An external third party is needed only when the two parties are not able to accomplish this mutual perspective taking, without help. Thus an important task of a third party is to help the two conflicting parties in finding their own internal third party.

EFFECTIVE MEDIATION

What constitutes effective mediation? Negotiation and third-party intervention has been a popular area of research in the field of conflict resolution (e.g., Bercovitch, 1984a, 1984b, 1985, 1986; Butterworth, 1976; Holsti, 1966, 1983; Lall, 1966; Ott, 1972; Pruitt, Carnevale, Forcey, & Van Slyck, 1986; Pruitt & Drews, 1969; Pruitt & Johnson, 1970; Pruitt, Peirce, McGillicuddy, Welton, & Castroianno, 1993; Rubin & Brown, 1975; Rubin et al., 1994; Touval & Zartman, 1985), and some findings from these studies may be summarized as follows. Conflicts are more often resolved successfully with a mediating third-party than without. However, people seem to wish to manage their affairs without the help of outsiders, if possible, and it is, accordingly, important that the triadic relationship is perceived by all concerned as temporary only. Two conflicting parties tend to accept third-party intervention mainly when they reach a stalemate situation, and neither side is any longer prepared for an escalation of the dispute.

In cases of intergroup disputes, conflict resolution by third parties can occur only when the adversaries are legitimate spokespeople for their parties. The smaller the power differences between adversaries, the greater is the chance of success. When vital interests are at stake, mediation is extremely difficult. The longer the duration of a dispute and the more intense the conflict, the more problematic it will be to solve it. Mediation is more likely to succeed if attempted at an early stage, and it should start at a propitious moment. It is likely to succeed if each side shows a willingness to moderate and revise its expectations. The issues at stake are important. When they pertain to security or independence, chances for success are enhanced, whereas issues of honor and ideology are less easy to reach agreement upon.

The *becharaa'*, described by Robarchek (chapter 5) can be regarded as third-party intervention during optimal circumstances, with a very high likelihood of success. The whole community can be involved, and ideally the process does not end until there is virtually no problem left.

Bercovitch (1984) suggested that important qualities that the mediator should have are credibility, evenhandedness, and impartiality. But mediation is a matter of resources, not only of impartiality; a third-party with as high a status as possible in the eyes of the opponent stands the best chances of success. It is hardly a coincidence that the United States has been hosting the Israeli-Palestinian talks, for instance.

Bercovitch (1986) suggested that it helps if the mediator has attributes such as stamina, energy, and a sense of humor. Social intelligence is probably an important factor: Österman and her colleagues (chapter 17) suggested that women should be involved in international mediation more often than they presently are, and that their potential in this respect has been neglected so far.

FINAL WORDS

We conclude that the source of conflict lies in the minds of people. External, social conflict is a reflection of intrapsychic conflict. External control does not solve the roots of the problem: If we wish a conflict really to disappear, then a change in attitude is needed. Only when people learn to understand and respect each other can peaceful coexistence begin. In the words of Montagu (1976, p. 299): "A genuinely healthy society is maintained and sustained not by the competitive struggle for existence to achieve a factitious success, but by a striving for that human cooperativeness which is the true dignity of humankind, and the respect that humans owe to each other."

REFERENCES

Avruch, K. (1991). Introduction: Culture and conflict resolution. In K. Avruch, P. W. Black, & J. A. Scimecca (Eds.), *Conflict resolution: Cross-cultural perspectives* (pp. 1–17), Westport, CT: Greenwood Press.

Bercovitch, J. (1984a). Problems and approaches in the study of bargaining and negotiation. *Political Science, 36,* 125–144.

Bercovitch, J. (1984b). *Social conflict and third parties: Strategies of conflict resolution.* Boulder, CO: Westview.

Bercovitch, J. (1985). Third parties in conflict management. *International Journal, 40,* 736–752.

Bercovitch, J. (1986). International mediation: A study of incidence, strategies and conditions of successful outcomes. *Cooperation and Conflict, 11,* 155–168.

Björkqvist, K. (in press). Learning aggression from models: From a social learning towards a cognitive theory of modeling. In S. Feshbach & J. Zagrodzka (Eds.), *Human aggression: Biological and social roots.* New York: Plenum.

Björkqvist, K., & Österman, K. (1992). Parental influence on children's self-estimated aggressiveness. *Aggressive Behavior, 18,* 411–423.

Black, D. (1984). Social control as a dependent variable. In Black, D. (Ed.), *Towards a general theory of social control* (pp. 1–36). Orlando, FL: Academic.

Black, D. (1993). *The social structure of right and wrong.* San Diego, CA: Academic.

Butterworth, R. (1976). *Managing interstate conflict 1945–1974.* Pittsburgh, PA: University of Pittsburgh Press.

Chagnon, N. A. (1992). *Yanomanö.* New York: Harcourt Brace Javanovich.

Farnsworth, E., & Kwong, J. (Producers). (1984). *Justice without law* [videotape]. (Available from Community Boards, 149 Ninth Street, San Francisco, CA 94103)

Flavell, J. H. (1979). Metacognitive development and cognitive monitoring: A new area of cognitive development inquiry. *American Psychologist, 34,* 906–342.

Gregor, T. (1994). Symbols and rituals of peace in Brazil's Upper Xingu. In L. E. Sponsel & T. Gregor (Eds.), *The anthropology of peace and nonviolence* (pp. 241–257). Boulder, CO: Lynne Rienner Publishers.

Höglund, B., & Ulrich, J. W. (1972). Peace research and the concepts of conflict: Summary and criticism. In B. Höglund & J. W. Ulrich (Eds.), *Conflict control and conflict resolution* (pp. 13–35). Copenhagen, Denmark: Munksgaard.

Holsti, K. (1966). Resolving international conflict: A taxonomy of behavior and some figures on procedures. *Journal of Conflict Resolution, 10,* 272–297.

Holsti, K. (1983). *International politics: A framework for analysis.* Englewood Cliffs, NJ: Prentice-Hall.

Huesmann, R. L., & Eron, L. D. (Eds.). (1986). *Television and the aggressive child: A cross-national comparison.* Hillsdale, NJ: Lawrence Erlbaum Associates.

Kuschel, R. (1988). *Vengeance is their reply: Blood feuds and homicides on Bellona Island. Part I: Conditions underlying generations of bloodshed. Language and culture of Rennell and Bellona Islands.* Copenhagen, Denmark: Dansk Psykologisk Forlag.

Kuschel, R. (1992). "Women are women and men are men": How Bellonese women get even. In K. Björkqvist & P. Niemelä (Eds.), *Of mice and women: Aspects of female aggression* (pp. 173–185). San Diego, CA: Academic.

Lall, A. (1966). *Modern international negotiation.* New York: Columbia University Press.

Lederach, J. P. (1991). Of nets, nails, and problems: The folk language of conflict resolution in a Central American setting. In K. Avruch, P. W. Black, & J. A. Scimecca (Eds.), *Conflict resolution: Cross-cultural perspectives* (pp. 165–186). Westport, CT: Greenwood.

Mason, W. A., & Mendoza, S. P. (Eds.). (1993). *Primate social conflict.* Albany, NY: State University of New York Press.

Miller, G. A., Galanter, E., & Pribram, K. H. (1960). *Plans and the structure of behavior.* New York: Holt, Rinehart & Winston.

Montagu, A. (1976). *The nature of human aggression.* New York: Oxford University Press.

Nader, L. (1969). Styles of court procedure: To make the balance. In L. Nader (Ed.), *Law and culture in society* (pp. 69–91). Chicago, IL: Aldine-Atherton.

Ott, M. C. (1972). Mediation as a method of conflict resolution. *International Organisation, 26,* 595–618.

Pruitt, D. G., Carnevale, P. J. D., Forcey, B., & Van Slyck, M. (1986). Gender effects in negotiation: Constituent surveillance and contentious behavior. *Journal of Experimental Social Psychology, 22,* 264–275.

Pruitt, D. G., & Drews, J. L. (1969). The effect of time pressure, time elapsed, and the opponent's concession rate on behavior in negotiation. *Journal of Experimental Social Psychology, 5,* 43–60.

Pruitt, D. G., & Johnson, D. F. (1970). Mediation as an aid to face saving in negotiation. *Journal of Personality and Social Psychology, 14,* 239–246.

Pruitt, D. G., Peirce, R. S., McGillicuddy, N. B., Welton, G. L., & Castroianno, L. M. (1993). Long-term success in mediation. *Law and Human Behavior, 17,* 313–330.

Robarchek, C. A. (1979). Conflict, emotion and abreaction: Resolution of conflict among the Semai Senoi. *Ethos, 7,* 104–123.

Robarchek, C. A. (1994). Ghosts and witches: The psychocultural dynamics of Semai peacefulness. In L. E. Sponsel & T. Gregor (Eds.), *The anthropology of peace and nonviolence* (pp. 183–196). Boulder, CO: Lynne Rienner Publishers.

Ross, M. H. (1993). *The management of conflict.* New Haven, CT: Yale University Press.

Rubin, J. & Brown, B. (1975). *The social psychology of bargaining and negotiation.* New York: Academic.

Rubin, J. Z., Pruitt, D. G., & Kim, S. H. (1994). *Social conflict: Escalation, stalemate, and settlement.* New York: McGraw-Hill.

Schank, R., & Abelson, R. (1977). *Scripts, plans, goals and understanding: An inquiry into human knowledge.* Hillsdale, NJ: Lawrence Erlbaum Associates.

Selman, R. L. (1980). *The growth of interpersonal understanding. Developmental and clinical analyses.* New York: Academic.

Shook, E. V., & Ke'ala Kwan, L. (1991). *Ho'oponopono:* Straightening family relationships in Hawaii. In K. Avruch, P. W. Black, & J. A. Scimecca (Eds.), *Conflict resolution: Cross-cultural perspectives* (pp. 213–229). Westport, CT: Greenwood.

Touval, S., & Zartman, I. (Eds.). (1985). *Mediation in theory and practice.* Boulder, CO: Westview.

Ury, W. L., Brett, J. M., & Goldberg, S. B. (1988). *Getting disputes resolved: Designing systems to cut the costs of conflict.* San Francisco, CA: Jossey-Bass.

White, G. M. (1991). Rhetoric, reality, and resolving conflicts: Disentangling in a Solomon Islands society. In K. Avruch, P. W. Black, & J. A. Scimecca (Eds.), *Conflict resolution: Cross-cultural perspectives* (pp. 187–212). Westport, CT: Greenwood.

Author Index

Subject Index